A Rational Expectations
Approach to
Macroeconometrics

A National Bureau
of Economic Research
Monograph

A Rational Expectations Approach to Macroeconometrics

Testing Policy Ineffectiveness and Efficient-Markets Models

Frederic S. Mishkin

The University of Chicago Press

Chicago and London

FREDERIC S. MISHKIN is associate professor of economics at the University of Chicago and research associate at the National Bureau of Research.

The University of Chicago Press, Chicago 60637
The University of Chicago Press, Ltd., London

Library of Congress Cataloging in Publication Data

Mishkin, Frederic S.
   A rational expectations approach to macroeconometrics.

   (A National Bureau of Economic Research monograph)
   Bibliography: p.
   Includes index.
   1. Rational expectations (Economic theory)
2. Macroeconomics. 3. Econometrics. I. Title.
II. Series.
HB172.5.M57   1983   339'.0724   82-20049
ISBN 0-226-53186-4 (pbk.)

Relation of the Directors to the
Work and Publications of the
National Bureau of Economic Research

1. The object of the National Bureau of Economic Research is to ascertain and to present to the public important economic facts and their interpretation in a scientific and impartial manner. The Board of Directors is charged with the responsibility of ensuring that the work of the National Bureau is carried on in strict conformity with this object.

2. The President of the National Bureau shall submit to the Board of Directors, or to its Executive Committee, for their formal adoption all specific proposals for research to be instituted.

3. No research report shall be published by the National Bureau until the President has sent each member of the Board a notice that a manuscript is recommended for publication and that in the President's opinion it is suitable for publication in accordance with the principles of the National Bureau. Such notification will include an abstract or summary of the manuscript's content and a response form for use by those Directors who desire a copy of the manuscript for review. Each manuscript shall contain a summary drawing attention to the nature and treatment of the problem studied, the character of the data and their utilization in the report, and the main conclusions reached.

4. For each manuscript so submitted, a special committee of the Directors (including Directors Emeriti) shall be appointed by majority agreement of the President and Vice Presidents (or by the Executive Committee in case of inability to decide on the part of the President and Vice Presidents), consisting of three Directors selected as nearly as may be one from each general division of the Board. The names of the special manuscript committee shall be stated to each Director when notice of the proposed publication is submitted to him. It shall be the duty of each member of the special manuscript committee to read the manuscript. If each member of the manuscript committee signifies his approval within thirty days of the transmittal of the manuscript, the report may be published. If at the end of that period any member of the manuscript committee withholds his approval, the President shall then notify each member of the Board, requesting approval or disapproval of publication, and thirty days additional shall be granted for this purpose. The manuscript shall then not be published unless at least a majority of the entire Board who shall have voted on the proposal within the time fixed for the receipt of votes shall have approved.

5. No manuscript may be published, though approved by each member of the special manuscript committee, until forty-five days have elapsed from the transmittal of the report in manuscript form. The interval is allowed for the receipt of any memorandum of dissent or reservation, together with a brief statement of his reasons, that any member may wish to express; and such memorandum of dissent or reservation shall be published with the manuscript if he so desires. Publication does not, however, imply that each member of the Board has read the manuscript, or that either members of the Board in general or the special committee have passed on its validity in every detail.

6. Publications of the National Bureau issued for informational purposes concerning the work of the Bureau and its staff, or issued to inform the public of activities of Bureau staff, and volumes issued as a result of various conferences involving the National Bureau shall contain a specific disclaimer noting that such publication has not passed through the normal review procedures required in this resolution. The Executive Committee of the Board is charged with review of all such publications from time to time to ensure that they do not take on the character of formal research reports of the National Bureau, requiring formal Board approval.

7. Unless otherwise determined by the Board or exempted by the terms of paragraph 6, a copy of this resolution shall be printed in each National Bureau publication.

(Resolution adopted October 25, 1926, as revised through September 30, 1974)

To My Father

Contents

Acknowledgments

This book developed from a line of research that I have pursued for several years. In the process I built up an intellectual debt to many individuals who provided me with comments on my work and, by so doing, improved it substantially. My former colleague, Andrew Abel, is owed the greatest debt. Part of this book—Chapter 3 and Appendix 2.1 to Chapter 2—is based on joint research we worked on together at the University of Chicago. Andy not only stimulated my thinking in this line of research but also showed me how much fun joint work can be. I also thank the following other individuals who gave me valuable comments: Ben Bernanke, John Bilson, Olivier Blanchard, Edwin Burmeister, Dennis Carlton, Eugene Fama, Robert Flood, Jacob Frenkel, David Galenson, Peter Garber, Clive Granger, Nathaniel Gregory, Lars Hansen, Fumio Hayashi, Dennis Hoffman, John Huizinga, Stephen LeRoy, Robert Lucas, Thomas Mayer, Bennet McCallum, Merton Miller, Ronald Michener, Michael Mussa, A. R. Nobay, Charles Plosser, Thomas Sargent, Don Schlagenhauf, William Schwert, Steven Sheffrin, Robert Shiller, Kenneth Singleton, Gary Skoog, and Mark Watson. I benefited from comments at seminars where I presented preliminary versions of this work—at the American Economic Association winter meetings; Cornell University; the University of California at Berkeley, at Davis, and at San Diego; the University of Chicago; the University of Pennsylvania; the University of Michigan; the Université de Montreal; the University of Virginia; the Massachusetts Institute of Technology; the National Bureau of Economic Research; and New York University. The students in my Economics 431 course during the Winter of 1982 at the University of Chicago performed the role of human guinea pigs by subjecting themselves to my teaching of this book. Their reactions and comments are greatly appreciated.

I thank June Nason and Alyce Monroe for their typing services, and Alan Brazil and Douglas McTaggart for excellent research assistance.

This book makes use of material from my articles published in *American Economic Review, Journal of Finance, Journal of Monetary Economics*, and *Journal of Political Economy*. I am grateful to each of these journals for permission to use material from these articles.

Research support from the National Science Foundation (NSF grants SES-7912655 and SES-8112004) is gratefully acknowledged. This work is part of the National Bureau of Economic Research's Program in Economic Fluctuations. The usual disclaimer applies.

1   Introduction

The recognition in recent years that expectations are extremely important to economic decision making has led to a major revolution in macroeconomic analysis. The rational expectations hypothesis developed initially by Muth (1961) has played a critical role in this revolution. Simply put, it states that expectations reflected in market behavior will be optimal forecasts using all available information. (A more precise definition will be developed in Chap. 2.) When this hypothesis is employed to describe expectations formation, serious doubts arise about the use of existing large-scale macroeconometric models for policy analysis (Lucas 1976). With additional assumptions about labor market behavior, the effectiveness of any deterministic policy rule to promote macroeconomic stabilization is even called into question (Sargent and Wallace 1975).

The rational expectations hypothesis has significant implications as well for the way macroeconometric models should be estimated. It leads to serious doubts about the traditional criteria for identifying and estimating these models—the exclusion of variables from some behavioral equations and not from others (Sims 1980). Yet we are not left helpless, because it does provide restrictions of a different sort which do allow identification and estimation, restrictions applying across equations (Sargent 1981).

This book pursues a rational expectations approach to macroeconometrics, yet it is not a comprehensive treatment of the subject. Instead it explores a particular class of models, widely discussed in the macroeconomics literature, which emphasize the effects from unanticipated, rather than anticipated, movements in variables. In these models, cross-equation restrictions implied by rational expectations are of central importance. These restrictions can be a powerful tool of analysis, making it easier to isolate the phenomenon we want to study. The following chapters will discuss and develop theoretically a unified econometric treatment of these models, and the resulting empirical analysis, based on Mishkin (1981a, 1981b, 1982a, 1982b, 1982c), will provide evidence on some of the more important macro issues debated today.

How does the econometric methodology in this book fit into the overall subject of rational expectations macroeconometrics? Other econometric methodology recently developed is designed to analyze models where more structure has been imposed than in the class of models discussed here. For example, see Chow (1980), Hansen and Sargent (1980), Sargent (1978), Taylor (1979), and Wallis (1980), all of which can be found in the Lucas and Sargent (1981) collection. Hansen and Sargent (1980) provide a prominent example of this alternative approach to estimating rational expectations models. Their techniques can be used to look at the "deep structure" of economic relationships by estimating parameters describing tastes and technology. This allows the researcher to analyze problems that are out of reach of the techniques described in this book.

However, there are advantages to the econometric approach here. Estimation is simple to execute with the techniques of this book and readily available computer packages, as the following chapter makes clear; this is less true of techniques such as Hansen and Sargent's. Fewer identifying assumptions are required to implement the econometric models analyzed here because the models are less structural. Because economists disagree strenuously about what is the appropriate structure of the economy (see the discussion in Sims 1980), empirical results obtained with fewer identifying assumptions are worth studying. The main conclusion to be drawn from these remarks is not that one set of econometric methodology is preferable to another; rather, all these techniques are needed for us to obtain a better understanding of how the economy works.

Because the investment in reading a book is far greater than that in reading a short journal article, the reader deserves to be convinced that he or she will be involved in a productive activity. The first step in this process is to show that the methodology in this book is well worth studying because it is applicable to a wide range of research problems. With the increasing prominence of rational expectations in the last few years, there has been a veritable explosion in the number of empirical studies that either use or can use the methodology outlined in this book. These include studies of consumption behavior (Bilson 1980; Flavin 1981), the question whether government bonds are net wealth (Plosser 1982), the behavior of foreign exchange markets (Dornbusch 1980; Frenkel 1981; Hartley 1983; Hoffman and Schlagenhauf 1981b), the demand for money (Carr and Darby 1981), money and interest rates (Makin 1981; Mishkin 1981a, 1982c; Shiller 1980), money and stock prices (Rozeff 1974), the rationality of inflation and interest rate forecasts (Mishkin 1981*b*), asset returns and inflation (Bodie 1976; Fama and Schwert 1977, 1979; Jaffee and Mandelkar 1976; Nelson 1976; Schwert 1981), relative price variability and inflation (Fischer 1981), the effects of nominal contracting on stock returns (French, Ruback, and Schwert 1981), stock exchange seats as capital assets (Schwert 1977*a*), regulatory effects of the securities exchange commission (Schwert 1977*b*), costs of financial intermediation and the Great Depression (Bernanke 1982), and the policy ineffectiveness proposition (Barro 1977, 1978, 1979; Barro and Hercowitz 1980; Barro and Rush 1980; Björklund and Holmlund 1981; Germany and Srivastava 1979; Gordon 1979; Grossman 1979; Hoffman and Schlagenhauf 1981*a*; Leiderman 1979, 1980; Makin 1982; Mishkin 1982*a*, 1982*b*; Sargent 1976*a*; Sheffrin 1979; Small 1979; Wogin 1980).

This broad list of empirical topics above should persuade the reader that future research can profit from use of the methodology developed in the following chapters. However, the reader may still want to ask, What specifically is to be gained by reading this book? It is designed to be read on several levels and a brief "road map" of the analysis should help answer this question and save the reader both time and effort. The main body of the book is divided into two parts. Part 1 on econometric theory and methodology is the more technical. It will be of particular interest to the reader already convinced that the class of models analyzed in this book is worth studying, and who may want to pursue empirical work along these lines.

The opening chapter of Part 1 describes the models to be analyzed in this book and discusses the details of their estimation. It covers such theoretical statistical issues as the consistency and efficiency of different estimation procedures. However, it is primarily a practical "how to" chapter that should help the interested researcher to apply the book's econometric techniques. To aid in the applications, an appendix to this chapter contains an annotated computer program that has been used to generate empirical results in Part 2 of the book. This program makes use of a standard econometric package available on many universities' computers and the techniques outlined here should be easily accessible to most researchers. Another purpose of this chapter is to provide sufficient information on the techniques used in the empirical work in the following chapters, so that this work is opened to scientific scrutiny. This chapter, however, also is intended to be a fairly general treatment because the techniques discussed are applicable to many empirical issues not analyzed in this book.

The next chapter treats theoretically the relationship among tests of rationality, market efficiency, and the short-run neutrality of policy. It provides information about how the tests conducted in this book relate to other tests in the literature, and it discusses the circumstances in which the resulting test statistics are generally valid. This chapter is useful in understanding both the empirical tests in this book and some of the previous literature on rational expectations models.

Part 2 is much less technical and contains empirical studies on topics of potentially widespread interest. Chapters in Part 2 will be sufficiently self-contained so as not to require knowledge of Part 1 to be understood. Readers who are interested in the macroeconomic issues studied here but who are not technically inclined, or who are not yet convinced of the value of the econometric techniques, should read this section first. They may then find it worth investing in a careful reading of Part 1.

The opening chapter of Part 2 provides information on the question of whether market forecasts are rational. Recent studies have found that forecasts of interest rates and inflation derived from well-known surveys are not consistent with the rational expectations hypothesis. For reasons discussed in this chapter, the survey measures may not reflect market behavior. We then want to know whether markets display rationality of expectations in contrast to the survey measures. If they do, doubt is cast on the survey measures as a description of market behavior. Tests similar to those conducted on survey data are used to provide evidence on this issue for the bond market. They do cast doubt on the usefulness of these survey measures and indicate for the most part that bond market forecasts are rational.

Chapter 5 explores the relationship of monetary policy with both long- and short-term interest rates. The impact of a money stock increase on nominal interest rates has been hotly debated in the monetary economics literature. The view most commonly held—also a feature of most structural macroeconometric models—has an increase in the money stock leading, at least in the short run, to a decline in interest rates. Monetarists dispute this view because they believe it ignores the dynamic effects of a money stock increase. The use of the rational expectations (or equivalently, the efficient markets) hypothesis in this analysis imposes a theoretical structure on the relationship that permits easier interpretation of the empirical results as well as more powerful statistical tests. In the interest of ascertaining the robustness of the results, many different empirical tests are conducted, and they do not support the proposition that increases in the money supply are correlated with declines in interest rates.

Recent equilibrium business cycle models, which incorporate features of the natural-rate model with the assumption that expectations are rational, lead to an important neutrality result: Anticipated changes in aggregate demand will not evoke an output or employment response. One deterministic policy rule is, therefore, as good as any other from the point of view of stabilizing the economy. Chapter 6 conducts an empirical investigation of this policy ineffectiveness proposition. Not only do the results strongly reject the proposition, but, in addition, unanticipated movements in aggregate demand policy are not found to have a larger impact on output and unemployment than anticipated movements.

The final chapter furnishes some concluding remarks and a general perspective on the empirical results and the econometric methodology.

1 Econometric Theory and Methodology

2   The Econometric Methodology

2.1   The Models

The rational expectations hypothesis asserts that the market's subjective probability distribution of any variable is identical to the objective probability distribution of that variable, conditional on all available past information. Following the literature, we will restrict our attention to linear models and focus only on the first moments of distributions; this yields models which are analytically and empirically more tractable. The rational expectations implication central to this book's analysis is the following: the expectation assessed by the market equals the true conditional expectation using all available past information. For a variable X, this can be written as

$$(1) \qquad E_m(X_t|\phi_{t-1}) = E(X_t|\phi_{t-1}),$$

where

$$\phi_{t-1} = \text{the set of information available at time } t - 1,$$
$$E_m(\ldots|\phi_{t-1}) = \text{the subjective expectation assessed by the market,}$$
$$E(\ldots|\phi_{t-1}) = \text{the objective expectation conditional on } \phi_{t-1}.$$

The application of rational expectations to financial markets—where it is referred to as market efficiency—shows why the rational expectations hypothesis should be taken seriously in explaining empirical phenomena. Tests of market efficiency usually focus on either holding period returns or prices of securities. For example, let y_t denote the return from holding a particular security from $t - 1$ to t, where the return includes both capital gains and intermediate cash income such as dividends or interest payments. Rational expectations, as in equation (1), then implies the following condition:

$$(2) \qquad E[y_t - E_m(y_t|\phi_{t-1})\,|\phi_{t-1}] = 0.$$

The condition above is too general to be testable. To give it empirical content we must specify a model of market equilibrium that relates $E_m(y_t|\phi_{t-1})$ to some subset of past information, Ω_{t-1},

$$(3) \qquad E_m(y_t|\phi_{t-1}) = f(\Omega_{t-1}) = \tilde{y}_t,$$

where Ω_{t-1} is contained in ϕ_{t-1}. For ease of exposition, $f(\Omega_{t-1})$, the representation of the model of market equilibrium, will be denoted by $\tilde{y}_t$. Combining equations (2) and (3) yields the efficient markets condition

$$(4) \qquad E(y_t - \tilde{y}_t|\phi_{t-1}) = 0.$$

This condition implies that $y_t - \tilde{y}_t$ should be uncorrelated with any past available information. When $\tilde{y}$, the equilibrium return (or, in loose parlance, a "normal" return), is viewed as determined by such factors as risk and the covariance of y_t with the overall market return (see Fama 1976a), the above condition can be stated in a slightly different way. Market efficiency, or equivalently rational expectations, implies that no unexploited profit opportunities will exist in securities markets: at today's price, market participants cannot expect to earn a higher than normal return by investing in that security.

The condition in (4) is analogous to an arbitrage condition. Arbitrageurs who are willing to speculate may perceive unexploited profit opportunities and will purchase or sell securities until the price is driven to the point where this condition holds approximately. An example may clarify the intuition behind this argument. Assume that for a security, $y_t - \tilde{y}_t$, which is sometimes called an "excess" return, is positively correlated with some piece of past information known at time $t - 1$, let us say the company's past earnings. If today the company's past earnings are known to be high, then a higher return than normal for this security is to be expected over the subsequent period. This is a contradiction because an unexploited profit opportunity would now exist. Market efficiency implies that, if this opportunity occurred, the security would be bid up in price until the expected return fell to the normal return. The positive correlation between past earnings and the "excess" return for this security would then disappear.

Several costs involved in speculating could drive a wedge between the left- and right-hand side of (4). Because the collection of information is not costless, arbitrageurs would have to be compensated for that cost and others incurred in their activities, as well as for the risk they bear. (Indeed, as Grossman and Stiglitz (1976) point out, if (4) held exactly, efficient-markets theory would imply a paradox. If all information were fully reflected in a market as eq. [4] specifies, obtaining information would have a zero return. Since there would be no incentive to collect information, it would remain uncollected and unknown. The market would then not reflect this information.) Transaction and storage costs would also result in violations of equation (4). Yet financial securities have the key feature of homogeneity, for they are merely paper claims to income on real assets. Transactions and storage costs will then be small, while compensation of arbitrageurs and the cost of collecting information should not be large relative to the total value of securities traded. Thus deviations from the condition in (4) should not be large.

There are two conclusions to be drawn from the discussion above. First, although the efficient markets or rational expectations condition in (4) may not hold exactly, it is an extremely useful approximation for macroeconomic analysis. Second, this condition should be a useful approximation even if not all market participants have expectations that are rational. Indeed, even if most market participants were irrational, we would still expect the market to be rational as long as some market participants stand ready to eliminate unexploited profit opportunities. It is important to emphasize this point when discussing whether survey forecasts should be used in analyzing market behavior, as Chapter 4 indicates.

A model that satisfies the efficient-markets condition in (4) is

$$(5) \qquad y_t = \widetilde{y}_t + (X_t - X_t^e)\beta + \epsilon_t,$$

where

ϵ_t = a disturbance with the property $E(\epsilon_t|\phi_{t-1}) = 0$—thus ϵ_t is serially uncorrelated and uncorrelated with X_t^e;

X_t = the vector containing variables relevant to the pricing of the security at time t;

X_t^e = the vector of one-period-ahead rational forecasts of X_t, that is, $X_t^e = E_m(X_t|\phi_{t-1}) = E(X_t|\phi_{t-1})$;

β = vector of coefficients.

That the model above satisfies (4) is easily verified by taking expectations conditional on ϕ_{t-1} of both sides of (5). This yields

$$(6) \qquad E(y_t|\phi_{t-1}) = E(\widetilde{y}_t|\phi_{t-1}) + E(X_t - X_t^e|\phi_{t-1})\beta$$
$$+ E(\epsilon_t|\phi_{t-1}) = \widetilde{y}_t$$

which clearly satisfies (4).

For expositional convenience, we refer to model (5) as "the efficient-markets model." Note, however, that the model embodies not only market efficiency (or, equivalently, rational expectations) but also a model of market equilibrium. This model stresses that only when new information hits the market will y_t differ from $\widetilde{y}_t$. This is equivalent to the proposition that only unanticipated changes in X_t can be correlated with $y_t - \widetilde{y}_t$.

As the empirical work later in the book demonstrates, the efficient-markets model is useful in attacking such interesting questions as the rationality of interest rate and inflation forecasts in the bond market and the relationship of monetary policy to interest rates. The econometric methodology outlined here is worth studying for this reason alone. Yet it is also worth studying because there are many other applications of the efficient markets model (e.g., Dornbusch 1980; French, Ruback, and Schwert 1981; Frenkel 1981; Hartley 1983; Hoffman and Schlagenhauf 1981*b*; Plosser 1982; Rozeff 1974; Schwert 1977*a*, 1977*b*).

The other model analyzed in the empirical section of this book displays the neutrality property that only unanticipated and not anticipated countercyclical policy will have an effect on business cycle fluctuations. This model displays the policy ineffectiveness proposition of Sargent and Wallace (1975) that a constant money growth rule is not dominated by any rule with feedback. As usually estimated, it has the form

$$(7) \qquad y_t = \widetilde{y}_t + \sum_{i=0}^{N} \beta_i (X_{t-i} - X_{t-i}^e) + \epsilon_t,$$

where

> y_t = unemployment or real output at time t;
> $\widetilde{y}_t$ = natural or equilibrium level of unemployment or real output at time t;
> X_t = an aggregate demand variable, such as money growth, inflation or nominal GNP growth;
> X_t^e = anticipated X_t conditional on information available at $t - 1$;
> β_i = coefficients;
> ϵ_t = error term which might be serially correlated but is assumed to be uncorrelated with the right-hand-side variable.

In the case where the number of lags, N, equals zero and $\widetilde{y}_t$ is a distributed lag on past y_t, this is the model estimated by Sargent (1976*a*). The Barro (1977, 1978) model has $N > 0$ and $\widetilde{y}_t$ is represented as a time trend or a linear combination of such variables as the minimum wage and a measure of military conscription. Other empirical applications of this model include Barro 1979; Barro and Hercowitz 1980; Barro and Rush 1980; Björkland and Holmlund 1981; Germany and Srivastava 1979; Gordon 1979; Grossman 1979; Hoffman and Schlagenhauf 1981*a*; Leiderman 1979, 1980; Makin 1982; Sheffrin 1979; Small 1979; and Wogin 1980. Following Modigliani (1977), this model will be referred to as the Macro Rational Expectations (MRE) model.

The methodology discussed here is also worth studying for its useful applications in many recent empirical studies which analyze the differential effects of anticipated versus unanticipated movements in explanatory variables. These studies make use of the general model

$$(8) \qquad y_t = \widetilde{y}_t + \sum_{i=0}^{N} \beta_i (X_{t-i} - X_{t-i}^e) + \sum_{i=0}^{N} \delta_i X_{t-i}^e + \epsilon_t$$

for different definitions of y_t, $\tilde{y}_t$, and X_t. They include Bernanke 1982; Bilson 1980; Bodie 1976; Carr and Darby 1981; Fama and Schwert 1977, 1979; Fischer 1981; Flavin 1981; Jaffee and Mandelkar 1976; Makin 1981; Nelson 1976; Schwert 1981; and Shiller 1980.

2.2   The Methodology

2.2.1   Estimation and Testing

The form of the efficient-markets equation is just a special case of the MRE equation where $N = 0$; hence the discussion here needs to focus only on the estimation and testing methodology for equations (7) and (8). To simplify the exposition, we will limit ourselves to the case where X_t is a single variable. Modifications of the analysis for the case where X_t is a vector of variables is straightforward.

Rational expectations implies that the anticipations of X_t will be formed optimally, using all available information, and, as is usual in the literature, forecasting models are assumed to be linear. A forecasting equation that can be used to generate these anticipations is

$$(9) \qquad X_t = Z_{t-1}\gamma + u_t,$$

where

Z_{t-1} = a vector of variables used to forecast X_t which are available at time $t - 1$ (this includes variables known at $t - 1, t - 2, t - 3$, etc.),

γ = a vector of coefficients,

u_t = an error term which is assumed to be uncorrelated with any information available at $t - 1$ (which includes Z_{t-1} or u_{t-1} for all $i \geq 1$, and hence u_t is serially uncorrelated).

An optimal forecast for X_t then simply involves taking expectations of equation (2) conditional on information available at $t - 1$. Hence

$$(10) \qquad X_t^e = Z_{t-1}\gamma,$$

and, substituting into equation (7), we have

$$(11) \qquad y_t = \tilde{y}_t + \sum_{i=0}^{N} \beta_i(X_{t-i} - Z_{t-1-i}\gamma) + \epsilon_t.$$

Two identification problems occur in the equation (11) model. Some assumption about the correlation of the error term, ϵ, and the right-hand-side variables is necessary in order to identify the β coefficients. The usual assumption—the one that is used in the tests here as well as in previous empirical work on this subject—holds that all the right-hand-side variables are exogenous and are uncorrelated with the error term. This assumption, that (11) is a true reduced form, implies that least-squares estimation methods will yield consistent estimates of the β's.

The other identification problem has been raised by Sargent (1976b). If Z_{t-1} includes only lagged values of X_t and there are no restrictions on the lag length N, the MRE model in (11) is observationally equivalent to "an unnatural rate model" where anticipated aggregate demand policy also matters. Hence, in this case, we cannot distinguish between the two competing hypotheses. To see Sargent's point, we can write the forecasting equation where only lagged X's are explanatory variables as,

$$(12) \qquad X_t = \gamma(L)X_{t-1} + u_t,$$

where

$$\gamma(L) = \text{polynomial in the lag operator } L = \sum_{i=1}^{\infty} \gamma_i L^i.$$

Taking expectations of (12) conditional on ϕ_{t-1} and substituting into (7) where N is not restricted, we have the MRE model

$$(13) \qquad y_t = \tilde{y}_t + \sum_{i=0}^{\infty} \beta_i[X_{t-i} - \gamma(L)X_{t-i-1}] + \epsilon_t,$$

and this can be written as

$$(14) \qquad y_t = \tilde{y}_t + \sum_{i=0}^{\infty} \psi_i X_{t-i} + \epsilon_t,$$

where

$$\psi_o = \beta_o,$$
$$\psi_i = \beta_i - \sum_{j=0}^{i-1} \beta_j \gamma_{i-j-1} \text{ for } i \geq 1.$$

If the forecasting equation in (12) is used to derive expectations in equation (8) where anticipated as well as unanticipated aggregate demand matters, we have

$$(15) \qquad y_t = \tilde{y}_t + \sum_{i=0}^{\infty} \beta_i[X_{t-i} - \gamma(L)X_{t-i-1}]$$
$$+ \sum_{i=0}^{\infty} \delta_i \gamma(L)X_{t-i-1} + \epsilon_t$$

which also can be written as (14), where

$$\psi_o = \beta_o$$
$$\psi_i = \beta_i + \sum_{j=0}^{i-1} (\delta_j - \beta_j)\gamma_{i-j-1} \text{ for } i \geq 1.$$

Because both models can be written down as (14), the two models are observationally equivalent: that is, the data cannot discriminate between them because parameters are unidentified.

The problem of observational equivalence has arisen in empirical work on whether anticipated aggregate demand policy matters, in particular, Grossman (1979). Grossman analyzes the MRE model where the aggregate demand variable is nominal GNP growth. His forecasting equation, however, includes only lags of nominal GNP growth as explanatory variables. Because of the resulting observational equivalence problem, Grossman cannot and does not test whether the anticipated nominal GNP growth variables have significant additional explanatory power. Instead, he reports results supporting the MRE hypothesis which rely on flimsy grounds for identification, namely, the assumption that the lag length on nominal GNP growth cuts off at six quarters.

It is possible to discriminate between the two competing models by means of identifying restrictions. These are derived by checking what conditions must be imposed to keep the MRE model and the model in which anticipated aggregate demand matters from being observationally equivalent. This exercise is carried out in Appendix 2.1. The observational equivalence problem is overcome, parameters are identified, and tests of the MRE model are feasible, by either of two conditions particularly important in this book's empirical applications. They are: (1) N is known to be zero, as in the efficient markets model; or (2) Z_{t-1} includes lagged values of at least one other variable besides X which does not enter equation (11) separately from the $\beta_i(X_{t-i} - Z_{t-1-i}\gamma)$ terms.

The method for estimating the MRE model involves joint, nonlinear estimation of the equations (9) and (11) system, which we rewrite as

(16)
$$X_t = Z_{t-1}\gamma + u_t,$$
$$y_t = \tilde{y}_t + \sum_{i=0}^{N} (X_{t-i} - Z_{t-1-i}\gamma)\beta_i + \epsilon_t.$$

System (16) embodies two sets of constraints. Rationality of expectations is imposed since the coefficient γ which appears in the equation for X_t also appears in the equation for y_t. The neutrality property, that anticipated policy is not correlated with $y_t - \tilde{y}_t$, is also imposed because the δ coefficients on X_{t-i}^e are constrained to be zero. Relaxing the neutrality and rationality constraints, the system (16) becomes

(17)
$$X_t = Z_{t-1}\gamma + u_t,$$
$$y_t = \tilde{y}_t + \sum_{i=0}^{N} (X_{t-i} - Z_{t-1-i}\gamma^*)\beta_i$$
$$+ \sum_{i=0}^{N} Z_{t-1-i}\gamma^*\delta_i + \epsilon_t.$$

A likelihood ratio test comparing both the constrained system (16) and the unconstrained system (17) provides a joint test of both the rationality constraints $\gamma = \gamma^*$ and the neutrality constraints $\delta_i = 0$, conditional on the maintained hypothesis of the model of equilibrium output. Note that (17) can also be written as

(18)
$$X_t = Z_{t-1}\gamma^* + u_t,$$

$$y_t = \tilde{y}_t + \sum_{i=0}^{N} \beta_i'(X_{t-i} - Z_{t-1-i}\gamma) + \sum_{i=0}^{N} \delta_i X_{t-i} + \epsilon_t,$$

where $\beta_i' = \beta_i - \delta_i$. This is the form used by Barro (1977) in his tests of neutrality.

As an alternative to relaxing both the neutrality and the rationality constraints, we can relax one set of constraints only. For example, maintaining the hypothesis of rationality but relaxing the assumption of neutrality, system (16) becomes

(19)
$$X_t = Z_{t-1}\gamma + u_t,$$

$$y_t = \tilde{y}_t + \sum_{i=0}^{N} (X_{t-i} - Z_{t-1-i}\gamma)\beta_i + \sum_{i=0}^{N} Z_{t-1-i}\gamma\delta_i + \epsilon_t.$$

Under the maintained hypothesis of rational expectations, the null hypothesis of neutrality, that is, $\delta_i = 0$, can be tested by comparing the estimated systems (16) and (19).

Rather than maintain the hypothesis of rationality of expectations and then test for neutrality, one can maintain the hypothesis of neutrality and then test for rationality. The unconstrained system used to perform this test is:

(20)
$$X_t = Z_{t-1}\gamma + u_t,$$

$$y_t = \tilde{y}_t + \sum_{i=0}^{N} (X_{t-i} - Z_{t-1-i}\gamma^*)\beta_i + \epsilon_t.$$

A comparison of the estimated systems (16) and (20) provides a test of the null hypothesis of rationality, that is, $\gamma = \gamma^*$, under the maintained hypothesis of neutrality. In the efficient-markets case where $N = 0$, neutrality is a reasonable maintained hypothesis since the absence of neutrality would indicate the presence of unexploited profit opportunities. It must be noted, however, that a rejection of the null hypothesis that $\gamma = \gamma^*$ may result from a breakdown of rationality, neutrality, or the model of market equilibrium. Furthermore, as is demonstrated in Appendix 2.1, when $N = 0$ this test is equivalent to that generated by comparing the systems (16) and (17), which jointly tests $\delta_0 = 0$ and $\gamma = \gamma^*$.

The χ^2 statistic for the joint hypothesis of rationality and neutrality can be partitioned into the contribution from each component hypothesis by relaxing the constraints sequentially. These constraints can be relaxed in two different orders. A priori economic reasoning may suggest an appropriate sequence for relaxing constraints. For example, in testing whether anticipated policy is correlated with output, it seems appropriate first to relax $\delta_i = 0$ and test neutrality under the maintained hypothesis of rationality. Then, without maintaining neutrality, the constraint $\gamma = \gamma^*$ can be relaxed, and rationality can be tested. This is the procedure that is followed in tests of the MRE hypothesis in Chapter 6.

Under the alternative sequence for relaxing constraints, we first relax the constraint $\gamma = \gamma^*$ and test for rationality under the maintained hypothesis of neutrality. The next step in relaxing constraints permits a test of neutrality without maintaining the hypothesis of rational expectations. Yet neutrality has meaning only if we have a theory of expectations such as rational expectations. Realize that the test of neutrality is conducted on the assumption that the expectations of X_t in the second equation of the system (17) are formed with the same information set Z_{t-1} as the time-series model of X_t in the first equation. Yet, if we are not willing to assume that expectations are rational, there seems to be no reason to assume that the same set of variables belongs in Z in both equations in (17). Therefore, it is not clear that this test yields useful information.

One way to generate the likelihood ratio statistics for the above tests is to estimate both the constrained and unconstrained systems with full-information-maximum-likelihood (FIML). Estimation proceeds under the identifying assumption used in previous research on the MRE hypothesis, that the y equation is a true reduced form.[1] This assumption implies that the covariance of the error terms in the two equations of the system is zero. The estimated variance-covariance matrix of the residuals is then

(21)
$$\hat{\Sigma} = \begin{bmatrix} \dfrac{\mathrm{SSR}_X}{n} & 0 \\[2mm] 0 & \dfrac{\mathrm{SSR}_y}{n} \end{bmatrix}$$

where

SSR_X = the sum of squared residuals of the X equation,
SSR_y = the sum of squared residuals of the y equation,
n = the number of observations.

The systems analyzed here are triangular, so FIML involves maximizing the concentrated log likelihood function,

(22)
$$\log L = \text{constant} - \frac{n}{2} \log (\det \hat{\Sigma}),$$

---

1. In the case where $N = 0$, even if the asumption is untrue, its imposition will not invalidate the test statistics (see Chap. 3). However, it is not clear that this desirable result—that the assumption does not matter to the tests of interest here—carries over to the case where $N > 0$.

where det $\hat{\Sigma}$ = determinant of $\hat{\Sigma}$. The resulting likelihood ratio statistic

(23) $$-2 \log \left[\frac{L^c(\hat{\Sigma}^c)}{L^u(\hat{\Sigma}^u)} \right] = n \log (\det \hat{\Sigma}^c / \det \hat{\Sigma}^u)$$

is distributed asymptotically as $\chi^2(q)$, where

q = the number of constraints (Appendix 2.1 discusses how to count them),
L^c = maximized likelihood of the constrained system,
L^u = maximized likelihood of the unconstrained system,
$\hat{\Sigma}^c$ = the resulting estimated $\hat{\Sigma}$ for the constrained system,
$\hat{\Sigma}^u$ = the resulting estimated $\hat{\Sigma}$ for the unconstrained system.

Comparison of this statistic with the critical $\chi^2(q)$ then tests the null hypothesis.

Test procedures used in this book proceed in a slightly different way from that described above, in that they make use of nonlinear least-squares estimation. Estimation is conducted with nonlinear least squares primarily for algorithmic reasons. FIML computer packages are usually not capable of handling large numbers of parameters, and this is required in some of the models analyzed empirically in this book. In addition, FIML packages do not allow us easily to impose the necessary covariance restrictions in (21) or to make a desirable degree of freedom correction, described below, which results in more conservative likelihood ratio statistics. In contrast, the nonlinear least-squares procedure outlined here easily implements the covariance restriction and degrees-of-freedom correction and makes use of a computer package (SAS Institute 1979) that can estimate systems with large numbers of parameters.

The procedure is as follows. Given an initial estimate for the variance-covariance matrix of the residuals, $\hat{\Sigma}$, estimate the system with nonlinear generalized least-squares (GLS). (The initial $\hat{\Sigma}$ can be obtained from unconstrained ordinary least-squares estimates of the X and y equations or from previously estimated systems.) Given the particular diagonal form of the $\hat{\Sigma}$ matrix, nonlinear GLS is equivalent to nonlinear weighted least squares (WLS) using the estimates from $\hat{\Sigma}$: that is, the observations for the X forecasting equation are weighted by $\sqrt{SSR_X/SSR_y}$. Appendix 2.2 contains an annotated computer program describing this procedure in great detail. A new $\hat{\Sigma}$ matrix can be estimated using the resulting residuals and the system reestimated again with nonlinear WLS. This iterative procedure is continued until there is little change in the $\hat{\Sigma}$ matrix. Because the system is triangular, this procedure will converge to maximum-likelihood estimates, since theorems showing that iterative three-stage-least-squares is equivalent to FIML then apply to this nonlinear case as well. High computation costs required that iterations were continued only until the estimated variance of all the weighted equations in the system differed by less than 5 percent. Some experimentation indicated that further iterations would have altered the likelihood ratio statistics in the book by at most 1 or 2 percent. This would only lead to a negligible effect on the inference drawn from these statistics.[2]

If the same procedure is followed for estimating the unconstrained system, then the likelihood ratio statistic in (23) is easily calculated and can be used to test the null hypothesis. Although (23) yields valid asymptotic tests, it could be misleading in a small sample like that used here. The problem is that, in the maximum-likelihood calculation of the $\hat{\Sigma}^u$ matrix of the unconstrained system, no correction is made for substantial relative differences in the degrees of freedom in estimates of each unconstrained equation. Thus the finite sample distribution of the test statistic might differ substantially from the asymptotic distribution. For example, in Chapter 6, model 2.1 (see tables 6.1 and 6.2), the unconstrained money growth equation is estimated with 79 degrees of freedom, while the unconstrained output equation is estimated with only 70 degrees of freedom. This is a difference of over 10 percent. The problem is even more severe in the case of model A16.1 (see tables 6.A.16 and 6.A.17) in Appendix 6.3 of Chapter 6: the degrees of freedom for the unconstrained money growth and output equations are now 79 and 32, respectively, a difference of 50 percent. Another way of stating this problem is to say that the weighting matrix for GLS will have a biased estimate of the variance of one equation relative to another. The bias occurs because the estimated variances are the maximum-likelihood estimates (the sum of squared residuals divided by the number of observations in each equation) rather than the unbiased estimates (the sum of squared residuals divided by the degrees of freedom).

The likelihood ratio statistics reported here are corrected for the small sample problem as follows: the constrained system is estimated with the iterative procedure, and the resulting $\hat{\Sigma}^c$ matrix from the constrained system is then again used with nonlinear WLS to estimate the unconstrained system. This corrects the degrees-of-freedom problem because, in the systems where there are cross-equation constraints, the degrees of freedom do not differ across equations. Thus $\hat{\Sigma}^c$ does not suffer from the degrees-of-freedom problem of $\hat{\Sigma}^u$. The resulting likelihood ratio statistic, which is also distributed asymptotically as $\chi^2(q)$ under the null hypothesis, is (Goldfeld and Quandt 1972)

$$(24) \qquad -2 \log \left[\frac{L^c(\hat{\Sigma}^c)}{L^u(\hat{\Sigma}^c)} \right] = 2n \log (\text{SSR}^c/\text{SSR}^u),$$

---

2. In the empirical analysis in this book, when Goldfeld-Quandt (1965) tests revealed the presence of heteroscedasticity within an equation, the time-trend procedure outlined by Glesjer (1969) was used to weight each observation to eliminate this heteroscedasticity.

where the superscripts on the $\hat{\Sigma}$ indicate that the maximized likelihoods of both the constrained and unconstrained systems were estimated with the same weighting matrix $\hat{\Sigma}^c$ and

SSR^c = the sum of squared residuals from the constrained weighted system,

SSR^u = the sum of squared residuals from the unconstrained weighted system.

Although asymptotically the two test statistics are equivalent, in finite samples the likelihood ratio statistic in (24) is smaller than the alternative in (23) and is more conservative on rejecting the null hypothesis.[3] To see this, realize that $L^u(\hat{\Sigma}^u) \geq L^u(\hat{\Sigma}^c)$, which implies

$$(25) \qquad -2 \log \left[\frac{L^c(\hat{\Sigma}^c)}{L^u(\hat{\Sigma}^c)} \right] \leq -2 \log \left[\frac{L^c(\hat{\Sigma}^c)}{L^u(\hat{\Sigma}^u)} \right].$$

Using (24) rather than (23) will thus give more credibility to rejections if they occur.

One issue concerning estimation remains to be discussed. Since the standard test statistics assume serially uncorrelated error terms, we need to eliminate serial correlation from the residuals. If this is not done, then, as Granger and Newbold (1974) and Plosser and Schwert (1978) have pointed out, we are likely to encounter the spurious regression phenomenon, where significant relationships appear in the data only because there has been no correction for serial correlation. As long as we include lagged dependent variables in the forecasting equation there should be little serial correlation in the u_t residuals and no serial correlation correction will be needed. In the case of the efficient-markets model, theory specifies that $E(\epsilon_t | \phi_{t-1}) = 0$ and hence ϵ_t should be serially uncorrelated. Again no serial correlation correction is needed. However, in the MRE output or unemployment model there is no theoretical argument guaranteeing that the error term is serially uncorrelated. To correct for potential serial correlation and thus avoid the spurious regression problem, the

---

3. The likelihood ratio statistics here are frequently not appreciably different whether they are calculated using (23) or (24). E.g., in Chapter 6's model 2.1 the likelihood ratio statistic for the joint hypothesis calculated from (23) is 22.81 vs. the value 22.69 reported in table 6.1. In the models found in Appendix 3 (Chapter 6), which use up more degrees of freedom, the difference between statistics calculated from (23) and (24) is more appreciable: e.g., in model A.16.1 the likelihood ratio statistic for the joint hypothesis calculated from (23) is 76.33 vs. the value 66.90 reported in table 6.A.13. Note that the statistic in (24) is essentially the statistic for a Lagrange multiplier test where the percentage change in the sum of squares is approximated by a change in the logs. It is well known that the Lagrange multiplier test is less likely to reject the null hypothesis than a likelihood ratio test, so these results are not surprising. For a further discussion of the Lagrange multiplier test, see Engle (1980).

error term in the MRE output or unemployment models estimated later is assumed to be a fourth-order autoregressive process. This specification for the error term was chosen because fourth-order autoregressions usually eliminate most serial correlation in quarterly, macro time series. Indeed, Durbin-Watson statistics and the residual autocorrelations of the estimated models indicate that this correction for serial correlation is successful in reducing the residuals to white noise.

2.2.2   Specification of the Forecasting Equation

Rational expectations theory implies that X_t^e is an optimal, one-period-ahead forecast, conditional on available information. Thus an appropriate forecasting equation for X_t should rely only on lagged explanatory variables. Economic theory may not be very valuable in generating an accurate model of expectations formation because it is difficult on theoretical grounds to exclude any piece of information available at time $t - 1$ from the Z vector as a useful predictor of a policy variable. Any particular variable may be a useful predictor of X_t even if there is no strong theoretical reason to include it in the Z_{t-1} vector, because the personalities involved in policymaking may be such that they react to this variable nonetheless. For example, if the Board of Governors of the Federal Reserve System were to link monetary policy to the level of unemployment, even though there is no good reason for doing so in a world where the policy ineffectiveness proposition holds, we would still expect to find that the unemployment rate would be highly useful in predicting money growth. This suggests that an atheoretical statistical procedure may be superior to economic theory for deciding on the forecasting equation's specification.

Two procedures are used in this book to specify the forecasting equations. The simplest uses univariate time-series models of the autoregressive type. In the empirical studies later in the book these models are usually subject to unstable coefficients and, more important, should only be used in the efficient-markets model where $N = 0$ because of the observational equivalence problem discussed earlier. Multivariate forecasting models are therefore needed. The Granger (1969) "causality" concept is a natural way to approach the specification of the multivariate models. A variable Z is said to Granger-cause another variable X, if X can be predicted better from past values of Z and X than from past values of X alone. Our forecasting equation for X should definitely include lagged values of X to eliminate any serial correlation in the residuals. If Z Ganger-causes X, then it should be used also in an optimal forecast of X. Hence, as is also argued in Sargent (1981), it belongs as an explanatory variable in the forecasting equation. Note that the issue here is the predictive content of information—which is what Granger-causality is really meant to analyze—and does not involve the tricky concept and issue of economic causality which has led to so much confusion in the literature (see Zellner 1979).

The Granger-criterion for specifying the multivariate forecasting equation is as follows. The X variable is regressed on its own four lagged values (four lags usually ensure white noise residuals in the quarterly data used in this study) as well as on four lagged values of a wide-ranging set of macro variables. The four lagged values of each of these variables are retained in the equation only if they are jointly significant at some marginal significance level (the 5 percent level is one choice). This procedure has the advantage of imposing a discipline on the researcher that prevents his searching for a forecasting equation specification that yields results confirming his prior on the validity of the null hypothesis. Note that a stepwise regression procedure might miss significant explanatory variables because of the order that it chooses to run the regressions. Some judgment must be used in conducting a more general search to find a specification that includes any variables with significant explanatory power.

2.2.3 Specification of the Lag Length, N

The theory of efficient markets indicates that only contemporaneous surprises will be correlated with $y_t - \tilde{y}_t$, and hence $N = 0$. However, the theoretical framework for the MRE model does not specify what the lag length, N, should be. For example, McCallum (1979a) argues that if all the state variables are included in the MRE output or unemployment equation, then the theory does imply that $N = 0$. However, since relevant state variables are almost surely excluded from estimated MRE equations, the lag length is not known. In studying the MRE model here, a primary objective is to obtain information on the robustness of results. As discussed in Leamer (1978), experimenting with plausible, less restrictive models is a necessary strategy for verifying robustness of results.

The addition of irrelevant variables to an estimated model only has the disadvantage of a potential decrease in power of the likelihood ratio tests so that we would be less likely to reject the null hypothesis if it were untrue. It will not result in invalid test statistics; that is, the test statistics will have the assumed asymptotic distributions. However, excluding relevant variables will render test statistics invalid. Furthermore, because rejections of the null hypothesis are less likely when the power of a test is reduced by the addition of irrelevant variables, a rejection in this case at a standard significance level is even stronger evidence against the null hypothesis. This is the rationale behind Leamer's (1978) suggestion that when the power of a test decreases—that is, the probability of Type II error increases—then the significance level used to signify rejection should be increased as well. The reasoning above suggests that less restrictive models with longer lags are worth studying, and they are a feature of the later empirical work.

2.2.4   Specification of $\tilde{y}$

Depending on the model studied, many different specifications of $\tilde{y}_t$ may be appropriate. This becomes apparent in the empirical analysis later in the book. Is a correct specification of $\tilde{y}_t$ always a necessary requirement for generating reliable tests of the models described here? This question is particularly important because some specifications of $\tilde{y}_t$ used in the empirical studies in this book are crude, which makes us suspect that they may not be entirely accurate.

The answer to this question is central to an understanding of much of the empirical literature on efficient markets and the policy ineffectiveness proposition. For example, tests of market efficiency have often assumed that $\tilde{y}_t$, the equilibrium nominal return on a security such as a stock or bond, is constant. This is clearly a very crude model of market equilibrium, and we might expect that it will result in a rejection of the efficient-markets model. Yet this often does not occur. Why? The answer is that as long as the variation of $\tilde{y}_t$ is small relative to the variation of $y_t - \tilde{y}_t$, then the specification of $\tilde{y}_t$ will have little impact on tests of the efficient-markets model. The reason in this case is that the correct $\tilde{y}_t$ model will only explain a small percentage of the variation in y_t and thus will have little explanatory power. Then alterations in the $\tilde{y}_t$ specification will make little difference to the fit of the model and hence to its test statistics. This is what we would expect to find in cases where the security is long-lived, such as a long-term bond or common stock, and the holding period is short, say three months. Then the actual return, y_t, has large variation, while any reasonable model of market equilibrium for $\tilde{y}_t$ indicates that it has only small variation. It is exactly in such cases as these where the crude model of the constancy of $\tilde{y}_t$ does not lead to rejections of market efficiency.

The interested reader can find a further discussion of this issue along with clarifying figures in Fama (1976a). The point raised here has been made in a different context by Nelson and Schwert (1977) in their comment on Fama (1975). They stress that, if $\tilde{y}_t$ has little variation relative to that of $y_t - \tilde{y}_t$, then tests for the specifications of $\tilde{y}_t$ have little statistical power.

Proponents of equilibrium or natural rate models in which the policy ineffectiveness proposition holds usually emphasize deviations from the natural rate in their explanations of unemployment or output. This emphasis makes sense because they believe that the bulk of the cyclical variation in unemployment or output can be attributed to these deviations. This is exactly the case in which the variation in $\tilde{y}_t$ (removing its trend, if there is one, as in the output case) is small relative to the variation in $y_t - \tilde{y}_t$. Then, as is argued above, tests of the policy ineffectiveness proposition are insensitive to the specification of the model for the natural rate of unemployment or output (as long as the trend is removed).

2.3   A Comparison with Previous Methodology

Previous empirical work has tested the neutrality implications of the MRE hypothesis. How does the methodology of this chapter compare with that used in the work cited earlier?

Barro (1977, 1979), Barro and Rush (1980), and Small (1979), among others, use a two-step procedure. They first estimate a forecasting equation by ordinary least squares (OLS) over the sample period and calculate the residuals, that is,

$$(26) \qquad \hat{u}_t = X_t - Z_{t-1}\hat{\gamma}$$

Then the residuals are used as the unanticipated aggregate demand variable in the MRE y equation,

$$(27) \qquad y_t = \tilde{y}_t + \sum_{i=0}^{N} \beta_i \hat{u}_{t-i} + \epsilon_t$$

which is then also estimated by OLS. Another way of describing this two-step procedure is to say that the γ in the y equation is assumed to equal the OLS estimate of γ from the forecasting equation. Tests of the neutrality proposition then involve adding current and lagged values of X to the y equation to yield an equation similar to (18),

$$(28) \qquad y_t = \tilde{y}_t + \sum_{i=0}^{N} \beta_i' \hat{u}_{t-i} + \sum_{i=0}^{N} \delta_i X_{t-i} + \epsilon_t,$$

and testing with a standard F test the null hypothesis that the δ coefficients of X_{t-i} are equal to zero.

This methodology raises several issues, the most important of which deal with the econometrics. The two-step procedure will yield consistent parameter estimates. However, it does not generate valid F test statistics. This procedure implicitly assumes that there is no uncertainty in the estimate of $\hat{\gamma}$. This results in inconsistent estimates of the standard errors of the parameters and hence test statistics that do not have the assumed F distribution. This can lead to inappropriate inference (see Pagan [1981] for a formal proof of this statement).

The joint estimation procedure generates valid test statistics because it does not ignore the uncertainty in the estimate of γ. It has two other advantages over the two-step procedure. The joint procedure will result in more efficient estimates of parameters because the X and y equations each make use of the other's information in the estimation process. The joint procedure also generates tests of both the neutrality and rationality implications of the MRE hypothesis, whereas the two-step procedure cannot test for rationality and is capable of testing only for neutrality.

What relationship exists between tests of neutrality using the joint versus the two-step procedure? Is the joint procedure more likely than the two-step procedure to lead to a rejection of neutrality? The answer is no: the opposite is true. By the nature of likelihood maximization in constrained systems, the joint procedure must attain as high or higher a likelihood than if the forecasting equation is forced to remain unchanged, as in the two-step procedure. The likelihood ratio statistic from the joint procedure should be smaller than the corresponding statistic from the two-step procedure. Therefore, the joint estimation procedure used in this book will be even more favorable to the neutrality hypothesis.

That the two-step procedure is biased toward rejecting neutrality and is less favorable to this null hypothesis than the joint procedure is borne out by a comparison of actual neutrality tests using both procedures. For example, in Chapter 6, model 4.1 (see table 6.4), the likelihood ratio statistic from the two-step procedure testing the neutrality constraints is $\chi^2(4) = 22.14$, with a marginal significance level of .0002 rejecting neutrality. The corresponding F statistic is $F(4,78) = 5.31$ with a marginal significance level of .0008. (The marginal significance level is the probability of obtaining as high a value of the test statistic or higher under the null hypothesis. A marginal significance level less than .01 indicates rejection of the null hypothesis at the 1 percent level.) In table 6.1, the test statistic using the joint procedure is only $\chi^2(4) = 15.45$, with a marginal significance level of .0039. Obviously, the bias of the two-step procedure against the neutrality null hypothesis is not negligible.

The two-step procedure suffers also from a conceptual problem more minor than the econometric criticisms of the procedure. It assumes that the OLS $\hat{\gamma}$, the estimate of γ which minimizes the mean-squared forecasting error, is used in forming expectations in the y equation. Rationality of expectations implies only that subjective probability distributions do not differ from the true probability distributions. This implies that the γ which is *expected* to minimize the mean-squared forecasting error is used in forming expectations and not the *actual* $\hat{\gamma}$ which minimizes the mean-squared error. Thus, in finite samples, the two-step procedure makes an overly strong assumption about expectations formation. This criticism is another way of stating the conceptual difficulty with using regression equations to measure anticipations of variable values early in the sample period when later data are used in estimating the regression relationship. Anticipations are made with information from the future as well as from the past, which clearly goes beyond the rational expectations principle. Note that the joint estimation procedure does not suffer from this problem. As rationality implies in this case, the γ which is expected to minimize the mean-squared forecasting error is used to form expectations in the y equation. As a practical matter, however, this criticism of the two-step procedure is not extremely important, because the OLS $\hat{\gamma}$'s are not very different from the jointly estimated $\hat{\gamma}$'s and asymptomatically they will not differ.

One last point about estimation methodology is worth discussing. Someone used to analyzing the neutrality proposition with the two-step procedure will tend to focus on the deterioration in fit from the imposition of the neutrality constraints of the y equation alone. Such a tendency will be highly misleading in the case of the estimated equations from the joint procedure. In the joint estimation procedure, if constraints are imposed on the y equation, the deterioration in fit is spread over both this equation and the forecasting equation. Thus the deterioration in the y equation fit will not be as severe as when the fit of the forecasting equation is not allowed to change, as in the two-step procedure. However, the likelihood ratio statistic in either (23) or (24) demonstrates that the deterioration of fit in both equations is involved in testing constraints. Therefore, strong rejections can occur even though there is only a small decline in R^2 (or rise in the standard error) of the y equation.[4]

The specification of the forecasting equation in previous empirical work sometimes violates a rational expectations principle. The theory of rational expectations implies that X_t^e in the y equation should be an optimal, one-period-ahead forecast conditional on information available at time $t - 1$. Thus, an appropriate forecasting equation should rely only on lagged explanatory variables. The procedure for specifying the forecasting equations here does satisfy this principle. However, this is not true in empirical studies which have used the Barro (1977) specification for the money growth forecasting equation. They include a contemporaneous variable (FEDV$_t$, the deviation of federal expenditures from the

---

4. The most striking example in Chapter 6 occurs when results of the model 2.1 (see tables 6.1 and 6.2) are compared with the 5.1 results (see table 6.5). The comparison is a little tricky because the model 2.1 is not strictly nested in model 5.1 because of the polynomial distributed lag specification, but it is still interesting to see what test statistics arise if we ignore this problem. The pseudolikelihood ratio statistic using (23) of the null hypothesis $\delta_o = \delta_1 \ldots = \delta_{20} = 0$ and $\beta_8 = \ldots \beta_{20} = 0$ equals 11.69 with a marginal significance level of .0199. Thus the hypothesis is rejected at the 5 percent level even though there is only a small change in the R^2 and standard error of the output equation in going from 2.1 to 5.1. A numerical explanation of the pseudolikelihood ratio statistic illustrates the point in the text. The maximum likelihood estimates of the standard errors of the 2.1 and 5.1 output equations are, respectively, .00796 and .00774. The percentage difference, calculated as the change in the logs, is 2.8 percent. The maximum likelihood standard errors for 2.1 and 5.1 money growth equations are, respectively, .00409 and .00394, with a percentage difference of 3.7 percent. Both of these percentage differences are added up in calculating the likelihood ratio statistic in (23), which is $92[2 (.028 + .037)] \approx 12$.

normal level) as an explanatory variable in the forecasting equation. Yet it is unlikely that the market has complete knowledge of this variable at time $t - 1$. That this is a possibly serious misspecification can be seen as follows. Denoting the contemporaneous variable by A_t, the forecasting equation can be written as

(29) $$X_t = Z_{t-1}\gamma + \xi A_t + u_t.$$

Using rational expectations and denoting $E(. . . |\phi_{t-1})$ by E_{t-1}, unanticipated X_t is

(30)
$$X_t - X_t^e = X_t - E_{t-1}X_t = X_t - (Z_{t-1}\gamma + \xi E_{t-1}A_t)$$
$$= (X_t - Z_{t-1}\gamma - \xi A_t) + \xi(A_t - E_{t-1}A_t)$$
$$= u_t + \xi(A_t - E_{t-1}A_t).$$

Expression (30) is not equivalent to the residual from the forecasting equation, for it differs by an expression involving unanticipated A_t. It is valid to use residuals from the forecasting equation to proxy for unanticipated X only if there are no errors in forecasting A_t. As is shown in the next chapter, this misspecification can render test statistics for rationality invalid. Note, however, the more accurately A_t can be predicted, the less serious this misspecification becomes.

This chapter's discussion of the specification of the lag length N suggests that MRE models with fairly long lags deserve study. The criterion for specifying the lag length N in earlier studies, on the other hand, results in a fairly short lag length—on the order of two years. The lag length is chosen by cutting off the lags when the coefficients on the unanticipated variables are no longer statistically significant in the MRE equation. If the MRE hypothesis is not valid, then choosing the lag length from an MRE equation is inappropriate for testing this hypothesis. This is then a further justification for experimenting with MRE models with longer lag lengths, as is done in Chapter 6.

Appendix 2.1:   Identification and Testing

The various tests discussed in this chapter depend on estimation of the parameters δ_i and γ^* in the unconstrained system (17). More specifically, neutrality requires that the estimate of δ_i not differ significantly from zero, and rationality requires that the estimate of γ^* not differ significantly from γ. These restrictions are testable only if the relevant parameters are identified, that is, if observational equivalence is avoided. If not all of the parameters are identified, then only some of the restrictions or linear combinations of restrictions are testable.

Appendix 2.1 is based on joint work with Andrew Abel (Abel and Mishkin 1983, sec. 5).

A procedure is outlined here for determining identification by analyzing an interesting special case of systems (16)–(20), where Z_{t-1} is rewritten as shown below in system (17):

(A1)
$$X_t = \sum_{i=1}^{M} Z_{t-i} \gamma_i + u_t$$

$$y_t = \tilde{y}_t + \sum_{j=0}^{N} \left(X_{t-j} - \sum_{i=1}^{M} Z_{t-j-i} \gamma_i^* \right) \beta_j$$

$$+ \sum_{j=0}^{N} \left(\sum_{i=0}^{M} Z_{t-j-i} \gamma_i^* \right) \delta_j + \epsilon_t,$$

where

X_t = a k-element row vector of variables relevant for determining y_t; $k \geq 1$.

Z_{t-i} = a $(p + k)$-element row vector of variables dated $t - i$ which are used in predicting X_t. It contains the k elements of X_{t-i} as well as p other variables; $p \geq 0$.

y_t = a scalar.

γ_i and $\gamma_i^* = (p + k)$ matrices of parameters.

β_i and $\delta_j = k \times 1$ column vectors of parameters.

Observe that this system embodies the exclusion restriction that Z_{t-i} does not enter the y equation except as it enters terms representing X_{t-i}^e. The exclusion restriction is crucial to the discussion of identification and hypothesis testing. Note that (A1) embodies the following simplifying assumptions: (*a*) the same lag length applies to all variables used to predict X_t in the first equation; and, (*b*) in the second equation the same lag length, N, is used for both anticipated and unanticipated X_t. These assumptions, which are made for expositional clarity, can be relaxed and the following discussion can be generalized in a straightforward manner. Note also that the row vector Z_{t-i}, which is used in the time-series model for predicting X_t, contains the k-element row vector X_{t-i}, since lagged values of the dependent variable are often useful in prediction. In addition, the row vector Z_{t-i} contains p other variables at time $t - i$, where $p \geq 0$. It is assumed that u_t and ϵ_t are uncorrelated and that $E(u_t|\phi_{t-1}) = E(\epsilon_t|\phi_{t-1}) = 0$. Finally, recall that the rationality restriction is $\gamma_i = \gamma_i^*$, $i = 1, \ldots, M$, and the neutrality restriction is $\delta_j = 0$, $j = 0, \ldots, N$.

The first step in determining identification is to analyze the order condition. Consider, for example, the most unconstrained system (A1) in which γ_i, γ_i^*, β_j, and δ_j are the free parameters to be estimated. Observe that γ_i can be estimated by OLS on the first equation in (A1). The remaining parameters γ_i^*, β_j, and δ_j are estimated from the second equation in (A1). The most constrained form of this second equation is

(A2)
$$y_t = \sum_{j=0}^{N} \hat{u}_{t-j}\beta_j + \sum_{l=1}^{M+N} Z_{t-l}\theta_l + \epsilon_t$$

where

$$\hat{u}_{t-j} = X_{t-j} - \sum_{i=1}^{M} Z_{t-j-i}\hat{\gamma}_i$$

$\theta_\ell = $ a $(p + k) \times 1$ column vector of parameters which is zero if
$\delta_j = 0, j = 0, \ldots, N$ and $\gamma_i^* = \gamma_i, i = 1, \ldots, M$

$$= \sum_{t+j=l} [(\gamma_i - \gamma_i^*)\beta_j + \gamma_i^*\delta_j], \ 1 \le i \le M \text{ and } 0 \le j \le N.$$

Note that for $j = 1, \ldots, N$, the residual $\hat{u}_{t-j}$ can be expressed as a linear combination of the other right-hand-side variables $Z_{t-1}, \ldots, Z_{t-M-N}$. That is, only the residual at time t, $\hat{u}_t$, is not perfectly correlated with the other right-hand-side variables. Hence, the most unconstrained form of this equation that can be estimated by OLS is

(A3)
$$y_t = \hat{u}_t\beta_o + \sum_{l=1}^{M+N} Z_{t-l}\theta_l + \epsilon_t.$$

Since there are k elements in β_o and $(M + N)(p + k)$ elements in the θ coefficients, equation (A3) can be used to estimate at most $k + (M + N)$ $(p + k)$ parameters. As long as this number of estimable parameters exceeds the number of free parameters contained in the β, δ, and γ^* coefficients, the order condition is satisfied.

Identification depends on the rank condition as well as the order condition. The rank condition is particularly important in the identification of (A3) because, in general, it need not be satisfied at the same time as the order condition. This failure to satisfy the rank condition becomes clear if we rewrite (A1) as

(A4)
$$X_t^1 = \sum_{i=1}^{M} Z_{t-i}\gamma_i^1 + u_t^1$$

$$\cdot$$
$$\cdot$$
$$\cdot$$

$$X_t^k = \sum_{i=1}^{M} Z_{t-i}\gamma_i^k + u_t^k$$

$$y_t = \sum_{s=1}^{k} \left[\sum_{j=0}^{N} (X_{t-j}^s\beta_j^s) + \sum_{j=0}^{N} (\delta_j^s - \beta_j^s) \sum_{i=1}^{M} Z_{t-i-j}\gamma_i^{*s} \right],$$

where X_t^s, γ_i^s, γ_i^{*s}, and u_t^s are the sth columns of X_t, γ_i, γ_i^*, and u_t, respectively. The scalars β_j^s and δ_j^s are the sth elements of β_j and δ_j, respectively.

Note that for any particular s, say s_o, the system will be unchanged by a doubling of all the elements of $\gamma_i^{*s_o}$ for all i and a halving of $\delta_j^{s_o} - \beta_j^{s_o}$ for all j. Because of this observational equivalence, the parameters $\delta_j^{s_o} - \beta_j^{s_o}$ and $\gamma_i^{*s_o}$ are not identified even when the order condition is satisfied. A restriction on any element of $\delta_j^{s_o}$ or $\gamma_i^{*s_o}$ is sufficient to identify these parameters. If we apply this argument to each of the k values of s, it is clear that k additional restrictions are needed for identification. The restrictions will be provided if either neutrality ($\delta_j = 0$) or rationality ($\gamma_i = \gamma_i^*$) is treated as a maintained hypothesis. Thus, only if neither neutrality nor rationality is maintained will the rank condition fail to be satisfied in situations when the order condition is satisfied.

Tests of hypotheses are conducted by comparing the residual sums of squares from constrained and unconstrained systems. The number of restrictions tested (and hence the number of degrees of freedom in the χ^2 statistic) equals the number of identified parameters estimated in the unconstrained system, less the number of identified parameters estimated in the constrained system. To illustrate this calculation using the procedures above, consider in the efficient-markets case in which $N = 0$, the test of rationality under the maintained hypothesis of neutrality. The last equation in the constrained system (where $\delta_o = 0$, $\gamma_i = \gamma_i^*$) contains k parameters (the elements of β), all of which are identified. The last equation in the unconstrained system (where $\delta_o = 0$) contains $k + Mk(p + k)$ parameters. However, as explained above, only $k + M(p + k)$ parameters can be estimated. Only if $k = 1$ will all of the parameters in the unconstrained system be identified. However, even if $k > 1$, there are $M(p + k)$ testable restrictions. These restrictions are linear combinations of the restrictions $\gamma - \gamma^* = 0$ (see the next chapter for an example).

Another test which may be conducted in the efficient-markets framework ($N = 0$) is a test of the null hypothesis of neutrality under the maintained hypothesis of rationality. Recall that the last equation of the constrained system ($\gamma_i = \gamma_i^*$, $\delta_o = 0$) contains k parameters (the elements of β), and observe that the last equation of the unconstrained system ($\gamma_i = \gamma_i^*$) contains $2k$ parameters (the elements of β and δ_o). In both the constrained and unconstrained systems, all parameters are identified and all k neutrality restrictions are testable.

A third test in the efficient-markets framework is a test of the joint hypothesis of neutrality and rationality. As in the first two tests, all k parameters of the last equation in the constrained system are identified. In the unconstrained system the last equation contains $2k + Mk(p + k)$ parameters (k elements of β, k elements of δ_o and $Mk(p + k)$ elements of γ_i^*, $i = 1, \ldots, M$), but, as explained above, only $k + M(p + k)$ parameters can be estimated. Therefore, under no circumstances will all parameters of this equation be identified. However, there are $M(p + k)$ testable restrictions that are linear combinations of the restrictions $\gamma - \gamma^* = 0$ and $\delta_o = 0$.

The interpretation of these efficient-markets tests depends on what hypothesis is maintained. In particular, the test statistic associated with the joint test of rationality and neutrality is identical to the test statistic for the test of rationality, under the maintained hypothesis of neutrality. This follows because, although the free parameters in the unconstrained systems are different, the estimated coefficients are identical. Furthermore, the constrained systems are the same. Because of the equivalence of the two tests, one cannot determine whether a rejection is due to a violation of rationality alone or a violation of both rationality and neutrality.

Tests of policy neutrality under the maintained hypothesis of rationality as in Barro (1977, 1978) and in Chapter 6 furnish another interesting case. These models assume that the deviation of current output from its natural level is affected only by the current and N lagged surprises in a single policy variable (i.e., $k = 1$ and $N > 0$). To obtain identification of the coefficients on surprises in the policy variable, these studies implicitly place restrictions on the covariance of ϵ_t with both u_t and with lagged disturbances. There are two alternative conditions sufficient for identification of the δ coefficients, that is, the coefficients on anticipated policy. One condition, discussed and used by Barro (1977, 1978, 1979), Leiderman (1980), and in Chapter 6, is the exclusion restriction $p \geq 1$. That is, the time-series model for the policy variable X_t contains at least one variable that is not directly included in the y equation. The y equation in the constrained system (where $\delta_i = 0$ and $\gamma_i = \gamma_i^*$) contains $N + 1$ parameters ($\beta_o, \ldots, \beta_N$), and in the unconstrained system (where $\gamma_i = \gamma_i^*$) it contains $2(N + 1)$ parameters ($\beta_o, \ldots, \beta_N$ and $\delta_o, \ldots, \delta_N$). In each of these systems, all of the parameters are identified because the number of free parameters is less than the number of estimable parameters, $1 + (M + N)(p + 1)$. Therefore all of the $N + 1$ neutrality restrictions are testable.

The alternative sufficient condition for identification is $M > N$; that is, the number of lags in the time-series model for the policy variable X_t exceeds the number of lagged surprises in the y equation. Although this condition formally leads to identification, it requires strong a priori knowledge of lag lengths. Without this prior knowledge we are faced with the observational equivalence problem raised by Sargent (1976b).

To identify δ_i at least one of the two conditions above must hold. One recent example in which this does not occur is in Grossman (1979). His specification of the time-series equation describing his policy variable (nominal GNP growth) does not include any variable other than lagged dependent variables. Moreover, the number of lags in the output equation exceeds that in the time-series equation for the policy variable. Therefore, the δ coefficients in his model are not identified, with the result that not all the neutrality constraints can be tested.

Appendix 2.2:   An Annotated Computer Program

The computer program here demonstrates how the models discussed in this book can be estimated. The particular example is chosen from Chapter 6 to illustrate the general principle of estimating models where (1) current and lagged values of *both* anticipated and unanticipated variables have explanatory power, and (2) the error term is specified to follow an autoregressive process. The program makes use of the PROC NLIN nonlinear estimation procedure in the widely available computer package SAS, described in the *SAS User's Guide* (1979). The detailed discussion of this sample program should not only allow a user of SAS to exploit the techniques described in this book, but also should provide enough of the program's logic so that it can be modified for use with other econometric packages with nonlinear estimation capabilities. It should be noted that the PROC NLIN procedure of SAS does have one major advantage: it can handle extremely large problems that are beyond the capability of other packages. This is not important for a small estimation problem, but it is crucial for estimation of models such as those found in Chapter 6 which have over fifty parameters. My experience with SAS's nonlinear estimation routine has been a happy one: it converges quickly and is not prohibitively expensive to use.

The program here estimates over the period 1954:1–1976:4 a model consisting of (A5), a forecasting equation for money growth, and (A6), an output equation in which both anticipated and unanticipated money growth matter.

$$(A5) \qquad M1G = \gamma_o + \sum_{i=1}^{4} \gamma_i\, M1G_{t-i} + \sum_{i=1}^{4} \gamma_{i+4}\, \mathrm{RTB}_{t-i}$$

$$+ \sum_{i=1}^{4} \gamma_{i+8}\, \mathrm{SURP}_{t-i} + u_t,$$

$$(A6) \qquad \log\,(\mathrm{GNP}_t) = c + \tau\,\mathrm{TIME} + \sum_{i=0}^{7} \beta_i (M1G_{t-i} - M1G_{t-i}^{e})$$

$$+ \sum_{i=0}^{7} \delta_i\, M1G_{t-i}^{e} + \epsilon_t,$$

where

$$\epsilon_t = \rho_1 \epsilon_{t-1} + \rho_2 \epsilon_{t-2} + \rho_3 \epsilon_{t-3} + \rho_4 \epsilon_{t-4} + \eta_t,$$

$$M1G_t^{e} = \gamma_o + \sum_{i=1}^{4} \gamma_i\, M1G_{t-i} + \sum_{i=1}^{4} \gamma_{i+4}\, \mathrm{RTB}_{t-i} + \sum_{i=1}^{4} \gamma_{i+8}\, \mathrm{SURP}_{t-i}.$$

The cross-equation restrictions are that the γ_i are identical in (A5) and (A6). The variables are as defined in Chapter 6. Note that this example does not make use of the polynomial distributed lag (PDL) restriction. The interested reader is referred to Kmenta (1971) to see how the PDL restriction can be imposed by "scrambling" variables.

The basic idea of the program is to stack the data so that the system of the two linear equations, (A5) and (A6), can be written as one equation with the appropriate nonlinear constraints. Estimation with the nonlinear procedure PROC NLIN is then fairly straightforward.

Notes for Program Listing in Exhibit A1

The SAS data set ONE contains the data used in estimation. The 120 quarterly observations run from 1947:1 to 1976:4. A number appended to the variable name indicates how many times it is lagged. For example, $M1G$ is unlagged money growth while $M1G1$ is money growth lagged one period. LGNP equals log (GNP) and C is the constant term.

Lines 1–17: The new data set ONEA created from ONE weights the variables in the forecasting equation by HETA in order to correct for the heteroscedasticity across equations. The value of HETA is chosen so that the weighted sum of squared residuals in each equation approach each other. The procedure for doing this will be explained when the output from the program is discussed.

Lines 18–21: The LGNP variable is dropped from the data set and the $M1G$ variable is renamed as LGNP. This operation is necessary for the stacking operation conducted later.

Lines 22–24: The new data set ONER will correspond to the output equation and it adds the constant term to the data set ONE.

Lines 25–76: Here the stacking operation is conducted in order to create the data set EST used in estimation. The outcome of this operation will be discussed first so that we may more easily follow the steps taken to achieve it. Each variable will have 240 observations with the first 120 corresponding to the output equation and the second 120 corresponding to the forecasting equation. If the weighted variables are denoted by the superscript A, then the resulting LGNP variable written in matrix notation is:

$$
LGNP = \begin{bmatrix} LGNP_{1947:1} \\ \cdot \\ \cdot \\ \cdot \\ LGNP_{1976:4} \\ M1G^A_{1947:1} \\ \cdot \\ \cdot \\ \cdot \\ M1G^A_{1976:4} \end{bmatrix} \cdot
$$

Hence the first 120 observations correspond to the dependent variable of the output equation while the second 120 observations correspond to the dependent variable of the forecasting equation (appropriately weighted for heteroscedasticity). The variables with an A added to their names correspond to the appropriately weighted explanatory variables in the forecasting equation, while those without A (except for LGNP) correspond to the explanatory variables in the output equation. For example,

$$
M1G1 = \begin{bmatrix} M1G1_{1947:1} \\ \cdot \\ \cdot \\ \cdot \\ M1G1_{1976:4} \\ 0 \\ \cdot \\ \cdot \\ \cdot \\ 0 \end{bmatrix} \quad M1G1A = \begin{bmatrix} 0 \\ \cdot \\ \cdot \\ \cdot \\ 0 \\ M1G1^{A}_{1947:1} \\ \cdot \\ \cdot \\ \cdot \\ M1G1^{A}_{1976:4} \end{bmatrix}.
$$

In the case of $M1G1$, the 120 observations corresponding to the forecasting equation are set to zero, while in the case of $M1G1A$ the 120 observations corresponding to the output equation are set to zero.

Lines 25–26 conduct the first stacking operation to create data set TWO. All the variables have 240 observations. The operations in lines 18–21 result in a LGNP variable of the form shown above, with the first 120 observations containing the dependent variable of the output equation and the second 120 containing the dependent variable of the forecasting equation. For all other variables, the first 120 observations from the data set ONER correspond to the output equation, and the second 120 observations from the data set ONEA correspond to the forecasting equation. Lines 27–35 add to a new data set THREE the variables with an A which are identical to their counterparts without A. Lines 36–37 have data set EST created from data set THREE. Lines 38–63 set to zero the second 120 observations of the variables with no A, and lines 64–76 set to zero the first 120 observations of the variables with an A. The stacked variables described above are the outcome of these operations.

Lines 77–78: These lines set the first twenty-eight observations of both sets of 120 observations in LGNP to a missing value. This ensures that when PROC NLIN is used in the following lines, the 1947:1–1953:4 observations are excluded from the sample period and estimation over the 1954:1–1976:4 sample period results.

Lines 79–247: Here the actual estimation is carried out with PROC NLIN. The parameters have slightly different names than in (A5) and (A6) above: CO corresponds to c, T to τ, M0–M7 to β_0–β_7, E0–E7 to δ_0–δ_7, A0–A12 to γ_0–γ_{12}, and RH01–RH04 to ρ_1–ρ_4.

Lines 79–80: The convergence criterion is set and the residuals from the estimation are stored as the variable RESID in the data set DRESID.

Lines 81–117: The starting values for the parameters are provided.

Lines 118–135: Variables are generated here to facilitate calculations of the derivatives in lines 193–247. If these derivatives are not needed, then these lines can be deleted.

Lines 136–139: Anticipated money growth, *EM*, is generated.

Lines 140–151: Unanticipated money growth, *UM*, and its lags are generated.

Lines 152–162: Lags of *EM* are generated.

Lines 163–178: The fourth-order autoregressive correction for serial correlation in the output equation (A6) requires the transformation here of the *UM* and *EM* variables into *RUM* and *REM*, as shown.

Lines 179–192: The model consisting of both the output and forecasting equation is written down here. Note that it incorporates the necessary transformation to allow for the serial correlation correction. The stacking operation in previous lines ensures also that this model captures the cross-equation restrictions and the appropriate heteroscedasticity correction.

Lines 193–247: The derivatives of the model in lines 179–192 are calculated here. The version of SAS used to estimate this model required these derivatives. Later versions of SAS may not require them, in which case these lines and lines 118–135 can be deleted.

Lines 248–259: Here the standard errors of both output and forecasting equations are calculated. They are used, as will be shown below, to calculate HETA for the heteroscedasticity correction and to decide when the last iteration is reached. Lines 248–250 retain only the residuals in the data set DRESID. Lines 251–259 use PROC MEANS to calculate the standard error first of the output equation and then of the weighted forecasting equation.

Discussion of the Output in Exhibit A2

The first page of the SAS output shows the convergence to the minimum sum of squared residuals, and pages 3–5 show the asymptotic correlation matrix of the parameter estimates. Only pages 2, 6, and 7 are displayed as they are of the greatest interest. Page 2 contains the parameter estimates, their asymptotic standard errors, and the sum of squared residuals of the system. For example, the coefficient of the constant term in the output equation is 6.18857905 with an asymptotic standard error of .04752109. The sum of squared residuals of the system, which is needed to calculate the likelihood ratio tests discussed in the chapter, is .01012971. Pages 6 and 7 show the standard errors of the output equation and the weighted forecasting equation, respectively, in the standard deviation column. The standard error of the output equation is .00738342, and the standard error of the weighted forecasting equation is .00753653.

The iterative procedure that corrects for heteroscedasticity across the equations continues as follows. The variables in the forecasting equation are weighted by the ratio from the previous iteration of the standard error of the forecasting equation to the standard error of the output equation. This means that the weighting variable HETA from the previous iteration needs to be multiplied by the standard error of the *weighted* forecasting equation divided by the standard error of the output equation. In the example here, the next iteration would therefore multiply the previous iteration's HETA by .00753653 ÷ .00738432, which equals 1.020612595. That is, line 3 of the program would be modified to insert *1.020612595 just before the semicolon, and the program would then be run. Note that computational costs have been lowered by using the last iteration's parameter estimates as starting values in lines 81–117. The criterion for terminating the iterative procedure can be varied but, in the empirical work reported in this book, if the standard errors of the weighted forecasting equation and the output equation differed by less than 2½ percent, then no further iterations were performed. Thus the results reported in Exhibit A2 are the final iteration.

Procedures for Calculating the Likelihood Ratio Tests

To carry out the tests in Chapter 6, the first system estimated was the most constrained where anticipated money has no effect on output but rationality is still imposed. The only changes needed in the computer program are to eliminate terms involving *REM* and *EM* from the model and derivative statements and to delete lines 92–99 and 203–210. The next, less constrained system estimated has anticipated money affecting output and makes use of the program in Exhibit A1. The first iteration uses the same HETA value used in the final iteration of the most constrained system. The likelihood ratio test of neutrality described in Chapter 2 is conducted by comparing the sum of squares of the less constrained system obtained from the first iteration, with the sum of squares for the final iteration of the most constrained system. Further iterations are then performed for this system in which anticipated money matters until the termination criterion is reached.

The most unconstrained system is subject neither to rationality nor to neutrality, and as there are now no binding constraints across the two equations of the system, each can be estimated separately. The forecasting equation can be estimated by OLS while the output equation is estimated by deleting lines 1–21, 25–76, 78, and 188–191 from the program in Exhibit A1 and modifying the derivatives statements appropriately. Note that the *CO* and *AO* parameters are not identified and so one of them should be set to a constant. As discussed in Appendix 2.1, at least one other parameter will not be identified and PROC NLIN will automatically set it to a constant in estimation. In some cases when more parameters are unidentified, the most unconstrained output equation is even more linear, and so takes an even simpler form.

The likelihood ratio tests of neutrality and rationality jointly, or of rationality alone, compare the sum of squared residuals of the appropriately weighted most unconstrained system with those of the more constrained systems, estimation of which is discussed above. The appropriately weighted sum of squared residuals for the most unconstrained system equals the sum of squared residuals from the most unconstrained output equation, added to the sum of squared residuals from the OLS estimated forecasting equation, divided by the square of the HETA value used in the constrained system's final iteration.

Line No.

```
 1.     DATA ONEA;
 2.     SET ONE;
 3.     HETA = .4204183267*1.200367097*1.02580668*1.06044268;
 4.     M1G = M1G/HETA;
 5.     M1G1 = M1G1/HETA;
 6.     M1G2 = M1G2/HETA;
 7.     M1G3 = M1G3/HETA;
 8.     M1G4 = M1G4/HETA;
 9.     RTB1 = RTB1/HETA;
10.     RTB2 = RTB2/HETA;
11.     RTB3 = RTB3/HETA;
12.     RTB4 = RTB4/HETA;
13.     SURP1 = SURP1/HETA;
14.     SURP2 = SURP2/HETA;
15.     SURP3 = SURP3/HETA;
16.     SURP4 = SURP4/HETA;
17.     C = 1/HETA;
18.     DATA ONEA;
19.     SET ONEA;
20.     DROP LGNP;
21.     RENAME M1G=LGNP;
22.     DATA ONER;
23.     SET ONE;
24.     C = 1;
25.     DATA TWO;
26.     SET ONER ONEA;
27.     DATA TWOA;
28.     SET TWO;
29.     RENAME
30.     M1G1=M1G1A M1G2=M1G2A M1G3=M1G3A M1G4=M1G4A
31.     RTB1=RTB1A RTB2=RTB2A RTB3=RTB3A RTB4=RTB4A
32.     SURP1=SURP1A SURP2=SURP2A SURP3=SURP3A SURP4=SURP4A
33.     C=CA;
34.     DATA THREE;
35.     MERGE TWO TWOA;
36.     DATA EST;
37.     SET THREE;
38.     IF _N_>=121 THEN M1G=0;
39.     IF _N_>=121 THEN C=0;
40.     IF _N_>=121 THEN TIME=0;
41.     IF _N_>=121 THEN TIME1=0;
42.     IF _N_>=121 THEN TIME2=0;
43.     IF _N_>=121 THEN TIME3=0;
44.     IF _N_>=121 THEN TIME4=0;
45.     IF _N_>=121 THEN M1G1=0;
46.     IF _N_>=121 THEN M1G2=0;
47.     IF _N_>=121 THEN M1G3=0;
48.     IF _N_>=121 THEN M1G4=0;
49.     IF _N_>=121 THEN M1G5=0;
50.     IF _N_>=121 THEN RTB1=0;
51.     IF _N_>=121 THEN RTB2=0;
52.     IF _N_>=121 THEN RTB3=0;
53.     IF _N_>=121 THEN RTB4=0;
54.     IF _N_>=121 THEN RTB5=0;
55.     IF _N_>=121 THEN SURP1=0;
56.     IF _N_>=121 THEN SURP2=0;
57.     IF _N_>=121 THEN SURP3=0;
58.     IF _N_>=121 THEN SURP4=0;
59.     IF _N_>=121 THEN SURP5=0;
60.     IF _N_>=121 THEN LGNP1=0;
61.     IF _N_>=121 THEN LGNP2=0;
62.     IF _N_>=121 THEN LGNP3=0;
63.     IF _N_>=121 THEN LGNP4=0;
64.     IF _N_<121 THEN M1G1A=0;
65.     IF _N_<121 THEN M1G2A=0;
66.     IF _N_<121 THEN M1G3A=0;
67.     IF _N_<121 THEN M1G4A=0;
68.     IF _N_<121 THEN RTB1A=0;
69.     IF _N_<121 THEN RTB2A=0;
70.     IF _N_<121 THEN RTB3A=0;
71.     IF _N_<121 THEN RTB4A=0;
72.     IF _N_<121 THEN SURP1A=0;
73.     IF _N_<121 THEN SURP2A=0;
74.     IF _N_<121 THEN SURP3A=0;
75.     IF _N_<121 THEN SURP4A=0;
```

```
76.      IF _N_<121 THEN CA=0;
77.      IF _N_<=28 THEN LGNP=.;
78.      IF _N_>120 AND _N_<=148 THEN LGNP=.;
79.      PROC NLIN CONVERGENCE=.0001;
80.      OUTPUT OUT=DRESID PREDICTED=PRED RESIDUAL=RESID;
81.      PARAMETERS
82.                           C0        =       6.18409321
83.                           T         =       0.00818261
84.                           M0        =       0.70203726
85.                           M1        =       1.02226901
86.                           M2        =       1.96325236
87.                           M3        =       2.39452781
88.                           M4        =       2.81242963
89.                           M5        =       2.59002714
90.                           M6        =       2.28592198
91.                           M7        =       1.31723568
92.                           E0        =       0.76382117
93.                           E1        =      -0.19910460
94.                           E2        =       0.24108277
95.                           E3        =      -0.40288643
96.                           E4        =      -0.07456418
97.                           E5        =      -0.59607729
98.                           E6        =       0.47914434
99.                           E7        =       0.95216249
100.                          A0        =       0.00210000
101.                          A1        =       0.73200405
102.                          A2        =       0.02305185
103.                          A3        =      -0.08331019
104.                          A4        =      -0.13184558
105.                          A5        =      -0.00226408
106.                          A6        =       0.00451728
107.                          A7        =      -0.00132287
108.                          A8        =      -0.00035536
109.                          A9        =      -0.00017881
110.                          A10       =       0.00019747
111.                          A11       =      -0.00000643
112.                          A12       =      -0.00012937
113.                          RHO1      =       1.19896060
114.                          RHO2      =      -0.42906225
115.                          RHO3      =       0.12553469
116.                          RHO4      =       0.03276445
117.      ;
118.      ZC = C*(1-RHO1-RHO2-RHO3-RHO4);
119.      MZC   = ZC*(-M0-M1-M2-M3-M4-M5-M6-M7);
120.      EZC=ZC*(E0+E1+E2+E3+E4+E5+E6+E7);
121.      ZM = M1G1 - RHO1*M1G2 - RHO2*M1G3 - RHO3*M1G4 - RHO4*M1G5;
122.      MZM   = -M0*ZM - M1*LAG1(ZM) -M2*LAG2(ZM) - M3*LAG3(ZM) -M4*LAG4(ZM)
123.      -M5*LAG5(ZM) - M6*LAG6(ZM) -M7*LAG7(ZM);
124.      ZR = RTB1 - RHO1*RTB2 - RHO2*RTB3 - RHO3*RTB4 - RHO4*RTB5;
125.      MZR   = -M0*ZR - M1*LAG1(ZR) -M2*LAG2(ZR) - M3*LAG3(ZR) -M4*LAG4(ZR)
126.      -M5*LAG5(ZR) - M6*LAG6(ZR) -M7*LAG7(ZR);
127.      ZH = SURP1 - RHO1*SURP2 - RHO2*SURP3 - RHO3*SURP4 - RHO4*SURP5;
128.      MZH   = -M0*ZH - M1*LAG1(ZH) -M2*LAG2(ZH) - M3*LAG3(ZH) -M4*LAG4(ZH)
129.      -M5*LAG5(ZH) - M6*LAG6(ZH) -M7*LAG7(ZH);
130.      EZM = E0*ZM + E1*LAG1(ZM) + E2*LAG2(ZM) + E3*LAG3(ZM) + E4*LAG4(ZM)
131.      + E5*LAG5(ZM) + E6*LAG6(ZM) + E7*LAG7(ZM) ;
132.      EZR = E0*ZR + E1*LAG1(ZR) + E2*LAG2(ZR) + E3*LAG3(ZR) + E4*LAG4(ZR)
133.      + E5*LAG5(ZR) + E6*LAG6(ZR) + E7*LAG7(ZR) ;
134.      EZH = E0*ZH + E1*LAG1(ZH) + E2*LAG2(ZH) + E3*LAG3(ZH) + E4*LAG4(ZH)
135.      + E5*LAG5(ZH) + E6*LAG6(ZH) + E7*LAG7(ZH) ;
136.      EM = A0*C + A1*M1G1  + A2*M1G2  + A3*M1G3  + A4*M1G4
137.      + A5*RTB1  + A6*RTB2  + A7*RTB3  + A8*RTB4
138.      + A9*SURP1  + A10*SURP2  + A11*SURP3  +
139.      A12*SURP4 ;
140.      UM = M1G - EM;
141.      UM1 = LAG1(UM);
142.      UM2 = LAG2(UM);
143.      UM3 = LAG3(UM);
144.      UM4 = LAG4(UM);
145.      UM5 = LAG5(UM);
146.      UM6 = LAG6(UM);
147.      UM7 = LAG7(UM);
148.      UM8 = LAG8(UM);
149.      UM9 = LAG9(UM);
150.      UM10 = LAG10(UM);
151.      UM11 = LAG11(UM);
152.      EM1 = LAG1(EM);
153.      EM2 = LAG2(EM);
154.      EM3 = LAG3(EM);
155.      EM4 = LAG4(EM);
156.      EM5 = LAG5(EM);
```

Line No.

```
157.    EM6 = LAG6(EM);
158.    EM7 = LAG7(EM);
159.    EM8 = LAG8(EM);
160.    EM9 = LAG9(EM);
161.    EM10  = LAG10(EM);
162.    EM11 = LAG11(EM);
163.    RUM= UM - RHO1*UM1 - RHO2*UM2  - RHO3*UM3  - RHO4*UM4 ;
164.    RUM1 = LAG1(RUM);
165.    RUM2 = LAG2(RUM);
166.    RUM3 = LAG3(RUM);
167.    RUM4 = LAG4(RUM);
168.    RUM5 = LAG5(RUM);
169.    RUM6 = LAG6(RUM);
170.    RUM7 = LAG7(RUM);
171.    REM= EM - RHO1*EM1 - RHO2*EM2  - RHO3*EM3  - RHO4*EM4 ;
172.    REM1 = LAG1(REM);
173.    REM2 = LAG2(REM);
174.    REM3 = LAG3(REM);
175.    REM4 = LAG4(REM);
176.    REM5 = LAG5(REM);
177.    REM6 = LAG6(REM);
178.    REM7 = LAG7(REM);
179.    MODEL LGNP =
180.    RHO1*LGNP1       + RHO2*LGNP2        + RHO3*LGNP3        + RHO4*LGNP4
181.    C0*C*(1-RHO1-RHO2-RHO3-RHO4)  +
182.    T*(TIME - RHO1*(TIME1) - RHO2*(TIME2) - RHO3*(TIME3)
183.    - RHO4*(TIME4))
184.    + E0*REM + E1*REM1  + E2*REM2  + E3*REM3  + E4*REM4
185.    + E5*REM5  + E6*REM6  + E7*REM7
186.    + M0*RUM + M1*RUM1  + M2*RUM2  + M3*RUM3  + M4*RUM4
187.    + M5*RUM5  + M6*RUM6  + M7*RUM7
188.    +    A0*CA  + A1*M1G1A  + A2*M1G2A  + A3*M1G3A  + A4*M1G4A
189.    + A5*RTB1A  + A6*RTB2A  + A7*RTB3A  + A8*RTB4A
190.    + A9*SURP1A  + A10*SURP2A  + A11*SURP3A  +
191.    A12*SURP4A
192.    ;
193.    DER.C0 = C*(1-RHO1-RHO2-RHO3-RHO4);
194.    DER.T= (TIME - RHO1*TIME1 -RHO2*TIME2 -RHO3*TIME3 -RHO4*TIME4);
195.    DER.M0 = RUM ;
196.    DER.M1 = RUM1;
197.    DER.M2 = RUM2;
198.    DER.M3 = RUM3;
199.    DER.M4 = RUM4;
200.    DER.M5 = RUM5;
201.    DER.M6 = RUM6;
202.    DER.M7 = RUM7;
203.    DER.E0 = REM ;
204.    DER.E1 = REM1;
205.    DER.E2 = REM2;
206.    DER.E3 = REM3;
207.    DER.E4 = REM4;
208.    DER.E5 = REM5;
209.    DER.E6 = REM6;
210.    DER.E7 = REM7;
211.    DER.A0 = MZC + EZC;
212.    DER.A1 = MZM + EZM + M1G1A;
213.:   DER.A2 = LAG1(MZM) + LAG1(EZM) + M1G2A;
214..   DER.A3 = LAG2(MZM) + LAG2(EZM) + M1G3A;
215.    DER.A4 = LAG3(MZM) + LAG3(EZM) + M1G4A;
216.    DER.A5 = MZR + EZR + RTB1A;
217.    DER.A6 = LAG1(MZR) + LAG1(EZR) + RTB2A;
218.    DER.A7 = LAG2(MZR) + LAG2(EZR) + RTB3A;
219.    DER.A8 = LAG3(MZR) + LAG3(EZR) + RTB4A;
220.    DER.A9 = MZH + EZH + SURP1A;
221.    DER.A10 = LAG1(MZH) + LAG1(EZH) + SURP2A;
222.    DER.A11 = LAG2(MZH) + LAG2(EZH) + SURP3A;
223.    DER.A12 = LAG3(MZH) + LAG3(EZH) + SURP4A;
224.    DER.RHO1 = LGNP1 - C0*C - T*(TIME1)
225.    -E0*EM1 - E1*EM2 - E2*EM3 - E3*EM4 - E4*EM5
226.    -E5*EM6 - E6*EM7 - E7*EM8
227.    -M0*UM1 - M1*UM2 - M2*UM3 - M3*UM4 - M4*UM5
228.    -M5*UM6 - M6*UM7 - M7*UM8
229.    ;
230.    DER.RHO2 = LGNP2 - C0*C - T*(TIME2)
231.    -E0*EM2 - E1*EM3 - E2*EM4 - E3*EM5 - E4*EM6
232.    -E5*EM7 - E6*EM8 - E7*EM9
233.    -M0*UM2 - M1*UM3 - M2*UM4 - M3*UM5 - M4*UM6
```

```
234.        -M5*UM7 - M6*UM8 - M7*UM9
235.        ;
236.        DER.RHO3 = LGNP3 - C0*C - T*(TIME3)
237.        -E0*EM3 - E1*EM4 - E2*EM5 - E3*EM6 - E4*EM7
238.        -E5*EM8 - E6*EM9 - E7*EM10
239.        -M0*UM3 - M1*UM4 - M2*UM5 - M3*UM6 - M4*UM7
240.        -M5*UM8 - M6*UM9 - M7*UM10
241.        ;
242.        DER.RHO4 = LGNP4 - C0*C - T*(TIME4)
243.        -E0*EM4 - E1*EM5 - E2*EM6 - E3*EM7 - E4*EM8
244.        -E5*EM9 - E6*EM10 - E7*EM11
245.        -M0*UM4 - M1*UM5 - M2*UM6 - M3*UM7 - M4*UM8
246.        -M5*UM9 - M6*UM10 - M7*UM11
247.        ;
248.        DATA DRESID;
249.        SET DRESID;
250.        KEEP RESID  ;
251.        DATA DRESID4;
252.        SET DRESID;
253.        IF _N_<29 THEN DELETE;          output eq^n
254.        IF _N_>120 THEN DELETE;
255.        PROC MEANS;
256.        DATA DRESID4;
257.        SET DRESID;
258.        IF _N_<149 THEN DELETE;     weighted forecasting eq^n
259.        PROC MEANS;
```

Exhibit A2 SAS Output

(Page 2 of Output)

NON-LINEAR LEAST SQUARES SUMMARY STATISTICS   DEPENDENT VARIABLE LGNP

SOURCE	DF	SUM OF SQUARES	MEAN SQUARE
REGRESSION	34	4265.59094289	125.45855714
RESIDUAL	150	0.01012971	0.00006753
UNCORRECTED TOTAL	184	4265.60107260	
(CORRECTED TOTAL)	183	2124.35825459	

SSR
SSE
SST

PARAMETER	ESTIMATE	ASYMPTOTIC STD. ERROR	ASYMPTOTIC 95 % CONFIDENCE INTERVAL LOWER	UPPER
CO	6.18857905	0.04752109	6.09468097	6.28247712
T	0.00817790	0.00075394	0.00668817	0.00966763
MO	0.67338908	0.25174720	0.17595567	1.17082248
M1	0.99052411	0.63419173	-0.26259075	2.24363898
M2	1.98333150	0.87999722	0.24452360	3.72213940
M3	2.42454230	1.09553356	0.25985090	4.58923371
M4	2.87331469	1.12105105	0.65820267	5.08842671
M5	2.67999149	1.07604971	0.55379870.	4.80618429
M6	2.40977049	0.92363811	0.58473149	4.23480950
M7	1.39301366	0.66200728	0.08493739	2.70108994
EO	0.75851491	0.68319790	-0.59143244	2.10846226
E1	-0.27845622	0.81563359	-1.89008646	1.33317402
E2	0.16799819	0.94744868	-1.70408870	2.04008508
E3	-0.49455089	0.87148992	-2.21654902	1.22744723
E4	-0.16589726	0.84832017	-1.84211370	1.51031918
E5	0.69837726	0.77518540	-2.23008493	0.83333042
E6	0.47054569	0.69561698	-0.90394081	1.84503220
E7	0.99845498	0.60581543	0.19859045	2.19550041
AO	0.00210000	0.00000000	0.00210000	0.00210000
A1	0.73786167	0.11300533	0.51457169	0.96115165
A2	0.01750937	0.14832346	-0.27556657	0.31058530
A3	-0.08423813	0.13137921	-0.34383350	0.17535724
A4	-0.13930343	0.10527634	-0.34732151	0.06871465
A5	-0.00201614	0.00083145	-0.00365903	-0.00037325
A6	0.00425483	0.00149704	0.00129679	0.00721287
A7	-0.00122770	0.00156798	-0.00432590	0.00187051
A8	-0.00041573	0.00089441	-0.00218303	0.00135156

A9	-0.00017315	0.00006205	-0.00029576	-0.00005055
A10	0.00020580	0.00007921	0.00004929	0.00036231
A11	-0.00001359	0.00008016	-0.00017199	0.00014480
A12	-0.00012975	0.00006598	-0.00026012	0.00000062
RHO1	1.19154724	0.12115199	0.95216009	1.4309340
RHO2	-0.42871113	0.18992137	-0.80398139	-0.05344087
RHO3	0.13010832	0.21066777	-0.28615525	0.54637190
RHO4	0.03918645	0.14039923	-0.23823180	0.31660470

(Page 6 of Output)

VARIABLE	N	MEAN	STANDARD DEVIATION	MINIMUM VALUE	MAXIMUM VALUE	STD ERROR OF MEAN	SUM	VARIANCE	C.V.
RESID	92	-0.00000250	0.00738342	-0.02660273	0.01635174	0.00076977	-0.00022995	0.00005451	-99999.000

(Page 7 of Output)

VARIABLE	N	MEAN	STANDARD DEVIATION	MINIMUM VALUE	MAXIMUM VALUE	STD ERROR OF MEAN	SUM	VARIANCE	C.V.
RESID	92	0.00003520	0.00753653	-0.02391151	0.01685502	0.00078574	0.00323822	0.00005680	21411.797

3   An Integrated View of Tests of Rationality, Market Efficiency, and the Short-Run Neutrality of Aggregate Demand Policy

3.1   Introduction

This chapter highlights the common elements in procedures for testing (1) rationality of forecasts in either market or survey data, (2) capital market efficiency, (3) the short-run neutrality of aggregate demand policy, and (4) Granger (1969) causality in macroeconometric models. It answers the following questions: How do the test statistics from these procedures relate to one another, and can they be used for inference under quite general conditions?

We will begin with the simplest case and then treat increasingly complex cases. The simplest case, discussed in Section 3.2, involves cross-equation tests of rationality when some measure of expectations is available. To make inferences about expectations in the absence of directly observable expectations, some model of market behavior is needed. This case is discussed in Section 3.3. Section 3.4 discusses cross-equation tests of short-run neutrality of aggregate demand policy. A final section summarizes the results.

3.2   Test of Rationality

As in Chapter 2, let ϕ_{t-1} denote the set of information available at the end of period $t-1$, and let $E(\ldots | \phi_{t-1})$ denote the objective expectation conditional on ϕ_{t-1}. Suppose that X_t is generated by the following linear model:

$$(1) \qquad X_t = Z_{1,t-1}\alpha_1 + Z_{2,t-1}\alpha_2 + u_t,$$

This chapter is based on joint work with Andrew Abel (Abel and Mishkin 1983).

where

$$Z_{1,t-1} \text{ and } Z_{2,t-1} = \text{vectors of variables known at time } t - 1,$$
$$\alpha_1, \alpha_2 = \text{coefficients,}$$
$$u_t = \text{error term which is assumed to have the property}$$
$$\text{that } E(u_t|\phi_{t-1}) = 0.$$

The distinction between $Z_{1,t-1}$ and $Z_{2,t-1}$ is that $Z_{2,t-1}$ includes variables relevant for forecasting X_t but ignored by the econometrician in conducting tests of rationality. Of course $Z_{2,t-1}$ could be empty. It is clear from (1) that the objective expectation of X_t, conditional on ϕ_{t-1}, is

$$(2) \qquad E(X_t|\phi_{t-1}) = Z_{1,t-1}\alpha_1 + Z_{2,t-1}\alpha_2.$$

Now consider a one-period-ahead forecast X_t^e, which is some observable measure of an expectation of X_t made at time $t - 1$. Rationality of expectations requires that the forecast X_t^e must equal the objective expectation of X_t conditional on ϕ_{t-1}: that is, $X_t^e = E(X_t|\phi_{t-1})$. Thus in the following equation,

$$(3) \qquad X_t^e = Z_{1,t-1}\alpha_1^* + Z_{2,t-1}\alpha_2^* + v_t,$$

rationality implies that $\alpha_1 = \alpha_1^*$, $\alpha_2 = \alpha_2^*$ and v_t is identically zero. However, in dealing with actual data on expectations, the following weaker definition of rationality is used which allows for a nonzero observation error v_t:

$$(4) \qquad E(X_t - X_t^e|\phi_{t-1}) = 0.$$

This definition still requires that $\alpha_1 = \alpha_1^*$ and $\alpha_2 = \alpha_2^*$, yet it allows the observation error v_t to be nonzero with the restriction that $E(v_t|\phi_{t-1}) = 0$. If v_t is identically zero, then X_t^e is a minimum-variance unbiased forecast of X_t. Replacing the restriction that v_t be identically zero with the restriction that $E(v_t|\phi_{t-1}) = 0$ will remove the minimum variance property of X_t^e but not the unbiasedness conditional on ϕ_{t-1}.

Observe that (4) implies that the forecast error is uncorrelated with information in ϕ_{t-1}. This implication of rational expectations is the basis for the following test procedure. The null hypothesis of rationality is tested by testing the coefficient $\omega = 0$ in the regression equation

$$(5) \qquad X_t - X_t^e = Z_{1,t-1}\omega + \eta_t,$$

when η_t = error term where $E(\eta_t|\phi_{t-1})$ is assumed to equal zero. This is the most common test of rationality used, for example, to study forward rate forecasts in the foreign exchange market (see Levich 1979).

The effect of ignoring relevant information in this test becomes clear when equation (3) is subtracted from (1) to obtain the following equation for the forecast error:

$$(6) \qquad X_t - X_t^e = Z_{1,t-1}(\alpha_1 - \alpha_1^*) + Z_{2,t-1}(\alpha_2 - \alpha_2^*) + u_t - v_t.$$

Recall that rationality implies that $\alpha_1 - \alpha_1^* = 0$, $\alpha_2 - \alpha_2^* = 0$, and $E(u_t - v_t | \phi_{t-1}) = 0$. Therefore, under the hypothesis of rationality, the coefficient $\hat{\omega}$ estimated from the OLS regression of $X_t - X_t^e$ on $Z_{1,t-1}$ in (5) will be a consistent estimate of $\alpha_1 - \alpha_1^*$ and should not be significantly different from zero. This follows directly from the orthogonality of Z_{t-1} and η_t [$\eta_t = Z_{2,t-1}(\alpha_2 - \alpha_2^*) + u_t - v_t$]. Note that under rationality $\hat{\omega}$ is a consistent estimate of $\alpha_1 - \alpha_1^*$ even if Z_2, which is the set of relevant variables excluded from the regression, is not empty. Thus leaving out relevant variables from the OLS regression (5) will not affect the rationality implication that $\hat{\omega}$ should not differ significantly from zero.

Another way of stating the point is that the test described here is a test of rationality no matter what available past information is included in Z_1 (or no matter what information is excluded from the regression equation). That is, plim $\hat{\omega}$ can differ from zero only if there is a violation of rationality. However, it is possible that plim $\hat{\omega}$ could equal zero even in the presence of irrationality. For example, suppose that $\alpha_1 = \alpha_1^*$, $E(u_t - v_t | \phi_{t-1}) = 0$ and Z_2 is orthogonal to Z_1, yet there is irrationality because $\alpha_2 \neq \alpha_2^*$. In this case, plim $\hat{\omega} = 0$. Therefore, a failure to reject the null hypothesis, even asymptotically, does not rule out irrationality because, in this case, the probability of Type II error does not go to zero as the sample size goes to infinity.

Studies that test for the rationality of survey forecasts (Pesando 1975; Carlson 1977; Mullineaux 1978; Friedman 1980) use the following alternative procedure. Consider the following least-squares regression equations:

(7) $$X_t = Z_{1,t-1}\gamma + u_{1t},$$

(8) $$X_t^e = Z_{1,t-1}\gamma^* + u_{2t},$$

where

γ, γ^* = coefficients
u_{1t}, u_{2t} = error terms where $E(u_{1t} | \phi_{t-1})$ and $E(u_{2t} | \phi_{t-1})$ are assumed to equal zero.

As is pointed out in Modigliani and Shiller (1973), rationality of expectations requires that plim $\hat{\gamma}$ = plim $\hat{\gamma}^*$. This implication of rationality becomes clear if we suppose that Z_2, the set of variables excluded from the regressions in (7) and (8), is empty; that is, the regressions in (7) and (8) contain all information in ϕ_{t-1} relevant for forecasting X_t. In this case, $\hat{\gamma}$ and $\hat{\gamma}^*$ are each consistent estimates of α_1 under the null hypothesis of rationality, and they should not differ significantly. One way to test $\gamma = \gamma^*$ is to stack (7) and (8) into a single regression and perform a Chow (1960) test for the equality of coefficients (see Pesando 1975). However, if the variance of residuals in (7) differs, as is likely, from the variance of residuals in (8), a correction must be made for this heteroscedasticity (see Mullineaux 1978). Note that testing the cross-equation restriction $\gamma = \gamma^*$ is equivalent to testing $\omega = 0$, in (5), since

(9) $$\hat{\omega} = (Z_1'Z_1)^{-1}Z_1'(X - X^e) = (Z_1'Z_1)^{-1}X$$
$$- (Z_1'Z_1)^{-1}Z_1'X^e = \hat{\gamma} - \hat{\gamma}^*,$$

where X_1 and X^e are $n \times 1$ vectors with X_t and X_t^e, respectively, in row t. Similarly Z_1 is a matrix of n rows with $Z_{1,t-1}$ in row t.

Now suppose that Z_2 is not empty, so that relevant variables are excluded from (7) and (8). In this case, the estimates $\hat{\gamma}$ and $\hat{\gamma}^*$ generally will not be consistent estimates of α_1 and α_1^*, respectively, even if expectations are rational. However, rationality of expectations still implies that plim $\hat{\gamma} =$ plim $\hat{\gamma}^*$ because, as shown above, $\hat{\gamma} - \hat{\gamma}^*$ is numerically equal to $\hat{\omega}$ and plim $\hat{\omega} = 0$. Another way to understand this finding is to calculate the plims of $\hat{\gamma}$ and $\hat{\gamma}^*$. They are

(10) $$\text{plim } \hat{\gamma} = \alpha_1 + (Z_1'Z_1)^{-1}Z_1'Z_2\alpha_2,$$

(11) $$\text{plim } \hat{\gamma}^* = \alpha_1^* + (Z_1'Z_1)^{-1}Z_1'Z_2\alpha_2^*.$$

Rationality implies that $\alpha_1 = \alpha_1^*$, $\alpha_2 = \alpha_2^*$, and hence plim $\hat{\gamma} =$ plim $\hat{\gamma}^*$. As is obvious from (10) and (11), the equality of plim $\hat{\gamma}$ and plim $\hat{\gamma}^*$ reflects the equal asymptotic bias in the two estimates.

This section has analyzed tests of rationality in the presence of some observable measure of expectations. The general conclusion is that a rejection of $\gamma = \gamma^*$ or, equivalently, of $\omega = 0$, is a rejection of rational expectations regardless of the completeness of the information set specified by Z_1. The two alternative procedures discussed here are thus tests of rationality under quite general conditions.

In the absence of direct observations of expectations, we must infer information on expectations from observed market behavior. The next section discusses the use of security price data to test for the rationality of expectations.

3.3   Test of Rationality and Market Efficiency

The most common tests of rationality (efficiency) in capital markets focus on the condition derived in the previous chapter:

(12) $$E(y_t - \widetilde{y}_t | \phi_{t-1}) = 0,$$

where y_t is a one-period return for a security and $\widetilde{y}_t$ is the expected return generated from a model of market equilibrium. Equation (12) above implies that $y_t - \widetilde{y}_t^*$ should be uncorrelated with any past information in ϕ_{t-1}. It is the basis for a common test of market efficiency (see Fama 1976a) in which the null hypothesis that $\alpha = 0$ is tested in the regression equation below:

(13) $y_t = \tilde{y}_t + Z_{t-1}\alpha + \mu_t$

where

Z_{t-1} = variables contained in ϕ_{t-1},
α = coefficients,
μ_t = error term where $E(\mu_t | \phi_{t-1})$ is assumed to equal zero.

A test of the null hypothesis that $\alpha = 0$ is a test of the joint hypothesis of market efficiency (rationality) and the model of market equilibrium, no matter what past information is included in Z.

The "efficient-markets model" of the previous chapter that satisfies (12) is:

(14) $y_t = \tilde{y}_t + (X_t - X_t^e)\beta + \epsilon_t,$

where

ϵ_t = a scalar disturbance with the property $E(\epsilon_t | \phi_{t-1}) = 0$—thus ϵ is serially uncorrelated and uncorrelated with X_t^e,
X_t = the k-element row vector containing variables relevant to the pricing of the security at time t,
X_t^e = the k-element row vector of one-period-ahead rational forecasts of X_t, that is, $X_t^e = E(X_t | \phi_{t-1})$,
β = $k \times 1$ vector of coefficients.

As in Chapter 2, the linear forecasting equation for the k variables in X_t is

(15) $X_t = Z_{t-1}\gamma + u_t,$

where

$\gamma = l \times k$ matrix of coefficients.
$u_t = k$-element row vector of disturbances where $E(u_t | \phi_{t-1})$ is assumed to equal zero.

When we apply rational expectations, (14) becomes

(16) $y_t = \tilde{y}_t + (X_t - Z_{t-1}\gamma^*)\beta + \epsilon_t,$

where $\gamma = \gamma^*$.

The system of (15) and (16) can be estimated with the methodology outlined in the previous chapter. The cross-equation constraints implied by market efficiency (rationality), $\gamma = \gamma^*$, can be tested with a likelihood ratio test and are analogous to the rationality constraints for the regressions (7) and (8). Although expectations are not directly observable, we can test their rationality by maintaining the equilibrium model of $\tilde{y}$ and the condition that only contemporaneous unanticipated movements in X_t are correlated with $y_t - \tilde{y}_t$. Any rejection of the constraint $\gamma = \gamma^*$ could indicate a failure either of the rationality of expectations about X_t or of the maintained equilibrium model. This interpretation of such a test is discussed in the previous chapter.

Two questions arise about the econometric properties of this procedure. First, does it provide a test of market efficiency (rationality) under the maintained model of $\tilde{y}_t$ even if Z_{t-1} excludes variables relevant to forecasting X_t? Second, what is the relation of this test to the common test for market efficiency using equation (13)? These questions are related; the following theorem provides answers.

3.3.1   Theorem

Consider the system of equations

(a)
$$X_t = Z_{t-1}\gamma + u_t,$$
$$y_t = \tilde{y}_t^* + (X_t - Z_{t-1}\gamma^*)\beta + \epsilon_t,$$

where X_t is a k-element row vector, Z_{t-1} is an l-element row vector, y_t and $\tilde{y}_t$ are scalars, γ and γ^* are $l \times k$ parameter matrices, β is a $k \times 1$ parameter vector, u_t is a k-element row vector, and ϵ_t is a scalar. Consider also the equation

(b)
$$y_t = \tilde{y}_t + Z_{t-1}\alpha + \mu_t,$$

where α is an $l \times 1$ parameter vector. The quasi-likelihood ratio test of the null hypothesis $\gamma = \gamma^*$ in (a) is asymptotically equivalent to a quasi-F test of the null hypothesis $\alpha = 0$ in (b). (The quasi-likelihood ratio and quasi–F tests are constructed as if the disturbances, u_t, ϵ_t, and μ_t are i.i.d. normal.)

Outline of Proof

(See Abel and Mishkin [1980] for a more detailed and formal proof.) The key insight in the proof of this theorem is to observe that the system (a) can be rewritten as

(17)
$$X_t = Z_{t-1}\gamma + u_t,$$
$$y_t = \tilde{y}_t + (X_t - Z_{t-1}\gamma)\beta + Z_{t-1}\theta + \epsilon_t,$$

where $\theta = (\gamma - \gamma^*)\beta$. The null hypothesis $\gamma = \gamma^*$ will be true only if $\theta = 0$, and this constraint can be tested using the nonlinear least-squares procedures described in the previous chapter. The constraint that γ is the same in both equations in (17) is not binding, so we can estimate the parameters in (17) by OLS on each equation. Specifically, the estimate $\hat{\gamma}$ is obtained by OLS on the first equation. Treating $\tilde{y}_t$ as known, $\hat{\beta}$ and $\hat{\theta}$ are obtained from an OLS regression of $y_t - \tilde{y}_t$ on $X_t - Z_{t-1}\hat{\gamma}$ and Z_{t-1}. Since the residuals from the first equation in (17), $X_t - Z_{t-1}\hat{\gamma}$, are orthogonal to Z_{t-1} by construction, the estimate of θ will not be affected if $X_t - Z_{t-1}\hat{\gamma}$ is omitted from the list of regressors when OLS is applied to the second equation in (17). Thus the estimate of θ is numerically identical to, and has the same distribution as, the OLS estimate of α in (b). Although the test statistic associated with the null hypothesis $\alpha = 0$ may differ in small samples from the test statistic associated with the null hypothesis $\theta = 0$, these test statistics will be asymptotically equal.

3.3.2   Remarks

The theorem is valid regardless of the properties of the error terms u and ϵ. If they are not i.i.d., the two test procedures will be asymptotically equivalent, but neither will yield test statistics with the assumed asymptotic distributions. If the contemporaneous correlation of u and ϵ is zero, the OLS regression of y on $\hat{u}$ ($\hat{u} = X - Z\hat{\gamma}$) and Z will provide consistent estimates of both β and θ. If the contemporaneous correlation of u and ϵ is unknown, then β is unidentified. Nevertheless, in this case the OLS estimate of θ is still consistent and the theorem continues to apply. Since β is, in general, unidentified, there is an alternative demonstration of this theorem. The maximized value of the likelihood function is not affected by an arbitrary choice of β. Therefore, set β equal to zero, and observe that we now have a seemingly unrelated system (Zellner 1962) in which the right-hand-side variables are identical in each equation. The estimates of γ and θ thus can be obtained from OLS equation by equation.

Observe that the second equation in (17) contains a model of market equilibrium. The proof outlined above treats $\tilde{y}_t$ as known. If it is unknown and assumed to be a linear function of past variables W_{t-1}, then W_{t-1} must also be included as explanatory variables in the time series model for X_t. The orthogonality of the residuals in the equations for X_t with the other right-hand-side variables in the second equation of (17) is thus preserved, and the proof of the theorem may proceed as above. This becomes clear in the proof of the corollary in Section 3.4. Of course, if the coefficients of W_{t-1} in the model of market equilibrium are estimated, then we cannot test the rationality restriction that $y_t - \tilde{y}_t$ is uncorrelated with W_{t-1}. The question of the testability of such restrictions has been discussed in Appendix 2.1.

Observe also that $\theta = (\gamma - \gamma^*)\beta$ is an $l \times 1$ vector. Thus the test of $\theta = 0$ (or, equivalently, $\alpha = 0$) is a test of only l constraints. However, there are $l \times k$ constraints in $\gamma = \gamma^*$. Therefore, all these constraints are testable only if $k = 1$. Even when $k > 1$, imposing the constraint $\gamma = \gamma^*$ places only l binding restrictions on the system in (a). For example, consider the case in which $l = k = 2$. The system of equations can be written as

(18)
$$X_{1t} = \gamma_{11}Z_{1,t-1} + \gamma_{21}Z_{2,t-1} + u_{1t},$$
$$X_{2t} = \gamma_{12}Z_{1,t-1} + \gamma_{22}Z_{2,t-1} + u_{2t},$$
$$y_t = \beta_1 X_{1t} + \beta_2 X_{2t} - (\gamma_{11}^*\beta_1 + \gamma_{12}^*\beta_2)Z_{1,t-1}$$
$$- (\gamma_{21}^*\beta_1 + \gamma_{22}^*\beta_2)Z_{2,t-1} + \epsilon_t.$$

The four parameters γ_{ij} can be estimated from the first two equations. If $\text{Cov}(\epsilon_t, u_{it})$ is known to be zero, we can estimate β_1, β_2, $(\gamma_{11}^*\beta_1 + \gamma_{12}^*\beta_2)$, and $(\gamma_{21}^*\beta_1 + \gamma_{22}^*\beta_2)$ from the third equation. Since we cannot estimate the four elements γ_{ij}^*, separately, we cannot separately test the four restrictions $\gamma_{ij} = \gamma_{ij}^*$. However, we can test $l = 2$ linear combinations of the rationality restrictions.

(19) $$(\gamma_{i1} - \gamma_{i1}^*)\beta_1 + (\gamma_{i2} - \gamma_{i2}^*)\beta_2 = 0 \qquad \text{for } i = 1 \text{ and } 2.$$

If we do not know the covariances of ϵ_t and u_{it}, then β_1 and β_2 are not identified. However, we can still test whether the two linear combinations above are equal to zero. To see this, rewrite the third equation as

(20) $$y_t = [(\gamma_{11} - \gamma_{11}^*)\beta_1 + (\gamma_{12} - \gamma_{12}^*)\beta_2]Z_{1,t-1} + [(\gamma_{21} - \gamma_{21}^*)\beta_1$$
$$+ (\gamma_{22} - \gamma_{22}^*)\beta_2]Z_{2,t-1} + \beta_1 u_{1t} + \beta_2 u_{2t} + \epsilon_t.$$

Observe that the coefficients of $Z_{1,t-1}$ and $Z_{2,t-1}$ in the rewritten equation are the testable linear combinations of rationality restrictions.

3.3.3 Implications

The most interesting implication of the above theorem is similar to the finding in Section 3.2: a rejection of the cross-equation restriction $\gamma = \gamma^*$ is a rejection of market efficiency or, equivalently, rationality (maintaining the model of market equilibrium) whether or not the information set in Z_1 is complete. This is demonstrated by noting that the test of $\gamma = \gamma^*$ is asymptotically equivalent to the test of $\alpha = 0$, which is clearly a test of the efficient-markets condition (12), regardless of what past information is included in Z. However, if the model generating X_t is not correctly specified, then in general there is an errors-in-variables bias that leads to inconsistent estimates of β and γ. Nonetheless, any asymptotic bias in $\hat{\gamma}$ will be identical to that in $\hat{\gamma}^*$.

The theorem implies further that rationality (or market efficiency) does not rule out significant correlations of $y_t - \tilde{y}_t$ with current variables. Therefore, if information not available at time $t - 1$ is included in the Z_{t-1} vector—as in earlier work mentioned in Chapter 2—then neither procedure provides a test of rationality.

3.4 Tests of the Short-Run Neutrality of Aggregate Demand Policy

Sargent (1976a) discusses tests of a classical equilibrium macroeconometric model with a Lucas (1973) supply function of the form

(21) $$y_t = \tilde{y}_t + (X_t - X_t^e)\beta + \epsilon_t,$$

where

y_t = a scalar representing output or unemployment at time t,

$\tilde{y}_t$ = the equilibrium (natural rate) level of output or unemployment at time t,

X_t = a k-element vector of aggregate demand variables, such as the price level or the money supply at time t,

ϵ_t = scalar disturbance term with the property $E(\epsilon_t|\phi_{t-1}) = 0$.

This equation has the neutrality property that only unanticipated changes in X_t have an effect on $y_t - \tilde{y}_t$. Note that it is one form of the MRE equation discussed in the preceding chapter and has the same form as the efficient-markets model (14). As before, we must specify how $\tilde{y}_t$, the equilibrium level of output or unemployment, is calculated in order to give the supply function empirical content. A particular specification often used with the Lucas supply function is

$$(22) \qquad \tilde{y}_t = \sum_{i=1}^{L} \lambda_i y_{t-i}.$$

Suppose that X_t is generated by the forecasting model

$$(23) \qquad X_t = Z_{t-1}\gamma + \sum_{i=1}^{L'} \psi_i y_{t-i} + u_t,$$

where

Z_{t-1} = an l-element row vector of predetermined variables other than lagged y_t,

γ = an $l \times k$ matrix of coefficients,

ψ_i = a k-element row vector of coefficients.

Note that (23) has the same form as the forecasting model (15) in the preceding section, except that in (23) we distinguish between lagged values of y_t and other predetermined variables. We assume for the moment that $E(u_t|\phi_{t-1}) = 0$ and combine (21)–(23) to obtain the system

$$(24) \qquad X_t = Z_{t-1}\gamma + \sum_{i=1}^{L'} \psi_i y_{t-i} + u_t,$$

$$y_t = \left(X_t - Z_{t-1}\gamma^* - \sum_{i=1}^{L'} \psi_i^* y_{t-i}\right)\beta + \sum_{i=1}^{L} \lambda_i y_{t-i} + \epsilon_t$$

with the cross-equation rationality constraints $\gamma = \gamma^*$ and $\psi_i = \psi_i^*$, $i = 1,$ $\ldots, L'$. Any rejection of these constraints could indicate a violation of the null hypothesis of rationality, or of the maintained hypothesis of the equilibrium model.

Sargent (1976a) uses Granger (1969) causality tests to test the joint hypothesis of rationality of expectations and the equilibrium model described in (21) in (22) above, which embodies the neutrality of anticipated policy. Substituting (22) into (21) and taking expectations conditional on ϕ_{t-1}, we have

$$(25) \qquad E(y_t|\phi_{t-1}) = \sum_{i=1}^{L} \lambda_i y_{t-i} = E(y_t|y_{t-1}, y_{t-2}, \ldots, y_{t-L}).$$

In other words, the optimal linear forecast for y_t does not benefit from the use of other information besides past y's. Hence, the equilibrium model in Sargent (1976a) requires that any past information, Z_{t-1}, fails to Granger-cause y_t. Specifically, if OLS is used to estimate the parameters v_i and α in the regression equation,

$$(26) \qquad y_t = \sum_{i=1}^{L'} v_i y_{t-i} + Z_{t-1}\alpha + \mu_t,$$

where $L' \geq L$, the estimate of α should not differ significantly from zero.

The relationship between tests of the cross-equation constraints in (24) and the Granger-causality test in (26) is made clear by the following corollary.

Corollary

If $L' \geq L$, then a quasi-likelihood ratio test of the null hypothesis $\gamma = \gamma^*$ in (24) is asymptotically equivalent to a quasi–F test of the null hypothesis that $\alpha = 0$ in (26).

Outline of Proof

As in the proof of the theorem, the unconstrained system (24) can be rewritten as

$$(27) \qquad X_t = Z_{t-1}\gamma + \sum_{i=1}^{L'} \psi_i y_{t-i} + u_t,$$

$$y_t = \left(X_t - Z_{t-1}\gamma - \sum_{i=1}^{L'} \psi_i y_{t-i}\right)\beta + \sum_{i=1}^{L} \lambda_i y_{t-i}$$

$$+ Z_{t-1}\theta_o + \sum_{i=1}^{L'} \theta_i y_{t-i} + \epsilon_t,$$

where $\theta_o = (\gamma - \gamma^*)\beta$ and $\theta_i = (\psi_i - \psi_i^*)$ for $i = 1, \ldots, L'$, and it can be estimated by OLS on each equation. Note that since θ_i and λ_i are both coefficients of y_{t-i} in (27), the separate parameters θ_i and λ_i are not identified for $i \leq L$. Hence, the constraints $\psi_i = \psi_i^*$ for $i \leq L$ are not testable. In order to test the testable cross-equation restrictions, the system (27) can be estimated by OLS on each equation, as explained in the proof of the theorem in Section 3.3. Since the estimated residuals from the first equation will be orthogonal to Z_{t-1} and y_{t-i} for $i = 1, \ldots, L'$, the deletion of this residual vector from the second equation will not affect the OLS estimates of the coefficients on Z_{t-1} and y_{t-i}. Hence, as in the previous proof, the least-squares estimates of α and θ_o will be numerically identical, and the test statistics associated with the null hypotheses $\alpha = 0$ and $\theta_o = 0$ will be asymptotically equal.

Remarks

Obviously, OLS cannot be applied directly to the second equation of (27) as it is written since for $i \leq L$, y_{t-i} appears twice on the right-hand side because we must estimate the parameters of the $\tilde{y}_t$ model. OLS can be used after this equation has been rewritten to eliminate the perfect collinearity of right-hand-side variables. Thus we cannot obtain testable restrictions on ψ_i^* for $i = 1, \ldots, L$. However, the constraints $\theta_i = 0$ and hence $\psi_i = \psi_i^*$ for $i = L + 1, \ldots, L'$ are testable with the identifying restriction that the lag length L in (22) is shorter than the lag length L' in (23). This seems a rather strong assumption to impose on the basis of a priori knowledge, and one should be cautious in interpreting results based on estimates of θ_i in this case.

Implications

It is important to consider the effects of specifying the list of variables included in Z_{t-1} incorrectly. Irrelevant predetermined variables in Z_{t-1} will not lead to inconsistent parameter estimates but will, in general, reduce the power of tests. On the other hand, excluding relevant variables from Z_{t-1} will lead to a breakdown of the assumption that $E(u_t|\phi_{t-1}) = 0$, and will lead to inconsistent estimates of γ. Even in this case, however, any rejection of the constraint $\gamma = \gamma^*$ in (24) indicates a failure of rationality, or of the equilibrium model which embodies neutrality, since a rejection of this constraint indicates that Z Granger-causes y. As demonstrated above, this implication holds regardless of the information included in Z.

The procedure outlined therefore provides a test of the joint hypothesis of rationality and the equilibrium model, even if relevant predetermined variables are omitted from Z_{t-1}. This result can be used to show that Lucas's (1972) conjecture that tests of neutrality cannot be conducted when there is a change in policy regime is not always correct. If there are two policy regimes in the sample period 1 to T with the break occurring at T_1, then there is a separate forecasting equation for each regime: for example,

$$(28) \qquad \begin{aligned} X_t &= Z_{t-1}\gamma_1 + u_{1t} & \text{for } t = 1 \text{ to } T_1 - 1, \\ X_t &= Z_{t-1}\gamma_2 + u_{2t} & \text{for } t = T_1 \text{ to } T. \end{aligned}$$

Using dummy variables, we can write one forecasting equation for both regimes:

$$(29) \qquad X_t = Z_{t-1}\gamma_1 + Z_{t-1}^*\xi + u_t \qquad \text{for } t = 1 \text{ to } T,$$

where

$$Z_{t-1}^* = \begin{cases} 0 & \text{for } t = 1 \text{ to } T_1 - 1 \\ Z_{t-1} & \text{for } t = T_1 \text{ to } T \end{cases}$$

$$\xi = \gamma_2 - \gamma_1$$

$$u_t = \begin{cases} u_{1t} & \text{for } t = 1 \text{ to } T_1 - 1 \\ u_{2t} & \text{for } t = T_1 \text{ to } T \end{cases}$$

Neglecting to take account of a change in policy regime is, therefore, equivalent to omitting the relevant set of variables Z_{t-1}^* from the forecasting equation. But as we have seen, even if Z_{t-1} excludes this relevant information because its variables are chosen without considering the change in policy regime, a test of the cross-equation restriction $\gamma = \gamma^*$ continues to be a test of the joint hypothesis enbodying neutrality. An important caveat, however, needs to be mentioned. The change in policy regime could alter the population variances of the error terms in both the forecasting equation and the output or unemployment equations. Unless attention is devoted to correcting potential heteroscedasticity that can arise as a result, the test statistics may lead to misleading inference.

McCallum (1979a) and Nelson (1979) emphasize the point raised by Sargent (1973, 1976b) that the Granger-causality tests are tests of the neutrality of anticipated policy only if (1) lagged values of $X_t - X_t^e$ do not enter the supply function (21), or (ii) the disturbance ϵ_t in (21) is serially uncorrelated. That is, if either of these two conditions does not hold, then it is possible for Z to Granger-cause y even though anticipated policy is neutral.

The analysis in the present chapter demonstrates these points also. The corollary above breaks down if there are lagged surprises in (21) and hence in (24). Although the contemporaneous residual from the first equation in (27) is, by construction, orthogonal to Z_{t-1} and y_{t-i}, the lagged residuals are not. Thus, the test of $\gamma = \gamma^*$ will no longer be equivalent to a Granger-causality test. Granger-causality will no longer be a test of the joint hypothesis of rationality and the model of equilibrium output.

Now consider the case in which only contemporaneous innovations in X_t appear in (21) and (24), but ϵ_t is serially correlated, implying that μ_t is serially correlated. Here, the corollary holds and the Granger-causality test is asymptotically equivalent to the test of $\gamma = \gamma^*$. However, since the right-hand sides of both (24) and (26) include lagged dependent variables, the estimates of α and θ_o will no longer be consistent. Test statistics from both procedures are invalid in this case. To obtain valid test statistics for the joint hypothesis, we correct the supply function (21) for serial correlation by quasi-differencing and generate specification with a serially uncorrelated error. The resulting specification will contain lagged as well as current $X_t - X_t^e$. We are then dealing with the case above where the Granger-causality test is no longer a test of the joint hypothesis.

3.5   Summary and Conclusions

The framework in this chapter ties together a range of issues in testing rationality, financial market efficiency, and the short-run neutrality of aggregate demand policy. Two main themes stand out in this integrated framework:

1. The cross-equation tests of rationality, market efficiency, and short-run neutrality discussed here are asymptotically equivalent to more common single-equation regression tests.

2. The exact specification of the relevant information set used in rational forecasts is not necessary for the cross-equation tests of rationality, market efficiency, and short-run neutrality to have desirable asymptotic properties.

2 Empirical Studies

4   Are Market
       Forecasts Rational?

4.1   Introduction

This chapter presents tests of the rationality of both inflation and short-term interest rate forecasts in the bond market. These tests make use of security price data to infer information on market expectations. A closer look at whether market forecasts of inflation and interest rates are rational seems necessary in light of recent work (Pesando 1975; Carlson 1977; Mullineaux 1978; Friedman 1980) that evaluates the inflation and interest rate forecasts from the Livingston and Goldsmith-Nagan surveys. A frequent empirical result in these studies is that the survey forecasts are inconsistent with the restrictions implied by the theory of rational expectations. What conclusions about the behavior of market expectations should we draw from these results?

One view which associates survey forecasts with market forecasts takes these empirical results to be evidence that the market is not exploiting all information in generating its forecasts. The Friedman (1980) study is particularly disturbing in this regard because it uses data from the Goldsmith-Nagan interest rate survey which is made up of interest rate forecasts from actual participants in the market.

An alternative view, Pesando (1975) for example, holds that markets probably do display rationality of expectations. Irrationality in the Livingston and Goldsmith-Nagan survey data would then indicate that these data cannot be used in empirical work to describe market expectations.

The latter view receives support for two reasons. Survey data are frequently believed to be inaccurate reflections of the behavior of market participants and are considered unreliable. More important is a point emphasized in Chapter 2 that is often ignored in discussing the properties of expectations. *Not all market participants need be rational for a market to display rational expectations.* The behavior of a market is not necessarily the same as the behavior of the average individual. As long as unexploited profit opportunities are eliminated by some participants in a market, then the market will behave as though expectations are rational despite irrational participants in that market. Therefore, survey forecasts do not necessarily describe the forecasts inherent in market behavior, and the irrationality of survey forecasts does not in itself imply that market forecasts are also irrational.

One purpose of this chapter is to provide indirect evidence on the usefulness of survey data like Livingston's and Goldsmith-Nagan's for describing the expectations reflected by markets. In particular, this chapter contains direct tests of the rationality of the bond market's interest rate and inflation forecasts, tests similar to those found in the studies mentioned in the opening paragraph. Because these tests are designed to use actual price data to infer information on market expectations rather than relying on survey data, they can provide direct information on the rationality of a particular market. They permit a clearer interpretation of results that indicate irrationality in survey forecasts. The empirical work in this chapter thus will shed light not only on the value of these surveys for further research, but also on the rationality of expectations in such markets as those in which bonds are traded.

4.2   Tests of Forecast Rationality

Rationality of expectations requires that

$$(1) \qquad E(X_t - X_t^e | \phi_{t-1}) = 0,$$

where X_t^e is the one-period-ahead forecast of a variable X_t, generated at the end of period $t - 1$, and ϕ_{t-1} is the set of information available at the end of $t - 1$. This implies that the forecast error, $X_t - X_t^e$, should be uncorrelated with any information or linear combinations of information in ϕ_{t-1}.

This implication is the basis of the tests of rationality found in the studies of survey forecasts mentioned above. Consider the following regression equations where we assume that $E(u_{1t}|\phi_{t-1}) = E(u_{2t}|\phi_{t-1}) = 0$:

$$(2) \qquad X_t = b_o + \sum_{i=1}^{k} b_i X_{t-i} + u_{1t},$$

$$(3) \qquad X_t^e = c_o + \sum_{i=1}^{k} c_i X_{t-i} + u_{2t}.$$

These equations can be estimated with ordinary least squares (OLS), and under the hypothesis of rational expectations Modigliani and Shiller

(1973) point out that the estimated b_i coefficients should not differ significantly from the estimated c_i coefficients. This null hypothesis that

(4) $$b_i = c_i \text{ for all } i = 0, \ldots, k$$

is subjected to a conventional F test in the survey forecast studies. A more detailed discussion of the rationale behind this test can be found in Chapter 3.

The theory of efficient markets leads to restrictions similar to those in (4) which can also be easily tested. Market efficiency (or, equivalently, rational expectations) implies that securities prices in a capital market should reflect all available information, and hence an expectation assessed by the market should equal the true expectation conditioned on all available information, $E(\ldots |\phi_{t-1})$. To give this concept empirical content, we must specify the relationship between the probability distribution of future prices and current prices. This requires a model which describes how current equilibrium prices are determined. Here, the market is assumed to equate expected, one-period, holding returns across securities, allowing for risk (liquidity) premiums which are constant over time.

In the case of long-term bonds, for example, the one-period return denoted by y_t, is the nominal return from holding the long-term bond from $t - 1$ to t, including both capital gains plus interest payments. The model of market equilibrium implies that the equilibrium return $\tilde{y}_t$ is

(5) $$\tilde{y}_t = E_m(y_t|\phi_{t-1}) = r_{t-1} + d,$$

where

$$r_{t-1} = \text{the return on a one-period bond from } t - 1 \text{ to } t$$
$$\text{(which of course equals the expected one-period}$$
$$\text{return)—this is just the short-term interest rate,}$$
$$d = \text{the constant liquidity (risk) premium,}$$
$$E_m(\ldots |\phi_{t-1}) = \text{expectation assessed by the market at } t - 1.$$

As discussed in Chapter 2 market efficiency implies that

(6) $$E(y_t - \tilde{y}_t|\phi_{t-1}) = E(y_t - r_{t-1} - d|\phi_{t-1}) = 0.$$

If we call the equilibrium return of $\tilde{y}_t$ a "normal" return, then the equation above states that no unexploited profit opportunities exist in the bond market: at today's price, market participants cannot expect to earn a higher-than-normal return by investing in a long-term bond. The efficient markets equation (6) is analogous to an arbitrage condition. Arbitrageurs who are willing to speculate may perceive unexploited profit opportunities and purchase or sell bonds until the price is driven to the point where (6) holds. Thus market efficiency does not require that all participants in the market are rational and use information efficiently.

The average behavior of an individual in the market is not a reliable guide to the market's behavior.

Equation (6) above implies that $y_t - r_{t-1}$ should be uncorrelated with any past available information or linear combinations of this information. A model consistent with (6)—referred to as the efficient-markets model—is

(7) $$y_t = r_{t-1} + d + (X_t - X_t^e)\beta + \epsilon_t,$$

where an e superscript denotes expected values conditional on all past available information (i.e., $X_t^e = E(X_t|\phi_{t-1})$, a one-period-ahead rational forecast), and

X_t = a variable (or vector of variables) relevant to the pricing of long bonds,

β = a coefficient (or vector of coefficients),

ϵ_t = an error process where $E(\epsilon_t|\phi_{t-1}) = 0$ and hence ϵ_t is serially uncorrelated.

The efficient-markets model stresses that only when new information hits the market will y_t differ from $r_{t-1} + d$. As equation (7) makes clear, this is equivalent to the proposition that only unanticipated changes (surprises) in variables can be correlated with $y_t - r_{t-1}$.

The assumption that the coefficient on r_{t-1} equals one in equation (7) has been subjected to empirical test by Fama and Schwert (1977) and Mishkin (1978) and is not rejected. It has been tested also for the 1954–1976 sample period of this chapter. A quarterly bond returns series was regressed on the beginning of period, ninety-day Treasury Bill rate (also at quarterly rates) using weighted least squares to correct for heteroscedasticity. (Mishkin 1978 describes this procedure.) The coefficient on the bill rate was not significantly different from one at the 5 percent level ($t = .51$). In a recent paper, Shiller (1979) has found evidence suggesting that the liquidity premium is correlated with the spread between long rates and short rates. To test this proposition for the 1954–1976 sample period, $y_t - r_{t-1}$ was regressed on this spread, again using weighted least squares to correct for heteroscedasticity. The evidence supporting Shiller's proposition is even weaker in this sample period than in the regression results reported in Mishkin (1978): the coefficient on the spread variable did not differ significantly from zero even at the 10 percent significance level ($t = 1.01$). In addition, as is discussed in Chapter 2, as long as the equilibrium return $\bar{y}_t$ has small variation relative to other sources of variation in the actual returns, assumptions describing the equilibrium return are not critical to empirical tests of the efficient-markets model. This appears to be the case for the long-term bonds discussed here. For example, using the model of market equilibrium described above, over the 1954–1976 period the variation in

$\tilde{y}_t$ is less than 2 percent of the variation in the actual return stemming from other sources.

It is easy to show that this efficient-markets model is consistent with the expectations hypothesis of the term structure where predictions of future short-term interest rates are optimal forecasts. To be more concrete, if the long-term bond is an n-period security where the liquidity premium is a constant d, the expectations hypothesis of the term structure is approximated by

$$(8) \qquad RL_t = \frac{1}{n} \, E_t(r_t + r_{t+1} + \ldots + r_{t+n-1}) + d,$$

where

RL_t = the interest rate (yield to maturity) on the long bond,
$E_t = E_m(\ldots \, |\phi_{t-1})$,
n = number of periods until maturity.

When expectations of future short rates are rational, then with some algebraic manipulation the expectations hypothesis described by this equation yields the same implications as equation (7). Note also that the efficient-markets model does not imply causation from $X_t - X_t^e$ to $y_t - r_{t-1}$. It is equally plausible that causation runs in the other direction or that a third factor affects both of these variables simultaneously.

Given a forecasting equation for X_t of the form of equation (2), rationality of expectations implies that

$$(9) \qquad X_t^e = c_o + \sum_{i=1}^{k} c_i X_{t-i},$$

where $c_i = b_i$ for all i because X_t^e must equal the conditional expectation of equation (2). Substituting (9) into (7) we have an efficient-markets model of the following form:

$$(10) \qquad y_t = r_{t-1} + d + \beta \left[X_t - \left(c_o + \sum_{i=1}^{k} c_i X_{t-i} \right) \right] + \epsilon_t.$$

Equations (10) and (2) can then be stacked into one regression system and estimated by nonlinear least-squares as described in Chapter 2, imposing the restrictions in (4) implied by forecast rationality: that $b_i = c_i$ for all i. In the initial estimates of each equation, Goldfeld-Quandt (1965) tests usually indicate the presence of heteroscedasticity, which is corrected for by weighting observations, using a time-trend procedure outlined in Glesjer (1969). The rationality restrictions can now be tested in the efficient-markets framework with the likelihood ratio test described in Chapter 2.

Chapter 3 demonstrates that the tests of the rationality restrictions are equivalent to more common regression tests of the efficient-markets condition in equation (6). However, as we shall see, exploring the efficiency or rationality of the bond market by analyzing the relation of b_i in equation (2) to the c_i in (10) yields insights that the more common tests do not provide.

4.3 Empirical Results

The first set of tests conducted here will scrutinize Friedman's (1980) finding that the survey measures of interest rate forecasts are inconsistent with rationality. Friedman's results were obtained using thirty quarterly observations extending from September 1969 to December 1976. This sample period is used to estimate the equations (10) and (2) system using bond return and Treasury Bill rate data to be described. Friedman's choice of six lagged quarters in the autoregressive specification will be adapted also. An additional test conducted over the longer 1954–1976 sample period will provide more information about the rationality of the bond market's forecasts.

Tests of the rationality of the CPI inflation forecasts will be conducted in a similar manner using the nonlinear efficient-markets procedure. The 1959–1969 sample period used by Pesando, Carlson, and Mullineaux, where so many rejections of rationality have been found, will be used here, in addition to the longer 1954–1976 sample period.

4.3.1 The Data

The sources and definitions of data used in the empirical work are as follows:

y_t = quarterly return from holding a long-term U.S. government bond from the beginning to the end of the quarter. The data were obtained from the Center for Research in Security Prices (CRSP) at the University of Chicago, and are described in Fisher and Lorie (1977) and Mishkin (1978). Note that this return series is calculated from end-of-period price data to avoid the aggregation problem discussed later in this chapter.

r_t = the end of quarter ninety-day Treasury Bill rate at a quarterly rate. Bill rate data were obtained from the Board of Governors of the Federal Reserve Board.

π_t = the CPI inflation rate (quarterly rate) calculated from the change in the log of the CPI (seasonally adjusted) from the last month of the previous quarter to the last month of the current quarter. The CPI was collected from the U.S. Department of Commerce's *Business Statistics* and *Survey of Current Business*.

4.3.2 Results on the Rationality of Interest Rate Forecasts

Table 4.1 provides the tests for the rationality of forecasts in the bond market both in Friedman's 1969–1976 sample period and in the longer

		Sample Peri
	1969:3–1976:4	195
Likelihood ratio statistic	6.55	4.9(
Marginal significance level	.364	.5⸱

Table 4.1   **Test of Forecast Rationality: Interest Rates**

Note: Likelihood ratio statistic is distributed asymptotically as $\chi^2(6)$. Marginal significance level is the probability of getting that value of the likelihood ratio statistic or higher under the null hypothesis.

1954–1976 sample period, and table 4.2 provides the parameter estimates of the constrained efficient-markets model for both sample periods. The marginal significance levels in table 4.1 are the probability of obtaining that value of χ^2 or higher under the null hypothesis that the rationality constraints are valid. A marginal significance level less than .05 indicates a rejection of the null hypothesis at the 5 percent level and, therefore, a rejection of forecast rationality in the bond market.

As the likelihood ratio statistics in table 4.1 indicate, very little evidence in the bond market data supports irrationality of interest rate forecasts. Not only are there no significant rejections of the rationality restrictions in either Friedman's sample period or the longer 1954–1976 sample period, but the marginal significance levels of table 4.1 are quite high. In addition, the efficient-markets model from which these likelihood ratio statistics have been derived, whose parameter estimates are found in table 4.2, has several attractive properties. The coefficients on the unanticipated movements of the bill rate are significantly different from zero at the 1 percent level, indicating that movements in short-term interest rates are information relevant to the pricing of long-term bonds. As might be expected from the expectations hypothesis of the term structure, the sign of this coefficient is negative, indicating that an unanticipated rise in the bill rate is accompanied by higher long-term rates with a resulting lower bond return. Furthermore, the magnitude of this coefficient is extremely close to that found in another study (Mishkin 1978), where a different measure of short-rate expectations is used.[1]

The failure to reject the rationality of interest rate forecasts in the bond market provides some resolution of how to interpret Friedman's result that the Goldsmith-Nagan survey measures of interest rate forecasts are irrational. This finding suggests that the survey measures of interest rate forecasts are not an accurate description of the actual bond market

---

1. Note that Mishkin (1978) used Treasury Bill data which are at an annual rate rather than a quarterly rate. The coefficient on the unanticipated bill rate, in that case, must be multiplied by four when compared to the β coefficients in table 4.2.

Nonlinear Estimates of the Efficient-Markets Model:

$$y_t = r_{t-1} + d + \beta(r_t - b_0 - \sum_{i=1}^{6} b_i r_{t-i}) + \epsilon_t$$

$$r_t = b_0 + \sum_{i=1}^{6} b_i r_{t-i} + u_t$$

	Sample Period	
	1969:3–1976:4	1954:1–1976:4
d	.0055	− .0018
	(.0091)	(.0032)
β	− 3.3613	− 3.0950
	(1.1642)	(.4566)
b_0	.0240	.0022
	(.0090)	(.0012)
b_1	.6158	1.0706
	(.1750)	(.0869)
b_2	.0639	− .3123
	(.1913)	(.1287)
b_3	.3159	.2189
	(.1869)	(.1331)
b_4	− .1434	.0296
	(.1872)	(.1348)
b_5	− .3195	− .1473
	(.1911)	(.1324)
b_6	.0463	.0906
	(.1790)	(.0909)

Note: Asymptotic standard errors in parentheses.

forecasts. The value of these survey measures to other empirical work is thus suspect. The view that the bond market could have improved its forecasting behavior by exploiting the information in the past bill rate movements more efficiently is not supported. Of course, these results should not be surprising considering how large a body of evidence (e.g., see Fama 1970) supports efficiency in the bond market.

4.3.3 Results on the Rationality of Inflation Forecasts

The test of the rationality of inflation forecasts in the bond market can be found in table 4.3. The parameter estimates of the constrained efficient-markets model are in table 4.4. The efficient-markets model yields the expected result that an unanticipated rise in inflation is associated with higher long-term rates and lower bond returns, although the coefficients on unanticipated inflation are not as significant as the coefficients on unanticipated interest rate movements. However, the likelihood ratio test rejects the rationality restrictions for the 1959–1969 sample period at the 1 percent significance level—this is the sample period where other studies (Pesando 1975; Carlson 1977; Mullineaux 1978) also find the Livingston price expectations data to be irrational.

Table 4.3   **Test of Forecast Rationality:**
                                Inflation

	Sample Period	
	1959:1–1969:4	1954:1–1976:4
Likelihood ratio statistic	23.77	8.70
Marginal significance level	.001	.191

Note: See table 4.1.

A look at the unconstrained estimates of the autoregressive model of inflation and the efficient-markets model provides a clue to why this rejection of rationality occurs. The sum of the coefficients on the lagged inflation rates in the unconstrained autoregressive model of inflation is positive and greater than one, indicating that a rise in inflation would persist: the $\hat{b}_i$ starting with lag one are $-.06, .59, .19, -.03, .30$, and $.25$. On the other hand, the sum of these autoregressive parameters derived from the unconstrained efficient-markets model is negative, indicating that the bond market expected that a rise in inflation would be reversed:

Table 4.4   **Nonlinear Estimates of the Efficient-Markets Model:**

$$y_t = r_{t-1} + d + \beta(\pi_t - b_0 - \sum_{i=1}^{6} b_i \pi_{t-i}) + \epsilon_t$$

$$\pi_t = b_0 + \sum_{i=1}^{6} b_i \pi_{t-i} + u_t$$

	Sample Period	
	1959:1–1969:4	1954:1–1976:4
d	$-.0036$	$-.0019$
	$(.0034)$	$(.0032)$
β	-2.5189	-1.8685
	(1.3319)	$(.8436)$
b_0	$.0003$	$.0012$
	$(.0008)$	$(.0006)$
b_1	$-.0464$	$.3778$
	$(.1461)$	$(.1031)$
b_2	$.6047$	$.5173$
	$(.1210)$	$(.1100)$
b_3	$.2626$	$.2075$
	$(.1497)$	$(.1224)$
b_4	$-.0477$	$-.1555$
	$(.1206)$	$(.1219)$
b_5	$.2104$	$-.0392$
	$(.1147)$	$(.1100)$
b_6	$.1233$	$-.0374$
	$(.1242)$	$(.1035)$

Note: Asymptotic standard errors in parentheses.

the $\hat{c}_i$ starting with lag one are $-.27, .25, 1.04, -.30, -.94$, and -1.60. This discrepancy is what leads to the rejection of the rationality of the bond market's forecasts of inflation, and it should not be all that surprising considering the sample period. The period started with a low inflation rate that then rose to unusually high levels by the end of the period. The fact that this was an unusual period might well cause the rationality restrictions found in table 4.3 to be rejected, even though the bond market would normally have rational inflation forecasts. A similar problem has been found for the rationality of inflation forecasts (represented by forecasts of exchange rate changes) in the German hyperinflation (Frenkel 1977), another unusual inflationary episode. The likelihood ratio test of the rationality of the inflation forecasts in the longer 1954–1976 period provides some evidence for this conjecture. In this period there is no rejection of the rationality restrictions at the 5 percent significance level. The bond market thus appears to have had rational inflation forecasts when a longer time horizon is taken into account.

Because these rationality restrictions are generated under the maintained hypothesis that $y_t - r_{t-1}$ is uncorrelated with anticipated movements by X, the rejection may arise from the invalidity of the maintained hypothesis and not from the irrationality of inflation expectations. To explore this possibility, the hypothesis of the rationality of the X_t^e forecasts can be tested along the lines discussed in Chapter 2 without maintaining the hypothesis that $y_t - r_{t-1}$ is uncorrelated with X_t^e. This involves estimating the system

$$(11) \qquad X_t = b_o + \sum_{i=1}^{k} b_i X_{t-i} + u_{1t},$$

$$y_t = r_{t-1} + d + \beta \left[X_t - \left(c_o + \sum_{i=1}^{k} c_i X_{t-i} \right) \right]$$

$$+ \delta \left(c_o + \sum_{i=1}^{k} c_i X_{t-i} \right) + \epsilon_t,$$

and testing the null hypothesis that $b_i = c_i$ for all i. Note that this procedure tests $k - 1$ restrictions, one less than in the previous tests. When this test for the rationality of the inflation forecasts is conducted with the same 1959–1969 sample period, the data still strongly reject the rationality restrictions. The resulting likelihood ratio statistic [distributed asymptotically as $\chi^2 (5)$] equaled 16.65 with a marginal significance level of .005. This rejection at the 1 percent level adds additional support to the view that inflation forecasts were not rational for this sample period.

The efficient-markets model does not specify whether seasonally adjusted or unadjusted data should be used in these tests. The tests reported in the tables use seasonally adjusted data because they are more compa-

rable with the rationality tests of the Livingston data found in the literature. However, seasonal adjustment of the CPI with the X-11 program
tends to "smudge" the data, and thus the tests here have also been
conducted with seasonally unadjusted data. The results are similar to
those reported in tables 4.3 and 4.4. The likelihood ratio statistic for the
1959:1–1969:4 sample period was 23.25 (marginal significance level of
.001), and for the 1954:1–1976:4 sample period it was 12.32 (marginal
significance level of .055).

What do these results tell us about the accuracy of the Livingston price
expectations data? We must take some care in our interpretation of these
results. The Livingston survey does not sample participants in the bond
market specifically, but the following conclusion nevertheless seems to be
indicated: Because inflation forecasts in the bond market from 1959 to
1969 do not satisfy restrictions implied by rationality, the failure of survey
measures to satisfy these restrictions cannot be taken as evidence that
they are inaccurate measures of market expectations. Clearly, further
research into the rationality of the Livingston price expectations data
over longer sample periods is needed before we can pronounce on their
accuracy.

4.3.4   Joint Tests of the Rationality of Both
Inflation and Interest Rate Forecasts

A further application of these tests relates to the work of Modigliani
and Shiller (1973). Modigliani and Shiller's seminal paper postulates that
information on both short-term interest rates and inflation would influence the price of long-term bonds, along with the proposition that the
autoregressive lag structure on the one-period-ahead short-rate and inflation forecasts would be "rational" in the sense discussed here. They
present evidence supporting this position, yet the evidence is incomplete
in two ways. First, they do not actually apply formal statistical tests to the
proposition of rationality in the autoregressive lag structure. Second,
their use of averaged data in the empirical work leads to a potentially
severe aggregation problem.

A simple example from Mishkin (1978) illustrates Modigliani and
Shiller's argument and why it breaks down with averaged data. Assume
that the stochastic process generating the short-term interest rate r_t has an
ARIMA (0,1,1) characterization as follows:

(12) $$(1 - L)r_t = (1 - \lambda L)u_t$$

or, equivalently,

(13) $$r_t = \frac{1 - \lambda}{1 - \lambda L} r_{t-1} + u_t = (1 - \lambda) \sum_{i=1}^{\infty} \lambda^i r_{t-i} + u_t,$$

where

L = the lag operator,
u_t = error term with the property that $E(u_t|\phi_{t-1}) = 0$.

Assuming expectations are rational, the market's forecast of r_{t+1} at time t is:

(14)
$$E_t r_{t+1} = \frac{1-\lambda}{1-\lambda L} r_t$$

and since $r_{t+2} = r_{t+1} + u_{t+2} - \lambda u_{t+1}$

(15)
$$E_t r_{t+2} = E_t r_{t+1} = \frac{1-\lambda}{1-\lambda L} r_t$$

and, similarly,

(16)
$$E_t r_{t+j} = \frac{1-\lambda}{1-\lambda L} r_t \text{ for all } j \geq 1.$$

Rewriting equation (8), which characterizes the expectations hypothesis of the term structure, the long bond rate at time t, RL_t, is

(17)
$$RL_t = \frac{1}{n} E_t \left(r_t + r_{t+1} + \ldots + r_{t+n-1} \right) + d.$$

Substituting (14)–(16) into (17) we have

(18)
$$RL_t = \frac{r_t}{n} + \left(\frac{n-1}{n} \right) \left(\frac{1-\lambda}{1-\lambda L} \right) r_t + d = \frac{r_t}{n}$$

$$+ \left(\frac{n-1}{n} \right) (1-\lambda) \sum_{i=0}^{\infty} \lambda^i r_{t-i} + d.$$

Modigliani and Shiller postulate that if the bond market is rational then the lag structure in (13) must be consistent with (18): that is, the λ must be the same in the two equations.

Note that the r_t and RL_t are end-of-period variables so this proposition is necessarily valid only for end-of-period data. Indeed, it does not hold for averaged data. To see this, take the case where the short rate is a random walk: that is, $\lambda = 0$ in (12). Working (1960) has shown that a variable that is a random walk will, if it is averaged, have an ARIMA (0,1,1) time-series process with the correlation coefficient at lag one equal to .25. The appearance of the moving average term when the data is averaged is really quite intuitive. If a variable is a random walk, then a rise in its average value from the first period to the second is more likely if its value at the end of the second period is higher than its average for the second period. Then the average for the third and following periods is likely to be higher than the average in the second period. This is exactly what we would find for an ARIMA (0,1,1) time-series process.

With the random walk characterization of the short rate,

(19) $$E_t r_{t+j} = r_t \text{ for } j \geq 1.$$

It is easy to see that the expectations hypothesis implies that the long rate will be a random walk as well. Using Working's result, averages of both these variables should have the following ARIMA (0,1,1) characterization:

(20) $$(1 - L)r_t^a = (1 + .268L)u_t,$$

(21) $$(1 - L)RL_t^a = (1 + .268L)u_t,$$

where

r_t^a = the average value of r over the period $t - 1$ to t,
RL_t^a = the average value of RL over the period $t - 1$ to t.

Using the expectations hypothesis equation (17) where r and RL are replaced by r^a and RL^a, equation (20) implies that the averaged value of the long rate has the following time-series process

(22) $$(1 - L)RL_t^a = \left(1 + \frac{.268}{n} L\right)u_t.$$

This time-series process is different from (21) and is obviously incorrect. Indeed, for large n it will be very close to a random walk.

The above example thus indicates that, if the data are averaged, equation (17) cannot be used to derive the lag weights of short rates in a long equation. Modigliani and Shiller's evidence on the rationality of the term structure proceeds with exactly this derivation with averaged data, and then comparing these lag weights with those actually estimated from a long rate equation. Yet as the example shows, this procedure is not valid.

The efficient-markets model discussed in this paper leads to a formal statistical test of the Modigliani-Shiller results using end-of-period data. Including both short-term interest rate and inflation movements as relevant information to the pricing of long-term bonds as is done by Modigliani and Shiller, we can write the efficient-markets model as

(23) $$y_t = r_{t-1} + d + \beta_r(r_t - r_t^e) + \beta(\pi_t - \pi_t^e) + \epsilon_t,$$

where π_t = CPI inflation rate.
The autoregressive models for r and π are

(24) $$r_t = k_r + \sum_{i=1}^{k} d_i r_{t-i} + \sum_{i=1}^{k} e_i \pi_{t-i} + u_{1t},$$

$$\pi_t = k_\pi + \sum_{i=1}^{k} f_i r_{t-i} + \sum_{i=1}^{k} g_i \pi_{t-i} + u_{2t},$$

and using these autoregressive models to derive expectations,

(25)

$$y_t = r_{t-1} + d + \beta_r\left[r_t - \left(k_r + \sum_{i=1}^{k} d_i\pi_{t-i} + \sum_{i=1}^{h} e_i\pi_{t-i}\right)\right]$$
$$+ \beta_\pi\left[\pi_t - \left(k_\pi + \sum_{i=1}^{k} f_i r_{t-i} + \sum_{i=1}^{k} g_i\pi_{t-i}\right)\right] + \epsilon_t.$$

The equations of (24) and (25) can then be estimated jointly as before and tests of the rationality restrictions can be conducted with the likelihood ratio test. These tests then provide direct information on the Modigliani and Shiller rationality proposition.

These tests and estimates of the efficient-markets model can be found in tables 4.5 and 4.6. The term-structure equation in the MPS (MIT-Penn-SSRC) Quarterly Econometric Model and the Modigliani and Shiller paper both use a sample period extending from 1954:4 to 1966:4 and an eighteen-quarter lag on short rates and inflation estimated with a third-order Almon lag. Therefore both the 1954:4–1966:4 and the 1954:1–1976:4 sample period, as well as the Modigliani-Shiller procedure for estimating the lag structure, are used in the rationality tests conducted here.

The likelihood ratio tests in table 4.5 confirm Modigliani and Shiller's results. The restrictions implied by rationality in both the inflation and interest rate forecasts are not rejected at the 5 percent significance level and again the marginal significance levels are high. Seasonally unadjusted CPI inflation data rather than the seasonally adjusted data again leads to results like those reported in tables 4.5 and 4.6. The likelihood ratio statistic with the unadjusted data for the 1954:4–1966:4 period is 17.00 (marginal significance of .074) and for 1954:1–1976:4 it is 11.89 (marginal significance level of .292). Thus Modigliani and Shiller's contention that the term structure of interest rates displays rationality is supported in these tests, a finding we should have expected considering the results of the previous tests in this chapter and in Sargent (1979).

4.4   Conclusion

This chapter provides an answer to the question, Are market forecasts rational? Empirical tests conducted here, with one exception, indicate

Table 4.5   **Modigliani-Shiller Tests of Forecast Rationality**

	Sample Period	
	1954:4–1966:4	1954:1–1976:4
Likelihood ratio statistic	13.87	12.90
Marginal significance level	.179	.230

Note: Likelihood ratio statistic is distributed asymptotically as $\chi^2(10)$.

Table 4.6 Nonlinear Estimates of the Modigliani-Shiller Efficient-Markets Model

$$y_t = r_{t-1} + d + \beta_r\left(r_t - k_r - \sum_{i=1}^{18} d_i r_{t-i} - \sum_{i=1}^{18} e_i \pi_{t-i}\right) + \beta_\pi\left(\pi_t - k_\pi - \sum_{i=1}^{18} f_i r_{t-i} - \sum_{i=1}^{18} g_i \pi_{t-i}\right) + \epsilon_t$$

$$r_t = k_r + \sum_{i=1}^{18} d_i r_{t-i} + \sum_{i=1}^{18} e_i \pi_{t-i} + u_{1t}$$

$$\pi_t = k_\pi + \sum_{i=1}^{18} f_i r_{t-i} + \sum_{i=1}^{18} g_i \pi_{t-i} + u_{2t}$$

Sample Period 1954:4–1966:4

$d = -.0021$ (.0032) $\beta_r = -10.9928$ (2.4208) $\beta_\pi = -1.8397$ (.9752)

$k_r = .0001$ (.0010) $k_\pi = .0009$ (.0027)

d_i	e_i	f_i	g_i
$d_1 = .8908$ (.1072)	$e_1 = .0512$ (.1879)	$f_1 = .1579$ (.0730)	$g_1 = -.3029$ (.1407)
$d_2 = -.0640$ (.0743)	$e_2 = .0515$ (.1659)	$f_2 = .1236$ (.0502)	$g_2 = .1312$ (.1222)
$d_3 = -.0372$ (.0463)	$e_3 = .0132$ (.1094)	$f_3 = .0665$ (.0325)	$g_3 = .1103$ (.0830)
$d_4 = -.0147$ (.0308)	$e_4 = -.0158$ (.0897)	$f_4 = .0237$ (.0232)	$g_4 = .0859$ (.0657)
$d_5 = .0038$ (.0267)	$e_5 = -.0366$ (.0903)	$f_5 = -.0066$ (.0205)	$g_5 = .0593$ (.0621)
$d_6 = .0184$ (.0277)	$e_6 = -.0502$ (.0921)	$f_6 = -.0261$ (.0204)	$g_6 = .0317$ (.0614)
$d_7 = .0295$ (.0282)	$e_7 = -.0576$ (.0878)	$f_7 = -.0365$ (.0200)	$g_7 = .0045$ (.0581)
$d_8 = .0372$ (.0270)	$e_8 = -.0598$ (.0773)	$f_8 = -.0395$ (.0188)	$g_8 = -.0211$ (.0514)
$d_9 = .0419$ (.0248)	$e_9 = -.0579$ (.0636)	$f_9 = -.0369$ (.0172)	$g_9 = -.0436$ (.0428)
$d_{10} = .0438$ (.0229)	$e_{10} = -.0528$ (.0517)	$f_{10} = -.0303$ (.0164)	$g_{10} = -.0618$ (.0352)
$d_{11} = .0431$ (.0228)	$e_{11} = -.0456$ (.0478)	$f_{11} = -.0215$ (.0170)	$g_{11} = -.0744$ (.0322)
$d_{12} = .0401$ (.0247)	$e_{12} = -.0373$ (.0524)	$f_{12} = -.0123$ (.0187)	$g_{12} = -.0800$ (.0344)
$d_{13} = .0351$ (.0271)	$e_{13} = -.0289$ (.0588)	$f_{13} = -.0042$ (.0206)	$g_{13} = -.0775$ (.0381)
$d_{14} = .0284$ (.0287)	$e_{14} = -.0214$ (.0605)	$f_{14} = -.0008$ (.0217)	$g_{14} = -.0654$ (.0392)
$d_{15} = .0201$ (.0288)	$e_{15} = -.0159$ (.0541)	$f_{15} = -.0013$ (.0217)	$g_{15} = -.0424$ (.0356)
$d_{16} = .0105$ (.0285)	$e_{16} = -.0133$ (.0437)	$f_{16} = -.0047$ (.0215)	$g_{16} = -.0073$ (.0296)
$d_{17} = -.0001$ (.0324)	$e_{17} = -.0147$ (.0576)	$f_{17} = -.0188$ (.0248)	$g_{17} = -.0413$ (.0374)
$d_{18} = -.0114$ (.0468)	$e_{18} = -.0210$ (.1144)	$f_{18} = -.0427$ (.0358)	$g_{18} = -.1047$ (.0718)

Table 4.6 (continued)

Sample Period 1954:1–1976:4

$$k_r = .0007 \ (.0005) \qquad d = -.0013 \ (.0032) \qquad \beta_r = -12.1804 \ (1.9664) \qquad \beta_\pi = -1.3112 \ (.8497)$$

$$k_\pi = -.0016 \ (.0013)$$

$d_1 = .8013$ (.0841)	$e_1 = .1427$ (.1545)	$f_1 = .1277$ (.0563)	$g_1 = -.0298$ (.1075)
$d_2 = -.0520$ (.0544)	$e_2 = .0605$ (.1158)	$f_2 = .0435$ (.0362)	$g_2 = .2530$ (.0776)
$d_3 = -.0410$ (.0328)	$e_3 = .0334$ (.0693)	$f_3 = .0051$ (.0215)	$g_3 = .1889$ (.0457)
$d_4 = -.0296$ (.0208)	$e_4 = .0114$ (.0437)	$f_4 = -.0217$ (.0132)	$g_4 = .1348$ (.0281)
$d_5 = -.0179$ (.0179)	$e_5 = -.0061$ (.0398)	$f_5 = -.0383$ (.0113)	$g_5 = .0900$ (.0255)
$d_6 = -.0063$ (.0190)	$e_6 = -.0195$ (.0448)	$f_6 = -.0461$ (.0122)	$g_6 = .0537$ (.0288)
$d_7 = .0049$ (.0197)	$e_7 = -.0292$ (.0479)	$f_7 = -.0466$ (.0128)	$g_7 = .0253$ (.0306)
$d_8 = .0153$ (.0192)	$e_8 = -.0357$ (.0466)	$f_8 = -.0412$ (.0124)	$g_8 = .0042$ (.0295)
$d_9 = .0247$ (.0183)	$e_9 = -.0394$ (.0415)	$f_9 = -.0313$ (.0117)	$g_9 = -.0105$ (.0261)
$d_{10} = .0326$ (.0178)	$e_{10} = -.0409$ (.0340)	$f_{10} = -.0184$ (.0113)	$g_{10} = -.0195$ (.0219)
$d_{11} = .0389$ (.0183)	$e_{11} = -.0406$ (.0266)	$f_{11} = -.0040$ (.0115)	$g_{11} = -.0233$ (.0186)
$d_{12} = .0431$ (.0192)	$e_{12} = -.0388$ (.0220)	$f_{12} = .0106$ (.0121)	$g_{12} = -.0228$ (.0180)
$d_{13} = .0449$ (.0197)	$e_{13} = -.0362$ (.0219)	$f_{13} = .0239$ (.0125)	$g_{13} = -.0185$ (.0195)
$d_{14} = .0440$ (.0189)	$e_{14} = -.0331$ (.0241)	$f_{14} = .0345$ (.0121)	$g_{14} = -.0113$ (.0210)
$d_{15} = .0401$ (.0173)	$e_{15} = -.0300$ (.0254)	$f_{15} = .0409$ (.0122)	$g_{15} = -.0019$ (.0211)
$d_{16} = .0328$ (.0191)	$e_{16} = -.0273$ (.0254)	$f_{16} = .0418$ (.0124)	$g_{16} = .0092$ (.0207)
$d_{17} = .0218$ (.0301)	$e_{17} = -.0256$ (.0292)	$f_{17} = .0355$ (.0198)	$g_{17} = .0211$ (.0252)
$d_{18} = .0069$ (.0509)	$e_{18} = -.0252$ (.0460)	$f_{18} = .0208$ (.0337)	$g_{18} = .0332$ (.0408)

Note: The $d_2 - d_{18}, e_2 - e_{18}, f_2 - f_{18}$, and $g_2 - g_{18}$ have each been estimated with a third-order polynomial with no fore- or endpoint constraints. Asymptotic standard errors in parentheses.

that for the bond market the answer is yes. Bond market data provides no evidence that interest rate forecasts are irrational. Thus evidence of irrationality in the Goldsmith-Nagan survey of interest rate expectations can be interpreted as casting doubt on the accuracy of this survey measure for describing market expectations. The accuracy of the Livingston price expectations data, however, is still an open question since irrationality has been found in both the bond market and survey data for the 1959–1969 period. This issue cannot be resolved without further empirical research on the rationality of this survey data over longer sample periods.

5   Monetary Policy and Interest Rates: An Efficient Markets-Rational Expectations Approach

5.1   Introduction

The impact of a money stock increase on nominal interest rates is an important issue. The most commonly held view—also a feature of most structural macro models—has an increase in the money stock leading, at least in the short and medium runs, to a decline in interest rates. In these macro models (see Brainard and Cooper 1976; Modigliani 1974), the interest rate decline not only stimulates investment directly but also has a further expansionary impact on investment and consumer expenditure through its effect on the valuation of capital. The decline in interest rates is thus a critical element in the transmission mechanism of monetary policy. In addition, the view that increases in the money stock lead to an immediate decline in interest rates has important implications for the Federal Reserve System's conduct of monetary policy when a decline in interest rates is desired. This view is the basis for demands by government officials that the Fed not keep the rate of money growth too low and so induce an objectionable increase in interest rates.

Milton Friedman (1968, 1969) has criticized this view on the grounds that it ignores the dynamic effects of a money stock increase. Friedman concedes that a so-called liquidity effect—where an excess supply of money will create increased demand for securities, a rise in their price, and a resulting fall in interest rates—does work in the direction of a decline in interest rates when the money stock is increased. However, two other effects can counter this liquidity effect. The money stock increase will, over time, have an expansionary effect on both real income and the price level. This "income and price level effect" will, through the usual arguments in the money demand function, tend to reverse the decline in interest rates. More important for short-run effects on interest rates, increases in the money stock can also influence anticipations of inflation. Higher expected inflation as a result of money stock increases would, through a Fisher (1930) relation, increase nominal interest rates. This "price anticipations effect" can thus not only mitigate the decline in interest rates stemming from the liquidity effect but could also overpower it. That interest rates are highest in countries experiencing rapid rates of monetary growth is casual evidence for this proposition.

Early work on the issue of money supply increases and interest rates, such as Cagan (1972), Gibson (1970), and Gibson and Kaufman (1968), tended to stress the "income and price level effect" more than the "price anticipations effect" because these researchers believed that adjustments of inflationary expectations proceeded slowly. Recent work on the theory of rational expectations and market efficiency, starting with Muth (1961), indicates that inflationary expectations can adjust quite rapidly. Thus, the "price anticipations effect" should, and does, receive more weight in this chapter when the effect of money supply increases on interest rates is discussed.

Two lines of empirical work bear on the issue whether increases in the money stock lead to a decline or to a rise in interest rates. "Keynesian" macroeconometric models impose a fair amount of structure in their estimates of financial market and income-expenditure relationships. In these models, increases in the money stock do lead to a substantial decline in interest rates in the short and medium run, as, for example, in Modigliani (1974) and the simulation results in this chapter. This evidence is suspect, however, because these models ignore constraints that should be imposed if financial markets are efficient. Financial market efficiency cannot be ignored because evidence supporting it is quite strong (see Fama 1970). Furthermore, recent work (Mishkin 1978) indicates that a failure to impose financial market efficiency on macroeconometric models can yield highly misleading results.

An alternative empirical approach to this issue is to estimate reduced form relationships where changes in interest rates are regressed on past changes in the money stock. Evidence from this approach (Gibson and Kaufman 1968) does not support the view that increases in the money stock result in a fall in interest rates. Unfortunately, this evidence suffers from a problem endemic to reduced form empirical work: it is difficult to interpret the empirical results because the theoretical framework is obscure. Also, the absence of structure when changes in interest rates are regressed on changes in the money stock leads to a large number of parameters being estimated, and this results in statistical tests with low power.

Neither approach discussed above distinguishes between the effects from unanticipated versus anticipated monetary policy. Yet the theory of efficient capital markets and rational expectations does make this distinction, and this suggests an alternative approach to analyzing the relationship of money stock increases and interest rate movements. This chapter develops efficient-markets (or, equivalently, rational expectations) models for both long- and short-term interest rates and estimates them using postwar quarterly data. This approach has the advantage of imposing a theoretical structure on the problem that allows both easier interpretation of the empirical results and more powerful statistical tests of the proposition that increases in the money stock are correlated with declines in interest rates. Moreover, a Keynesian, liquidity preference view of interest rate determination can be embedded in the efficient-markets model and tested. Finally, as a side issue, attractive tests of bond market efficiency result from the approach used here.

5.2   The Model

The theory of efficient markets (or, equivalently, rational expectations) implies that interest rates in a bond market should reflect all available information. More precisely, it implies that the market uses available information correctly in assessing the probability distribution of all future interest rates and bond returns. Hence for long bond returns, y_t, and short-term interest rates, r_t,

(1) $$E_m(y_t|\phi_{t-1}) = E(y_t|\phi_{t-1})$$

and

(2) $$E_m(r_t|\phi_{t-1}) = E(r_t|\phi_{t-1}),$$

where

$y_t =$ the one-period (from $t - 1$ to t) nominal return from holding long-term bonds—it includes capital gains plus interest payments,
$r_t =$ the one-period (short-term) interest rate at time t,
$\phi_{t-1} =$ information available at time $t - 1$,
$E(. . .|\phi_{t-1}) =$ the expectation conditional on ϕ_{t-1},
$E_m(. . .|\phi_{t-1}) =$ the expectation assessed by the market at $t - 1$.

In order to give this concept empirical content we must specify models of market equilibrium. For the case of long-term bonds, we assume, as in the previous chapter, that the market equates expected one-period holding returns across securities, allowing for risk (liquidity) premiums which are constant over time. This model of market equilibrium implies that

(3) $$E_m(y_t|\phi_{t-1}) = r_{t-1} + d^l,$$

where $d^l = $ a constant liquidity premium for long-term bonds.

A more refined model of market equilibrium allowing the risk premium to vary over time is not used for long-term bonds because, as discussed in the previous chapter, it makes little difference to the empirical tests. Combining the model of market equilibrium above with market efficiency yields the same condition as in Chapter 4:

(4) $$E(y_t - r_{t-1} - d^l | \phi_{t-1}) = 0$$

and the same efficient-markets model

(5) $$y_t = r_{t-1} + d^l + (X_t - X_t^e)\beta^l + \epsilon_t^l,$$

where an e superscript denotes expected values on all past information [i.e., a rational forecast is defined as $X_t^e = E(X_t | \phi_{t-1})$], and

X_t = a variable (or vector of variables) relevant to the pricing of bonds,
β^l = a coefficient (or vector of coefficients),
ϵ_t^l = serially uncorrelated error process [because $E(\epsilon_t^l | \phi_{t-1}) = 0$].

In the analysis of short-term interest rates, we can no longer argue that the model of the market equilibrium has no effect on tests of the efficient-markets model. In this case, the model of the risk premium used here does contribute significantly to the explanation of the dependent variable. We assume, as in Fama (1976b), that the one-period-ahead forward rate equals the one-period-ahead expected short rate, plus a risk premium that now varies over time with the uncertainty in short-rate movements, that is,

(6) $$_{t-1}F_t = E_m(r_t | \phi_{t-1}) + d_t^s$$

and

(7) $$d_t^s = a_0 + a_1\,\sigma_t,$$

where

$_{t-1}F_t$ = forward rate for the one-period rate at time t implied by the yield curve at $t-1$,
d_t^s = risk (liquidity) premium for $_{t-1}F_t$,
σ_t = measure of uncertainty in short rate movements.

Combining this model of market equilibrium with the rationality or market efficiency condition of (2) yields

(8) $$E(r_t - _{t-1}F_t - a_0 - a_1\,\sigma_t | \phi_{t-1}) = 0$$

and the corresponding efficient-markets model

(9) $$r_t = _{t-1}F_t - a_0 - a_1\sigma_t + (X_t - X_t^e)\beta^s + \epsilon_t^s,$$

where the s superscript is used to differentiate the β and ϵ from their counterparts in the long-term bond model.

The research question posed in the first section of this chapter suggests that money growth is an interesting piece of information relevant to the pricing of bonds and interest rates. Substituting for X_t leads to the following efficient-markets models:

(10)
$$y_t = r_{t-1} + d^l + \beta_m^l (MG_t - MG_t^e) + \epsilon_t^l,$$

(11)
$$r_t = {}_{t-1}F_t - a_0 - a_1 \sigma_t + \beta_m^s (MG_t - MG_t^e) + \epsilon_t^s,$$

where MG_t = the money growth rate at time t.

As is found in the foreign exchange market (see Mussa 1979), spot and forward rates move together, so that changes in short-term interest rates are predominantly unanticipated. Because the long rate is closely linked to the price of a long bond, over periods as short as a quarter the correlation of changes in long rates with unanticipated bond returns, $y_t - r_{t-1} - d$, is very negative: $-.96$ in the sample period used in the following empirical work. Changes in long interest rates will thus also be predominantly unanticipated. We can see how the efficient-markets models above differ from earlier analysis: they stress that only unanticipated movements in money growth can have an effect on unanticipated movements in interest rates. Since changes in interest rates are predominantly unanticipated, these efficient-markets models emphasize the effects of unanticipated money growth movements on changes in interest rates. In contrast, the earlier work does not distinguish between the effects of anticipated and unanticipated money growth.

If unanticipated increases in money growth are associated with a decline in long rates (as might be expected from "Keynesian" macroeconometric models), the coefficient on unanticipated money growth should be significantly positive in the long bond equation above because $y_t - r_{t-1}$ and the change in long rates are negatively correlated: that is, $\beta_m^l > 0$. If unanticipated increases in money growth are associated with a decline in short rates, then the coefficient on unanticipated money growth in the short-rate equation should be significantly negative, that is, $\beta_m^s < 0$.

An important caveat is in order. As noted in Chapter 2, the efficient-markets model does not guarantee that $X_t - X_t^e$ is exogenous so that the estimates of β are consistent. Another way to make this point is to acknowledge that the efficient-markets model does not indicate whether a significant β coefficient implies causation from its unanticipated variable to bond prices and interest rates. As far as market efficiency is concerned, causation could just as well run in the other direction, or it could be nonexistent, as in the case where new information simultaneously affects both interest rates and the right-hand-side variable. Thus, we must be careful in interpreting empirical results on the β's, not to ascribe causation to the results without further identifying information.

The same caveat applies especially when we analyze the estimated β_m coefficient. If the money supply process is seen as exogenous, the interpretation of the estimated β_m's is straightforward. The finding of a significant positive β_m^l and negative β_m^s will then provide evidence supporting the "Keynesian" position that increased money growth leads, at least in the short run, to declines in interest rates; and a failure to find this result will cast doubt on this view. If the money supply process is not exogenous, however—the position taken by many critics of monetarist analysis—then the estimated β_m coefficients may suffer from simultaneous equation bias and give a misleading impression about how increases in the money supply affect interest rates. Because this chapter provides no evidence on the exogeneity of the money supply process, the β_m estimates must be viewed as providing information only on the correlations of unanticipated money growth and the movements in interest rates. Interpretation of these correlations is deferred to the concluding remarks at the end of the chapter.

The liquidity preference approach to the demand for money (see Goldfeld 1973; and Laidler 1977) indicates that interest rates are related not only to money growth but also to movements in real income, the price level, and inflation. Adding this information to the X vector of the efficient-markets models, noting that unanticipated inflation is equivalent to the unanticipated price level, leads to the following:

$$(12) \qquad y_t = r_{t-1} + d^l + \beta_m^l(MG_t - MG_t^e) + \beta_y^l(YG_t - YG_t^e)$$
$$+ \beta_\pi^l(\pi_t - \pi_t^e) + \epsilon_t^l$$

$$(13) \qquad r_t = {}_{t-1}F_t - a_0 - a_1\sigma_t + \beta_m^s(MG_t - MG_t^e)$$
$$+ \beta_y^s(YG_t - YG_t^e) + \beta_\pi^s(\pi_t - \pi_t^e) + \epsilon_t^s$$

where

$$YG_t = \text{growth rate of real income,}$$
$$\pi = \text{inflation rate,}$$
$$\beta_m, \beta_y, \beta_\pi = \text{coefficients.}$$

These equations are really efficient-markets analogs to the typical money demand relationship found in the literature. In addition, they capture elements of interest rate models of the Feldstein and Eckstein (1970) variety.

The magnitude and sign of the β coefficients in equations (10)–(13) depend on the time-series processes of the money supply, real income, and price level, even when the sign and magnitude of these coefficients are assumed to reflect an underlying structural theory such as liquidity preference. If the time-series processes of real income and the price level are such that an unanticipated rise in these variables is not followed by more than a compensating decline in these variables, then a liquidity preference view implies that the coefficients of unanticipated income growth and inflation should be negative in the long bond equation (12)— that is, $\beta_y^l < 0$, $\beta_\pi^l < 0$—and positive in the short-rate equation (13)—that is, $\beta_y^s > 0$, $\beta_\pi^s > 0$. In this case, an unanticipated increase in income growth should lead to higher interest rates, currently and in the future. The negative effect of an unanticipated increase in inflation on bond returns follows from the resulting reduction in real money balances, which also leads to rising interest rates. The unanticipated inflation effect should be further strengthened if, as in the Cagan (1956) adaptive expectations model, expected inflation rises when actual inflation is above its expected value. In this case, an unanticipated rise in inflation promotes a rise in nominal interest rates either through a Fisher (1930) relation or because expected inflation is a separate argument in the money demand function, as in Friedman (1956).

Note also that the more persistent the time-series process of inflation and income growth—that is, the more an unanticipated increase in these variables leads to further increases—the more powerful the unanticipated income and inflation effects on interest rates indicated by the theoretical structure discussed above. Clearly, the importance of the "income and price level" and "price anticipations" effects also depend on the time-series process of money growth. Thus the β_m coefficients also will not be invariant to changes in the money growth, time-series process.

We now turn to the actual estimation of the efficient-markets models of equations (10)–(13), with the warning that some caution must be exercised when interpreting results from estimates of these equations because the direction of causation cannot be established in this framework.

5.3   Empirical Results

5.3.1   The Data

Postwar quarterly data is used in the empirical work below. The long bond models are estimated over the sample period 1954–1976. However, six-month Treasury Bills were not issued before 1959, and since the six-month bill rate is needed to calculate the forward rate in the short rate models, these models are estimated over the 1959–1976 period. The data sources and definitions of variables used in these estimations are as follows:

> y_t = quarterly return from holding a long-term government bond from the beginning to the end of the quarter,
>
> r_t = the ninety-day Treasury Bill rate, the last trading day of the quarter in fractions at an annual rate in the short rate equations, but r_{t-1} is at a quarterly rate in the long bond equations,

$$_{t-1}F_t = 4\left[1 - \frac{(360 - 180\, rsix_{t-1})}{(360 - 90\, r_{t-1})}\right],$$

where

> $rsix_t$ = the six-month (180 days) bill rate at the end of quarter—in fractions at an annual rate,

$M1G_t$ = growth rate of $M1$ (quarterly rate) = the first differenced series of the log of the average level of $M1$ in the last month of the quarter,

$M2G$ = growth rate of $M2$ (quarterly rate) = the first differenced series of the log of the average level of $M2$ in the last month of the quarter,

IPG_t = growth rate of industrial production (quarterly rate) = the first differenced series of the log of industrial production in the last month of the quarter,

π_t = the CPI inflation rate (quarterly rate) = the first differenced series of the log of CPI in the last month of the quarter.

Unless otherwise noted, all these variables have been constructed from seasonally adjusted data except for r_t, $_{t-1}F_t$, and y_t, which do not require seasonal adjustments. The bond return series was obtained from the Center for Research in Security Prices (CRSP) at the University of Chicago and is described in Fisher and Lorie (1977) and Mishkin (1978). The Treasury Bill data was supplied by the Federal Reserve Board. The IPG, and π, variables were constructed from data in the Department of Commerce's *Business Statistics* and *Survey of Current Business*. The $M1$ and $M2$ data were obtained from the Board of Governors of the Federal Reserve, *Banking and Monetary Statistics*, and the *Federal Reserve Bulletin*. All other variables used to specify the forecasting equations were obtained from the NBER data bank.

As shown in Chapter 4, using averaged data in efficient-markets or rational expectations models can give misleading results. The data for bond returns and interest rates here are thus derived from security prices at particular points in time. For the same reason, the derivation of the other variables here uses data as close to being end of quarter as possible. Industrial Production is thus made a proxy for real income in estimating the models rather than the more broadly based national income accounts measure. Similarly, the CPI has been used to calculate the inflation variable rather than the GNP deflator. Endpoint data (or close to end-point) help unearth significant relationships between bond returns and unanticipated variables. Some experiments with quarterly averaged data led to worse fits for efficient-markets models, fewer significant coefficients, and no appreciable differences as to the statistical significance of the β_m coefficients.

5.3.2 The Estimation Procedure

To estimate the short and long rate models of equations (10)–(13), measures of anticipated money growth, industrial production growth and inflation are needed. Here, these anticipations are assumed to be rational forecasts obtained from linear forecasting equations. The model estimates are produced by estimating each short or long rate equation jointly with the forecasting equations, and imposing the cross-equation restrictions implied by rationality of expectations. See Chapter 2 for details of this procedure.

In Chapter 2 we saw that economic theory may not be a useful tool for deciding on the specification of the forecasting equations. Thus atheoretical statistical procedures are used here. If indeed economic theory is not particularly useful in evaluating the forecasting equations, it is all the more important to check for the robustness of results to changes in the specification of these equations. Therefore, two procedures for specifying the forecasting equations are used in the text, and results with several additional specifications are discussed in Appendix 5.2.

The simplest forecasting equations are univariate time-series models of the autoregressive type. Fourth-order autoregressions are usually successful in reducing residuals in quarterly data to white noise and are thus used here. Ordinary least-squares estimates for the $M1G$, $M2G$, IPG, and π equations for both sample periods used in estimation can be found in Appendix 5.1. There is a fair amount of persistence in the time-series models for money growth and inflation, indicating that "income and price level" and "price anticipation" effects of the sort that Friedman (1968, 1969) discusses are potentially important. Although less persistence is evident in the time-series process of industrial production growth, it has the characteristic that a positive innovation does lead to a permanently higher level of industrial production (although not in the rate of growth). Thus, as discussed in the preceding section, the unanticipated inflation and IPG coefficients may be expected to be negative in the long-rate bond equations and positive in the short-rate equations.

The univariate time-series models suffer from the problem of unstable coefficients. Chow (1960) tests reported in Appendix 5.1, where the sample period has been split into equal lengths, reject in five out of eight equations the hypothesis that the coefficients of the univariate models are equal in the two subperiods. Multivariate forecasting equations thus have been specified by the procedure outlined in Chapter 2 which makes use of Granger's (1969) concept of predictive content. Each of the four variables—$M1G$, $M2G$, IPG, and π—was regressed on its own four lagged values as well as on four lagged values of each of the other three variables and four lagged values of each of the following variables: the unemployment rate; the ninety-day Treasury Bill rate; the balance of payments on current account; the growth rate of real federal government expenditure, the high employment budget surplus; and the growth rate of federal government, interest bearing debt, in the hands of the public. (These other variables were selected because a reading of the literature on Federal Reserve reaction functions—see Fair 1978 and the references therein—indicated that they might help explain money growth.) The four lagged values of each variable were retained in the equation only if they were jointly significant at the 5 percent level or higher.

The resulting multivariate time-series models for both sample periods can be found in Appendix 5.1 along with F statistics of the joint significance test for whether the four lagged values of each variable should be included in the regression model. Not only do these models have a better fit than the corresponding univariate models, but Chow tests reported in Appendix 5.1 now reject stability of the coefficients in only one out of eight cases.

Before we turn to the empirical results, the measure of short-rate uncertainty, σ_t, used here requires some discussion. Fama (1976b) calculates σ_t as the average of the absolute value of the changes in the spot rate during the year before t and during the year following t. Because the risk (liquidity) premium must be set conditional on available information—in this case that known at $t-1$—allowing σ_t to be calculated from information not available at $t-1$ could be problematic. An alternative, though similar, measure of σ_t is used in this study. The difference between the forward rate and the spot rate, that is, $r_t - {}_{t-1}F_t$, was regressed on measures of σ_t, calculated as the average absolute change of the bill rate over a number of previous quarters, where the number of quarters was varied. The best fit was obtained with σ_t calculated from eight previous quarters of changes in the bill rate. The results are as follows:

$$(14) \qquad r_t - {}_{t-1}F_t = -.0001 - 1.0961\ \sigma_t + \epsilon_t$$
$$\phantom{(14) \qquad r_t - {}_{t-1}F_t = }(.0017)\quad (.2937)$$

$$R^2 = .1659 \quad \text{standard error} = .0068$$
$$\text{Durbin-Watson} = 1.90$$

where

$$\sigma_t = \frac{\sum_{i=1}^{8} |r_{t-i} - r_{t-i-1}|}{8}.$$

As in Fama (1976b), increased uncertainty in short-rate movements does lead to an increased risk premium, and this effect is statistically significant at the 1 percent level. In addition, the σ_t measure used here outperforms the Fama measure that is constructed from information unavailable at $t-1$. The above σ_t measure is used in the empirical tests that follow. Its specification is not a critical issue to the outcomes however: if we use a Fama measure of σ_t or exclude σ_t from the model altogether, the results do not alter appreciably.

5.3.3   The Results

There is no strong theoretical reason to estimate the long bond or short-rate model with one monetary aggregate versus another. Unanticipated growth rates of both $M1$ and $M2$ are therefore used and results with additional monetary aggregates are explored in Appendix 5.2. The resulting estimates of the models appear in tables 5.1 and 5.2. Panel A of

Table 5.1   **Nonlinear Estimates of the Long Bond Model Using Seasonally Adjusted Data**

	Coefficients of				
Model	$M1G - M1G^e$	$M2G - M2G^e$	$IPG - IPG^e$	$\pi - \pi^e$	Constant Term
	Panel A: Using Univariate Forecasting Models				
1.1	.0482				−.0014
	(.5961)				(.0032)
1.2	.0501		−.4242**	−1.8482*	−.0029
	(.5517)		(.1260)	(.8028)	(.0032)
1.3		.9174			−.0013
		(.5459)			(.0032)
1.4		.7174	−.4077**	−1.7691*	−.0027
		(.5063)	(.1243)	(.7880)	(.0031)
	Panel B: Using Multivariate Forecasting Models				
1.5	−.2621				−.0014
	(.7429)				(.0032)
1.6	.4108		−.5039**	−1.7529	−.0020
	(.7164)		(.1568)	(.9552)	(.0032)
1.7		.9199			−.0014
		(.6738)			(.0032)
1.8		1.0950	−.4987**	−1.8206	−.0020
		(.6283)	(.1492)	(.9353)	(.0032)

Note: Asymptotic standard errors of coefficients in parentheses.
* = Significant at the 5 percent level.
** = Significant at the 1 percent level.

these tables contains estimates which make use of the univariate forecasting equations, while panel B's estimates use the multivariate forecasting models of the form found in Appendix 5.1. The estimates of the γ coefficients are not presented here because they are not particularly interesting.

An issue basic to these results is whether the efficient-markets (rational expectations) model used here is valid. Previous evidence on the efficiency of the bond market indicates that efficient-markets models of the type used here are a reasonable characterization of bond market behavior. Table 5.3 contains likelihood ratio tests, described in Chapter 2, of the nonlinear constraints implied by both market efficiency (rational expectations) and the model of market equilibrium. The test statistics do not reject the constraints for any of the long bond models in table 5.1: the marginal significance level of the statistics are never lower than .05. These results then also provide additional evidence for the efficient-markets model of long bond behavior.

Table 5.2 **Nonlinear Estimates of the Short Rate Model Using Seasonally Adjusted Data**

			Coefficients of			
Model	$M1G - M1G^e$	$M2G - M2G^e$	$IPG - IPG^e$	$\pi - \pi^e$	Constant Term	σ
			Panel A: Using Univariate Forecasting Models			
2.1	.2788*				.0006	$-1.2266**$
	(.1088)				(.0015)	(.2714)
2.2	.2774**		.0352	.6211**	.0002	$-1.1514**$
	(.1075)		(.0275)	(.1989)	(.0014)	(.2618)
2.3		.1616			.0006	$-1.2563**$
		(.1085)			(.0015)	(.2851)
2.4		.1904	.0399	.6545**	.0002	$-1.1571**$
		(.1053)	(.0278)	(.2058)	(.0015)	(.2686)
			Panel B: Using Multivariate Forecasting Models			
2.5	.1677				.0006	$-1.2761**$
	(.1283)				(.0015)	(.2863)
2.6	.2512		$-.0455$	.5199	.0004	$-1.2109**$
	(.1381)		(.0493)	(.3272)	(.0016)	(.3015)
2.7		.2562			.0001	$-1.1807**$
		(.1341)			(.0016)	(.2917)
2.8		.3039*	$-.0770$	.6501*	$-.0004$	$-1.0779**$
		(.1409)	(.0471)	(.3314)	(.0016)	(.3069)

Note: See table 5.1.

The table 5.3 results for the short-rate models, however, reject the nonlinear constraints at the 5 percent level in six out of eight cases. How should we interpret these rejections? They can result from either the failure of rationality (market efficiency) or of the model of market equilibrium. Both models of market equilibrium used in the long bond and short-rate models are crude: neither risk premium is derived from utility maximizing behavior. A theoretically more justifiable risk premium would, for example, exploit the covariance of bill or bond returns with returns on alternative assets. Yet, as the regression results in equation (14) indicate, the model of market equilibrium is a significant element in explaining the movements of the dependent variable in the short-rate equation. In this situation, unlike that for the long-rate equation where the model of market equilibrium appears to be unimportant in explaining the dependent variable, its misspecification can lead to rejections of the nonlinear constraints. Thus, rejections of the nonlinear constraints occurring in the short-rate models, but not in the long bond models, can be attributed plausibly to misspecification in the model of market equilibrium.

Table 5.3   **Likelihood Ratio Tests of Nonlinear Constraints**

Model	Likelihood Ratio Statistic	Marginal Significance Level
1.1	$\chi^2(4) = 6.45$	.1680
1.2	$\chi^2(12) = 14.00$	.3007
1.3	$\chi^2(4) = 3.20$	.5249
1.4	$\chi^2(12) = 12.43$	.4118
1.5	$\chi^2(12) = 18.10$	.1127
1.6	$\chi^2(24) = 33.81$	.0881
1.7	$\chi^2(8) = 10.67$	.2211
1.8	$\chi^2(24) = 32.60$	.1128
2.1	$\chi^2(4) = 12.76^*$	.0125
2.2	$\chi^2(12) = 13.65$	.3235
2.3	$\chi^2(4) = 12.46^*$	.0143
2.4	$\chi^2(12) = 17.18$	.1430
2.5	$\chi^2(8) = 21.65^{**}$	.0056
2.6	$\chi^2(28) = 50.02^{**}$	.0067
2.7	$\chi^2(8) = 25.69^{**}$	.0012
2.8	$\chi^2(28) = 50.92^{**}$	.0051

Note: Marginal significance level is the probability of getting that value of the likelihood ratio statistic or higher under the null hypothesis.
*Significant at the 5 percent level.
**Significant at the 1 percent level.

A suitable transformation of the unconstrained system outlined in Chapter 2 yields additional evidence on the potential misspecification of the model of market equilibrium. The unconstrained system where the γ are not equal in the forecasting and short-rate equations can be rewritten as

(15) $$X_t = Z_{t-1}\gamma + u_t,$$

$$r_t = {}_{t-1}F_t - a_0 - \sigma a_1 - Z_{t-1}\alpha + (X_t - Z_{t-1}\gamma)\beta^s + \epsilon_t,$$

where the γ's are constrained to be equal in the two equations. Therefore, the nonlinear constraints tested in this paper are equivalent to $\alpha = 0$ in the above system. It is now easy to see the following point: if the risk premium is related to the variables in Z, yet they have been excluded from the model of the risk premium, then this may explain the rejections of the nonlinear constraints. To make this conjecture plausible, we should expect that a model of the risk premium which is related to Z would have reasonable characteristics. The Fama-type model, for example, does generate plausible values. The resulting risk premiums (at annual rates) have a mean of 57 basis points (1/100 of a percentage point) and a standard deviation of 30 basis points. They also move smoothly: their autocorrelations for lags of one through four are respectively .96, .91, .85, and .78. In the model which leads to the strongest rejection of the nonlinear constraints, model 2.7, we could attribute this rejection to the fact that a more appropriate specification of the risk premium is $d_t^s = a_o + a_1\sigma_t + Z_{t-1}\alpha$, where Z_{t-1} contains the four lagged values of money growth ($M2G$) and Treasury Bill rates (r). This latter specification leads to values for the risk premium that are somewhat more variable and less smooth than the equation (14) specification, but not appreciably so. The risk premium from this expanded specification has a mean of 57 basis points, a standard deviation of 46 basis points, and four lagged autocorrelations of .75, .56, .49, and .29.

Viewing the rejections with the benefit of the system (15) also has the advantage of providing us with potentially interesting information on the risk premium. The results indicate that the premium could be related to money growth and interest rates as well as the variability measure σ. However, they give no indication that the liquidity premium is in addition related to the other variables in table 5.A.2 of Appendix 5.1. The results here thus point out a direction for future research on the risk premium. Following Nelson (1972), I also conducted more direct experiments on the relation of the risk premium to lagged interest rates and unemployment with negative results. Experiments with lagged values of $r - F$ also did not add explanatory power to the model of the risk premium.

If a misspecified model of the risk premium is the source of the rejections of the nonlinear constraints, the efficient markets-rational expectations model used here is fortunately still a valid framework for analyzing the relationship of money growth and short rates. With rational expectations, the unanticipated $X_t - X_t^e$ variable will be uncorrelated with any past information, among which can be included the determinants of the risk premium which is set at $t-1$. Therefore, if some determinants of this risk premium have been excluded from the market equilibrium model, they will be orthogonal to $X_t - X_t^e$. The exclusion of these variables, and the resulting rejection of the nonlinear constraints, will not lead to inconsistent estimates of the β coefficients. Since it is not necessary to derive a better model of the risk premium to achieve reliable estimates of the β's, this tricky research issue, which is beyond the scope of this study, is left to future research.

The unanticipated $M1G$ coefficients in table 5.1 do not lend support to the view that an unanticipated increase in money growth is correlated with a fall in long bond rates. In panel A, although both of these coefficients have a positive sign, they are not significantly different from zero at the 5 percent level: asymptotic t statistics are less than .1. In addition these coefficients are quite small. The β coefficients here denote the percentage point change in the bond return from a 1 percent error in anticipations, and in our 1954–1976 sample period, a one percentage point rise in the quarterly bond return corresponds approximately to a 10 basis point (1/100 of a percentage point) fall in the long bond rate. Thus, the $M1G$ coefficients in panel A indicate that a 1 percent surprise increase in $M1$ is associated with only a .5 basis point decline in the long bond rate.

The panel B estimates of the $M1G$ coefficients indicate that the conclusion on the relationship of long rates and money growth is not altered by using multivariate versus univariate forecasting models in estimation. Again, neither of the unanticipated $M1G$ coefficients are significantly different from zero at 5 percent, and they continue to be small, with the largest of the coefficients indicating that a 1 percent surprise increase in $M1$ leads to only a 4.1 basis point decline in the long bond rate. Furthermore, one of the unanticipated $M1G$ coefficients is now negative.

The coefficients on unanticipated $M2$ growth in table 5.1 are more positive than the unanticipated $M1G$ coefficients, they nevertheless do not lend strong support to the view that unanticipated money growth should be negatively correlated with the change in long rates. They do not differ significantly from zero at the 5 percent level (although in 1.3 the unanticipated $M2G$ coefficient is significantly different from zero at the 10 percent level). Also note that the $M2$ results in panel A and in panel B are so similar that it is again clear that the results on unanticipated money growth are not particularly sensitive to specifications of the money growth forecasting model.

How different are these findings from those that might be inferred from "Keynesian," structural macroeconometric models? Using a simulation technique discussed in Mishkin (1979) we can examine the response of a macromodel to a 1 percent surprise increase in $M1$. Equation 1.1 was used to trace out the effect on $M1$ growth from a 1 percent innovation. The resulting $M1$ numbers were then used in a simulation experiment with the MPS (MIT-Penn-SSRC 1977) Quarterly Econometric Model in order to derive the response of this model to the 1 percent $M1$ innovation occurring in the 1967:1 quarter. The MPS model indicates that this 1 percent $M1$ innovation would lead to an immediate decline of 18.1 basis points in the long rate. Not only is this long-rate decline several times larger than the maximum 4.1 basis point decline implied by the empirical evidence in table 5.1, but also it is significantly larger at the 5 percent level for three of the four estimates in table 5.1 (and is almost significantly larger for the remaining estimate). Clearly, the coefficients on unanticipated $M1$ growth are quite low relative to what might be expected from a structural macroeconometric model.

The unanticipated inflation and industrial production coefficients in table 5.1 conform to our priors. In both the $M1$ and $M2$ efficient-market models, these coefficients are negative and are either significant or nearly significant at the 5 percent level. The results on the coefficients of unanticipated industrial production growth are especially strong, with both the panel A and panel B estimates significantly different from zero at the 1 percent level. Although the unanticipated inflation coefficients are very similar in both panels, their asymptotic standard errors rise somewhat from panel A to panel B. They are thus not quite significant at the 5 percent level in panel B, while they are significant at this level in panel A.

The similarity between the money growth as well as other coefficient estimates in panel A and panel B is encouraging, for it gives us confidence that these results are robust to changes in the models describing expectations. Further model estimates described in Appendix 5.2 with additional specifications for the forecasting equations yield similar results. This is an important finding. Poor specification of expectations formation appears to be a major concern in this line of research because it leads to errors-in-variables bias in the coefficient estimates. The important question is, How severe would this bias be? Denoting the measured $X_t - X_t^e$ by an m superscript and the true $X_t - X_t^e$ with a T superscript, we can write

$$(16) \qquad (X_t - X_t^e)^m = (X_t - X_t^e)^T + v_t,$$

where v_t is the measurement error. If such variables as money growth, industrial production growth, and inflation are hard to forecast—which seems likely—then the variance of the true $X_t - X_t^e$ forecast error will be substantial. If the incremental predictive power of other information besides the past history of the forecasted variable is not large, then the variance of the measurement error in expectations used here will be small in relation to the variance of the true forecast error: that is, Var $[(X_t - X_t^e)^T] >> Var(v_t)$. If this occurs, the errors-in-variables bias would be negligible and should not be an important problem in this research.

The similarity of the model estimates despite substantial changes in the specifications for the forecasting equations is found not only in this chapter, but also in the chapters preceding and following. This provides strong support for the view that unanticipated increases in money growth are associated with interest rate declines. Moreover, the smaller standard errors found for the coefficients estimated using univariate rather than multivariate forecasting equations provides some support for the position taken by Feige and Pearce (1976), that forecasts from univariate time-series models may be "economically rational" expectations.[1]

The results for the short-rate model in Table 5.2 are even more damaging to the view that associates a decline in interest rates with an unanticipated money growth increase.[2] All the coefficients on both unanticipated $M1$ and $M2$ growth are positive in table 5.5, and in three cases the coefficients are statistically significant. They indicate that a 1 percent

1. Note that Sims (1977) has raised some questions about the statistical techniques used by Feige and Pearce (1976), and this does cast some doubt on their evidence.

2. Urich and Wachtel (1981) obtain similar results using weekly data. Thus, reduction of the unit of observation in the analysis is likely to leave the findings here intact.

Table 5.4   **Nonlinear Estimates of the Long Bond Model**
                       Using Seasonally Unadjusted Data

Model	$M1G - M1G^e$	$M2G - M2G^e$	$IPG - IPG^e$	$\pi - \pi^e$	Constant Term
			Coefficients of		
		Panel A: Using Univariate Forecasting Models			
4.1	− .7339*				− .0017
	(.3631)				(.0031)
4.2	− .5879		− .2028*	− 2.5145**	− .0026
	(.3631)		(.0857)	(.6912)	(.0032)
4.3		.0001			− .0014
		(.3610)			(.0032)
4.4		.1426	− .2420**	− 2.4438**	− .0024
		(.3330)	(.0838)	(.7111)	(.0032)
		Panel B: Using Multivariate Forecasting Models			
4.5	− 1.2781**				− .0014
	(.4504)				(.0032)
4.6	− .8078		− .4105**	− 2.4472**	− .0020
	(.4339)		(.1371)	(.8089)	(.0032)
4.7		− .1404			− .0014
		(.4821)			(.0032)
4.8		.1534	− .4741**	− 2.6226**	− .0020
		(.4391)	(.1396)	(.8237)	(.0033)

Note: See table 5.1.

surprise increase in $M1$ or $M2$ is associated with a 16–30 basis point unanticipated increase in the bill rate. The simulation experiment with the MPS model that is described above indicates that a 1 percent $M1$ surprise leads to an immediate *decline* of 88 basis points in the bill rate. This finding contrasts strongly with the finding here that even the least positive $M1$ coefficient is more than eight of its standard errors away from this figure.

The results on the unanticipated inflation coefficients are similar to those in the long bond model. These coefficients are positive, as might be expected, and are significantly different from zero in three out of four cases. The results on the unanticipated industrial production growth coefficients are not quite as strong as in the earlier table. They are never statistically significant, and in panel B they even have the wrong sign.

The efficient markets–rational expectations model does not specify whether the $X - X^e$ variables should be described by seasonally adjusted or seasonally unadjusted data. This empirical issue cannot be settled easily on theoretical grounds because it is not clear whether market participants concentrate on seasonally adjusted versus unadjusted in-

Table 5.5   **Nonlinear Estimates of the Short Rate Model
Using Seasonally Unadjusted Data**

Model	$M1G - M1G^e$	$M2G - M2G^e$	$IPG - IPG^e$	$\pi - \pi^e$	Constant Term	σ
			Coefficients of			
			Panel A: Using Univariate Forecasting Models			
5.1	.3029**				.0003	−1.1255**
	(.0652)				(.0014)	(.2530)
5.2	.2458**		.0274	.4687**	.0001	−1.1267**
	(.0671)		(.0171)	(.1716)	(.0014)	(.2464)
5.3		.1926*			.0003	−1.1468**
		(.0644)			(.0015)	(.2765)
5.4		.1967**	.0440*	.5459**	.0001	−1.1260**
		(.0624)	(.0176)	(.1746)	(.0014)	(.2526)
			Panel B: Using Multivariate Forecasting Models			
5.5	.3431**				.0007	−1.2403**
	(.0831)				(.0015)	(.2639)
5.6	.2484**		.0386	.5079	.0004	−1.2037**
	(.0956)		(.0376)	(.2623)	(.0016)	(.2861)
5.7		.3285**			−.0007	−.9891**
		(.0918)			(.0015)	(.2841)
5.8		.2011*	.0400	.5788*	−.0003	−1.0791**
		(.0986)	(.0374)	(.2674)	(.0016)	(.3021)

Note: See table 5.1.

formation. For this reason, the table 5.1 and table 5.2 models have also been estimated with seasonally unadjusted data for the X's. The resulting estimates and test statistics appear in tables 5.4, 5.5, and 5.6 and were obtained by the same procedures as the previous estimates with seasonally adjusted data.

A comparison of tables 5.4–5.6 with tables 5.1–5.3 indicates that the choice of adjusted or unadjusted data is not a critical factor in this research. The likelihood ratio tests of the nonlinear constraints yield similar conclusions. In addition the coefficient estimates are similar, although their standard errors tend to be smaller in the seasonally unadjusted results. In the short-rate models, all the industrial production growth coefficients now have the "correct" positive sign.

The seasonally unadjusted data are even less favorable to the view that increased money growth is associated with a decline in interest rates. Now all the $M1$ coefficients in the long bond model are negative, implying a positive correlation of movements in money growth and long interest rates, and two of these coefficients are significantly different from zero at the 5 percent level. In addition, the $M2$ coefficients in the long-rate model

Table 5.6   **Likelihood Ratio Tests of Nonlinear Constraints**

Model	Likelihood Ratio Statistic	Marginal Significance Level
4.1	$\chi^2(4) = 5.08$	.2792
4.2	$\chi^2(12) = 20.83$	.0529
4.3	$\chi^2(4) = 3.27$	.5137
4.4	$\chi^2(12) = 19.53$	.0765
4.5	$\chi^2(12) = 12.10$	.4377
4.6	$\chi^2(24) = 28.48$	.2403
4.7	$\chi^2(8) = 7.23$	.5120
4.8	$\chi^2(24) = 27.11$	.2994
5.1	$\chi^2(4) = 9.14$	.0578
5.2	$\chi^2(12) = 14.81$	.2521
5.3	$\chi^2(4) = 12.02^*$	.0172
5.4	$\chi^2(12) = 15.01$	.2407
5.5	$\chi^2(8) = 19.30^*$	.0133
5.6	$\chi^2(28) = 49.71^{**}$	.0070
5.7	$\chi^2(8) = 24.90^{**}$	.0016
5.8	$\chi^2(28) = 49.96^{**}$	.0065

Note: See table 5.3.

are less positive. For the short-rate models, all the money growth coefficients in table 5.4 are positive and are now statistically significant at the 5 percent level, with six out of eight significant at the 1 percent level. The seasonally unadjusted data, then, lend support to the contrary view that unanticipated movements in money growth and interest rates are positively correlated.

5.4 Concluding Remarks

A wide range of empirical tests of the relationship between money growth and interest rates have been conducted in this chapter and in Appendix 5.2. A guiding principle of this research has been to use many different empirical tests of the model in order to provide information on the robustness of the results. In pursuit of this goal, model estimations have been varied along the following dimensions: (1) the choice of the monetary aggregate, (2) the choice of the relevant variables to include in the X vector, (3) the use of seasonally adjusted versus seasonally unadjusted data, (4) the specification of the forecasting models used to describe expectations formation, and (5) the sample period. The large number of estimates provide information on the sensitivity and reliability of the results reported here.

The results point to the following conclusions. There is no empirical support for the view that an unanticipated increase in the money stock is associated with a decline in interest rates. However, there are two aspects of the research methodology used here which raise questions about the general validity of this conclusion.

As we have seen, the β coefficients in the efficient markets–rational expectations models are not invariant to changes in the time-series processes of the money growth, income growth, and inflation variables. Thus the conclusions from the estimates in this chapter provide information on the relationship between money growth and interest rates only for the postwar sample period. However, realize that many structural macroeconometric models displaying a negative relationship between money growth and interest rates have been estimated using sample periods which overlap those used here. The results reported in this chapter are certainly of interest in evaluating these models.

A further difficulty with the present research methodology is that misspecification of the forecasting equations describing expectations formation can invalidate the results on the relationship between money growth and interest rates. Specifically, misspecification of expectations formation can lead to inconsistent and biased β coefficients. However, the robustness of results to different specifications of the time-series models describing expectations provides evidence that the misspecification problem is probably not very severe.

How should we interpret the conclusion reached above? If we are willing to accept exogeneity of the money supply process in the postwar period and the efficient-markets models as true reduced forms, the interpretation is clear-cut. The evidence here would then cast doubt on the commonly held view that an unanticipated increase in the money stock will lead to a decline in interest rates. Not only does this suggest that the Federal Reserve cannot lower interest rates by increasing the rate of money growth, but it also requires some modification of the monetary transmission mechanism embodied in structural macroeconometric models. It is plausible that an unanticipated increase in money growth will not induce a decline in interest rates because it leads to an immediate upward revision in expected inflation. Thus, there is still a potential effect on real interest rates from unanticipated money growth, and the evidence in no way denies that there are potent effects of money supply increases on aggregate demand.

As was mentioned in Section 5.2, if unanticipated money growth is not exogeneous, then the β_m coefficient estimates are inconsistent and can lead to misleading inference. Particularly disturbing in this regard is the case where the Federal Reserve smooths interest rates so that an unanticipated increase is interest rates causes the Federal Reserve to react by an unanticipated increase in money growth. The resulting correlation of $MG_t - MG_t^e$ with the ϵ_t error terms (negative with ϵ_t^l and positive with ϵ_t^s) tends to bias the results toward a positive association of money growth and interest rates. Thus, we cannot rule out the view in structural macroeconometric models that an exogenous increase in money growth leads to a decline in interest rates, despite the empirical results of this chapter.

Note, however, the nature of money growth endogeneity required for this reservation to hold. If money growth is endogenous in the sense that the Federal Reserve modifies money growth within a quarter only in response to past public information available at the start of the quarter, $MG_t - MG_t^e$ will not be correlated with ϵ_t^l or ϵ_t^s. Hence the existence of Granger (1969) "causality" running from interest rates to money growth does not imply that the estimates of β_m will be inconsistent. "Causality" tests of the Sims (1972) variety, therefore, cannot shed light on the consistency of the β_m estimates. If we are not to reject the common view that increases in money growth lead to interest rate declines, research of a fairly subtle sort is needed to demonstrate that unanticipated money growth is negatively correlated with ϵ_t^l and positively correlated with ϵ_t^s. Hence, this issue cannot be resolved without further research.

Appendix 5.1: Estimates of the Forecasting Equations

Table 5.A.1   Univariate Time-Series Models

Model: Dependent Variable: Sample Period:	A1.1 M1G 1954–1976	A1.2 M1G 1959–1976	A1.3 M2G 1954–1976	A1.4 M2G 1959–1976	A1.5 IPG 1954–1976	A1.6 IPG 1959–1976	A1.7 π 1954–1976	A1.8 π 1959–1976
Constant term	.0038 (.0013)	.0053 (.0019)	.0049 (.0017)	.0076 (.0024)	.0093 (.0283)	.0092 (.0035)	.0012 (.0066)	.0014 (.0008)
$M1G(-1)$	.3777 (.1078)	.3158 (.1234)						
$M1G(-2)$	.2205 (.1152)	.2166 (.1289)						
$M1G(-3)$	.0550 (.1151)	.0306 (.1275)						
$M1G(-4)$	-.0341 (.1076)	-.0371 (.1236)						
$M2G(-1)$			.6598 (.1080)	.6113 (.1220)				
$M2G(-2)$			-.0542 (.1280)	-.0412 (.1421)				
$M2G(-3)$			.1736 (.1286)	.1619 (.1408)				
$M2G(-4)$			-.0758 (.1094)	-.1525 (.1230)				

Table 5.A.1 (continued)

Model: Dependent Variable: Sample Period:	A1.1 M1G 1954–1976	A1.2 M1G 1959–1976	A1.3 M2G 1954–1976	A1.4 M2G 1959–1976	A1.5 IPG 1954–1976	A1.6 IPG 1959–1976	A1.7 π 1954–1976	A1.8 π 1959–1976
$IPG(-1)$					.4254 (.1003)	.3514 (.1187)		
$IPG(-2)$					−.2346 (.1091)	−.2100 (.1250)		
$IPG(-3)$					.1507 (.1091)	.1449 (.1238)		
$IPG(-4)$					−.2516 (.1003)	−.2025 (.1131)		
$\pi(-1)$							.4008 (.1044)	.3991 (.1209)
$\pi(-2)$							.5520 (.1112)	.6162 (.1268)
$\pi(-3)$							.1063 (.1119)	−.0179 (.1275)
$\pi(-4)$							−.1837 (.1033)	−.1613 (.1112)
R^2	.2952	.2023	.4563	.3766	.2148	.1496	.7305	.7555
SE	.0062	.0066	.0066	.0070	.0237	.0239	.0039	.0038
D-W	1.97	1.96	1.96	1.94	2.00	1.98	2.03	2.01

Note: Standard error of the coefficients in parentheses. Definitions of variables: $M1G$ = quarterly rate of growth of $M1$, $M2G$ = quarterly rate of growth of $M2$, IPG = quarterly rate of growth of industrial production, π = quarterly rate of growth of CPI, UN = unemployment rate, r = ninety-day bill rate, BOP = balance of payments on current account, G = quarterly rate of growth of real federal government expenditures, GDEBT = quarterly rate of growth of government debt, SURP = high employment surplus.

Table 5.A.2 Multivariate Time-Series Models

Model: Dependent Variable: Sample Period:	A2.1 M1G 1954–1976	A2.2 M1G 1959–1976	A2.3 M2G 1954–1976	A2.4 M2G 1959–1976	A2.5 IPG 1954–1976	A2.6 IPG 1959–1976	A2.7 π 1954–1976	A2.8 π 1959–1976
Constant term	−.0004 (.0017)	.0015 (.0021)	.0026 (.0016)	.0044 (.0027)	−.0148 (.0125)	.0017 (.0111)	.0053 (.0019)	.0033 (.0021)
M1G(−1)	.0906 (.1655)	−.1031 (.1875)			.6904 (.3938)			.1835 (.0635)
M1G(−2)	.5233 (.1680)	.5336 (.1906)			.6883 (.4089)			.0376 (.0649)
M1G(−3)	−.2765 (.1785)	−.3184 (.1990)			1.0207 (.4200)			−.0663 (.0657)
M1G(−4)	−.1757 (.1791)	.0052 (.1739)			.2745 (.4337)			.1600 (.0727)
M2G(−1)	.3590 (.1618)	.5998 (.1666)	.5050 (.1119)	.5211 (.1271)		.7132 (.3814)		
M2G(−2)	−.3972 (.1754)	.5612 (.1935)	.0985 (.1266)	.0955 (.1426)		.9460 (.4300)		
M2G(−3)	.3510 (.1757)	.4112 (.2077)	.1517 (.1167)	.1179 (.1325)		.7217 (.4122)		
M2G(−4)	.1396 (.1645)	.0240 (.1843)	−.0806 (.1036)	−.0838 (.1180)		−.2049 (.4182)		

Table 5.A.2 (continued)

Model: Dependent Variable: Sample Period:	A2.1 M1G 1954–1976	A2.2 M1G 1959–1976	A2.3 M2G 1954–1976	A2.4 M2G 1959–1976	A2.5 IPG 1954–1976	A2.6 IPG 1959–1976	A2.7 π 1954–1976	A2.8 π 1959–1976
$IPG(-1)$					-.0947 (.1622)	-.2778 (.1129)		
$IPG(-2)$					-.6171 (.1727)	-.3626 (.1089)		
$IPG(-3)$					-.0902 (.1709)	-.0457 (.1089)		
$IPG(-4)$					-.2807 (.1224)	-.1869 (.1010)		
$\pi(-1)$					-.5539 (.6501)	-2.277 (.793)	.2245 (.1079)	.1209 (.1273)
$\pi(-2)$					-.5186 (.6229)	-1.753 (.701)	.5527 (.1053)	.7705 (.1171)
$\pi(-3)$					-.8774 (.6533)	.398 (.846)	.2833 (.1090)	.3911 (.1339)
$\pi(-4)$					-.7464 (.6533)	1.252 (.591)	-.0636 (.1116)	-.2328 (.1176)
$UN(-1)$					-.0904 (.0096)		-.0036 (.0009)	-.0052 (.0014)
$UN(-2)$					-.0018 (.0120)		.0012 (.0016)	-.0016 (.0021)
$UN(-3)$					.0173 (.0114)		.0018 (.0015)	.0034 (.0021)
$UN(-4)$					-.0001 (.0091)		-.0004 (.0095)	-.0004 (.0013)

	(1)	(2)	(3)	(4)	(5)	(6)	(7)	(8)
$r(-1)$	-.2647		-.4966	-.5214		.9813		
	(.1067)		(.1000)	(.1221)		(.4501)		
$r(-2)$	.2086		.4853	.4827		.5253		
	(.1305)		(.1373)	(.1631)		(.4819)		
$r(-3)$	.1250		.0332	.0551		.3307		
	(.1396)		(.1472)	(.1669)		(.4793)		
$r(-4)$	-.0277		.0519	.0333		-1.830		
	(.1121)		(.1132)	(.1279)		(.437)		
$BOP(-1)$						.0058		.0001
						(.0035)		(.0006)
$BOP(-2)$						.0050		.0003
						(.0047)		(.0008)
$BOP(-3)$						.0016		-.0005
						(.0046)		(.0008)
$BOP(-4)$						-.0094		-.0010
						(.0037)		(.0006)
R^2	.5427	.4024	.6232	.5472	.5159	.7108	.7949	.8789
SE	.0053	.0059	.0056	.0061	.0200	.0160	.0035	.0029
D-W	1.97	2.01	1.96	1.95	2.03	2.00	1.96	2.21

Note: See table 5.A.1.

Table 5.A.3   **F Statistics for Significant Explanatory Power in Forecasting Equations of Four Lags of Each Variable**

				Model				
Variable	A2.1	A2.2	A2.3	A2.4	A2.5	A2.6	A2.7	A2.8
MIG	3.10*	2.44	2.32	2.17	6.53**	.09	1.66	4.14
M2G	3.98**	5.28**	15.37**	10.42**	.05	11.09**	1.12	1.13
IPG	.98	1.26	1.70	1.65	3.71**	4.70**	1.08	1.55
π	2.04	1.81	1.19	.40	7.61**	5.05**	79.32**	48.33**
UN	.77	1.42	.51	.25	3.00*	2.32	6.51**	5.88**
r	2.85*	2.46	9.19**	5.93**	1.95	5.62**	.69	.94
BOP	1.41	.79	1.04	.70	1.83	3.54*	2.32	2.87*
G	1.54	.47	.10	.22	.89	.46	2.25	1.59
GDEBT	.63	.43	.90	.44	.36	1.84	.57	1.33
SURP	.57	.62	1.09	1.28	.54	.70	1.57	2.01

Note: The F statistics test the null hypothesis that the coefficients on the four lags of each of these variables equals zero. The F statistics are distributed asymptotically as $F(4, x)$, where x runs from 47 to 83. The critical values of F at the 5 percent level are 2.5–2.6 and at the 10 percent level are 3.6–3.7.
*Significant at the 5 percent level.
**Significant at the 1 percent level.

Table 5.A.4   Chow Tests for the Models of Tables 5.A.1 and 5.A.2

Model	F Statistic	Marginal Significance Level
A1.1	$F(5,82) = 3.50^{**}$	.0064
A1.2	$F(5,62) = 2.73^{*}$	.0271
A1.3	$F(5,82) = 2.49$	.0377
A1.4	$F(5,62) = 1.24$	.3014
A1.5	$F(5,82) = 2.81^{*}$	.0216
A1.6	$F(5,62) = 3.80^{**}$	.0046
A1.7	$F(5,82) = 1.59$	.1721
A1.8	$F(5,62) = 1.83$	.1200
A2.1	$F(13,66) = 1.81$	.0597
A2.2	$F(9,54) = 2.94^{**}$	.0065
A2.3	$F(9,74) = 1.60$	.1310
A2.4	$F(9,54) = 1.80$	.0895
A2.5	$F(17,58) = 1.39$	.1753
A2.6	$F(21,30) = 1.76$	.0765
A2.8	$F(17,38) = 1.24$	.2824

Note: Tests that the coefficients are equal in the two halves of the sample period.
*Significant at the 5 percent level.
**Significant at the 1 percent level.

Appendix 5.2:   Additional Experiments Using the Two-Step Procedure

Because the two-step procedure used by Barro (1977) yields consistent parameter estimates and is far easier to execute than the joint nonlinear procedure used in the text, it is used in tables 5.A.5 and 5.A.6 to provide additional estimates of the long bond and short-rate models.

The two-step procedure here does not correct for heteroscedasticity within each long bond and short-rate equation even though Goldfeld-Quandt (1965) tests frequently reveal that it exists. This simplifies estimation and does not affect the consistency of the parameter estimates. However, this two-step procedure may yield incorrect standard errors and test statistics. Thus although tables 5.A.5 and 5.A.6 provide useful information, some caution about statistical inference is warranted.

The first four models of panels A and B in both tables reestimate the models in the text by the two-step procedure. As we might expect, the parameter estimates are similar to those génerated by the nonlinear procedures of the text and yield similar conclusions. This gives us some confidence that the two-step procedure can be used to gain further information on the robustness of this chapter's empirical results. Using the two-step procedure, long bond and short-rate models were also estimated with alternative specifications of the forecasting equations.

Table 5.A.5   Estimates of the Long Bond Model: Using Seasonally Adjusted Data and the Two-Step Procedure (Sample Period 1954–1976)

			Coefficients of					
Model	$M1G_t - M1G_t^e$	$M2G_t - M2G_t^e$	$MBG_t - MBG_t^e$	$URG_t - URG_t^e$	$UBG_t - UBG_t^e$	$IPG_t - IPG_t^e$	$\pi_t - \pi_t^e$	Constant Term
			Panel A: Using Residuals from Univariate Forecasting Models					
A5.1	.3507 (.5753)							-.0008 (.0034)
A5.2	.3658 (.5460)					-.4447 (.1412)	-2.136 (.8580)	-.0008 (.0033)
A5.3		1.113 (.530)						-.0008 (.0034)
A5.4		.8762 (.5007)				-.4265 (.1385)	-1.987 (.8455)	-.0008 (.0033)
A5.5			-.3502 (.5388)					-.0008 (.0034)
A5.6			.1974 (.5195)			-.4409 (.1418)	-2.295 (.8793)	-.0008 (.0033)
A5.7				.1955 (.1936)				-.0008 (.0034)
A5.8				.2214 (.1909)		-.3952 (.1437)	-2.487 (.8788)	-.0008 (.0033)
A5.9					.3703 (.4937)			-.0008 (.0034)
A5.10					.4196 (.4879)	-.4064 (.1436)	-2.410 (.8796)	-.0008 (.0033)

Panel B: Using Residuals from Multivariate Forecasting Models

A5.11	.2788 (.7149)							−.0008 (.0034)
A5.12	.6262 (.6958)					−.5626 (.1863)	−1.997 (.994)	−.0008 (.0033)
A5.13		1.105 (.642)						−.0008 (.0034)
A5.14		1.197 (.608)				−.5547 (.1795)	−1.973 (.977)	−.0008 (.0033)
A5.15			.3019 (.6563)					−.0008 (.0034)
A5.16			.1308 (.6229)			−.5339 (.1854)	−2.077 (1.008)	−.0008 (.0033)
A5.17				.1587 (.2204)				−.0008 (.0034)
A5.18				.1558 (.2164)		−.5063 (.1855)	−2.195 (1.016)	−.0008 (.0033)
A5.19					.3936 (.5875)			−.0008 (.0034)
A5.20					.6392 (.5657)	−.5219 (.1818)	−2.311 (1.018)	−.0008 (.0033)

Note: See table 5.A.1.

Table 5.A.6 Estimates of the Short-Rate Model: Using Seasonally Adjusted Data and the Two-Step Procedure (Sample Period 1959–1976)

Model	$M1G_t - M1G_t^e$	$M2G_t - M2G_t^e$	$MBG_t - MBG_t^e$	$URG_t - URG_t^e$	$UBG_t - UBG_t^e$	$IPG_t - IPG_t^e$	$\pi_t - \pi_t^e$	Constant Term	σ
					Coefficients of				
			Panel A: Using Residuals from Univariate Forecasting Models						
A6.1	.2777 (.1223)							.0002 (.0017)	-1.164 (.287)
A6.2	.2930 (.1131)						.6534 (.1968)	.0001 (.0016)	-1.102 (.266)
A6.3		.0766 (.1197)				.0538 (.0315)		.0000 (.0018)	-1.123 (.298)
A6.4		.1632 (.1133)				.0615 (.0324)	.6723 (.2081)	.0002 (.0016)	-1.079 (.276)
A6.5			.2291 (.1287)					-.0003 (.0017)	-1.078 (.290)
A6.6			.1390 (.1252)			.0601 (.0327)	.5094 (.2096)	-.0008 (.0016)	-1.003 (.277)
A6.7				.0095 (.0450)				-.0002 (.0017)	-1.093 (.296)
A6.8				.0111 (.0444)		.0646 (.0342)	.5527 (.2102)	-.0008 (.0016)	-1.005 (.280)
A6.9					.0752 (.1157)			-.0002 (.0016)	-1.097 (.295)
A6.10					.0934 (.1139)	.0703 (.0341)	.5310 (.2091)	-.0008 (.0016)	-1.003 (.278)

Panel B: Using Residuals from Multivariate Forecasting Models

	(1)	(2)	(3)	(4)	(5)	(6)	(7)	(8)	(9)
A6.11	.1990 (.1442)							.0001 (.0015)	−1.130 (.293)
A6.12	.2060 (.1451)					.3650 (.3147)	.0323 (.0609)	.0001 (.0018)	−1.139 (.296)
A6.13		.0894 (.1397)						.0001 (.0017)	−1.092 (.295)
A6.14		.1143 (.1429)				.3781 (.3272)	.0340 (.0619)	−.0001 (.0018)	−1.101 (.298)
A6.15			.2054 (.1617)					−.0003 (.0017)	−1.056 (.294)
A6.16			.1616 (.1569)			.6450 (.2398)	.0111 (.0427)	.0003 (.0017)	−1.126 (.289)
A6.17				.0168 (.0494)				−.0001 (.0017)	−1.091 (.296)
A6.18				−.0006 (.0549)		.6694 (.2443)	.0131 (.0435)	.0002 (.0017)	−1.158 (.290)
A6.19					.1493 (.1357)			−.0004 (.0017)	−1.046 (.296)
A6.20					.0901 (.1325)	.6377 (.2443)	.0161 (.0435)	−.0000 (.0017)	−1.121 (.293)

Note: See table 5.A.1.

Models were estimated with residuals from the eighth-order autoregressive forecasting equations, as well as from multivariate models which included the four lagged values of a variable even if it was significant only at the 10 percent level (rather than the 5 percent level as in the text). The results were quite close to those reported here and the results again appear robust to changes in the specification of the forecasting equation.

Because the Federal Reserve might have changed its reaction function in the 1970s by paying more attention to monetary aggregates than it did previously, it is possible that the results here might substantially change if the 1970s are excluded from the sample period. Two-step estimates of the long bond and short-rate models over the sample period ending in the 1969:4 quarter fail to support this conjecture. The unanticipated IPG and π coefficients remain similar to those in tables 5.A.5 and 5.A.6: for the long bond model, the IPG coefficients range from $-.36$ to $-.46$ and the π coefficients from -1.69 to -2.17; and for the short-rate model, the IPG coefficients range from $-.04$ to $.03$ and the π coefficients from $.37$ to $.57$. Similar conclusions about the relationship of money growth and interest rates result also from estimates using the shorter sample periods. For the long bond model, the unanticipated $M1G$ coefficients are now negative, ranging from $-.26$ to $-.54$ and the $M2G$ coefficients range from $.24$ to $.79$. For the short-rate model, the money growth coefficients remain positive, with the $M1G$ coefficients ranging from $.11$ to $.20$ and the $M2G$ coefficients from $.03$ to $.12$.

The most obvious choice for the monetary aggregate that is exogenously determined by the Federal Reserve are not $M1$ and $M2$. As becomes clear from such debates as those between Anderson and Jordan (1969) and De Leeuw and Kalchenbrenner (1969), other aggregates may be a more sensible control variable for the Fed. If these aggregates are more likely than $M1$ or $M2$ to be exogenous, their use in the models here should give a clearer picture of the effect of monetary policy on interest rates. For this reason, tables 5.A.5 and 5.A.6 also contain two-step estimates of the models using the following additional variables:

MBG = growth rate of the monetary base (quarterly rate),
URG = growth rate of unborrowed reserves (quarterly rate),
UBG = growth rate of the unborrowed base (quarterly rate).

These variables are constructed analogously to $M1G$ and $M2G$ from the same data source, and the specifications for the forecasting equations were obtained with the same procedures used for $M1G$ and $M2G$.

In some applications the monetary base has been chosen as the Fed's control variable (e.g., see Anderson and Jordan 1968), while in monetary sectors of the large structural macroeconometric models such as the MPS (see Modigliani 1974) unborrowed reserves are often the exogenous control variable. On the other hand, the unborrowed base is the monetary aggregate corresponding most closely with open market operations. All three of the monetary aggregates are thus worthy candidates to be included in the long bond and short-rate models.

The results from using alternative monetary aggregates do not alter the conclusions or the relationship of monetary policy and interest rates. In the long bond models, the coefficients for the alternative aggregates are somewhat less positive than those for $M1$ or $M2$. They provide even less support for the view that an increase in monetary aggregates is associated with a fall in long interest rates. The coefficients in the short-rate models are almost always positive, and this is consistent with the results for $M1$ and $M2$, that a surprise increase in the monetary aggregate is associated with a rise in short rates.

6   Does Anticipated Aggregate Demand Policy Matter?

6.1   Introduction

Recent theorizing has focused on business cycle models that incorporate features of the natural rate model of Friedman (1968) and Phelps (1967) with the assumption that expectations are rational in the sense of Muth (1961). An important neutrality result from this research (Lucas 1973; Sargent and Wallace 1975) is that anticipated changes in aggregate demand policy will have been taken into account already in the behavior of economic agents and will evoke no further output or employment response. Therefore, deterministic, feedback policy rules will have no effect on output fluctuations in the economy. This policy ineffectiveness proposition of what Modigliani (1977) has dubbed the Macro Rational Expectations (MRE) hypothesis runs counter to much previous macroeconomic theorizing (and to views prevailing in policymaking circles). This proposition is of such importance that it demands a wide range of empirical research for verification or refutation.

This chapter applies the econometric methodology developed in Chapter 2 to the important question whether anticipated aggregate demand policy matters to the business cycle. It begins with a brief review of the methodology in Section 6.2, then follows with the empirical results in Section 6.3, and ends with a section of concluding remarks.

6.2   A Review of the Methodology

The tests here are based on the MRE model of the form

(1) $$ y_t = \tilde{y}_t + \sum_{i=0}^{N} \beta_i (X_{t-i} - X_{t-i}^e) + \epsilon_t , $$

where

y_t = unemployment or real output at time t,
$\tilde{y}_t$ = natural level of unemployment or real output at time t,
X_t = aggregate demand policy variable, such as money growth, inflation, or nominal GNP growth,
X_t^e = anticipated X conditional on information at time $t-1$,
β_i = coefficients,
ϵ_t = error term.

A forecasting equation that can be used to generate these anticipations of X_t is

(2) $$X_t = Z_{t-1}\gamma + u_t,$$

where

Z_{t-1} = a vector of variables used to forecast X_t available at time $t-1$,
γ = a vector of coefficients,
u_t = an error term which is assumed to be uncorrelated with any information available at $t-1$ (which includes Z_{t-i} or u_{t-i} for all $i \geq 1$, and hence u_t is serially uncorrelated).

A rational forecast for X_t then involves simply taking expectations of equation (2) conditional on information available at $t-1$:

(3) $$X_t^e = Z_t\gamma.$$

Substituting into equation (1), we have

(4) $$y_t = \tilde{y}_t + \sum_{i=0}^{N} \beta_i(X_{t-i} - Z_{t-i}\gamma) + \epsilon_t.$$

The MRE hypothesis embodies two sets of constraints. The neutrality proposition implies that deviations of output and unemployment from their natural levels are not correlated with the anticipated movements in aggregate demand policy. That is, $\delta_i = 0$ for all i in

(5) $$y_t = \tilde{y}_t + \sum_{i=0}^{N} \beta_i(X_{t-i} - X_{t-i}^e) + \sum_{i=0}^{N} \delta_i X_{t-i}^e + \epsilon_t.$$

Rationality of expectations implies that (5) can be rewritten as

(6) $$y_t = \tilde{y}_t + \sum_{i=0}^{N} \beta_i(X_{t-i} - Z_{t-i}\gamma^*) + \sum_{i=0}^{N} \delta_i Z_{t-i}\gamma^* + \epsilon_t,$$

where $\gamma = \gamma^*$.

The joint nonlinear estimation procedure outlined in Chapter 2 is used here to estimate both the constrained (2) and (4) system and the unconstrained (2) and (6) system where $\gamma = \gamma^*$ is not imposed. It corrects for serial correlation with a fourth-order autoregressive (AR) specification for the ϵ_t error term, and this is successful in reducing the residuals to white noise.[1] The conventional identifying assumption found in previous research on this topic is made that the output or unemployment equation is a true reduced form. The joint MRE hypothesis of rationality and neutrality is then tested with a likelihood ratio statistic constructed from a comparison of the two estimated systems. It is distributed asymptotically as $\chi^2(q)$ under the null hypothesis where q is the number of constraints.

If the joint hypothesis of rationality and neutrality is rejected, we can obtain information on how much the rationality versus the neutrality constraints contributes to this rejection. The neutrality constraints are tested under the maintained hypothesis of rational expectations by constructing a likelihood ratio statistic as above where the constrained system is (2) and (4), and the unconstrained system is (2) and (6) subject to the rationality constraints, $\gamma = \gamma^*$. A separate test for the rationality constraints proceeds similarly: the constrained system is (2) and (6) imposing $\gamma = \gamma^*$, and the unconstrained system is (2) and (6) where $\gamma = \gamma^*$ is not imposed.

In the results to follow, rejections of the MRE hypothesis occur when the number of lags (N) in the unemployment or output equation is large. However, although many degrees of freedom are used up in these estimations, there is no allowance for the loss of degrees of freedom in the likelihood ratio statistics. The danger thus arises that spurious rejections of the null hypothesis may occur because the small sample distributions of the test statistics differ substantially from the asymptotic distributions.

The nature of the problem here becomes more obvious if we look at the following analogous example. In an OLS regression, a test of restrictions can be carried out with a finite sample test, the F, or with an asymptotic test, the likelihood ratio. Asymptotically, the test statistics have the same distribution, but misleading inference with the likelihood ratio statistics can easily result in small samples. The F statistic is calculated as

(7) $$F(q, df) = \left[\left(\frac{\text{SSR}^c - \text{SSR}^u}{\text{SSR}^u} \right) \frac{df}{q} \right]$$

while the likelihood ratio statistic is

(8) $$n[\log(\text{SSR}^c/\text{SSR}^u)],$$

1. In the output and unemployment equations estimates here, the Durbin-Watson statistics range from 1.82 to 2.26, and none indicates the presence of first-order serial correlation. Furthermore, the Ljung and Box (1978) adjusted Q statistics for the first twelve autocorrelations of the residuals cannot reject the null hypothesis that these autocorrelations are zero. The $Q(12)$ statistics range from 5.84 to 15.0 for all the models except those in Appendix 6.1, while the critical $Q(12)$ at 5 percent is 15.5. For the models in Appendix 6.1, the $Q(12)$ statistics range from 8.26 to 15.90, while the critical $Q(12)$ at 5 percent is 18.2.

where

> df = the degrees of freedom of the unconstrained model,
> n = the number of observations,
> q = the number of constraints.

For over 100 degrees of freedom $qF(q,df)$ is nearly distributed as $\chi^2(q)$, and for small percentage differences, $(SSR^c - SSR^u)/SSR^u$ is approximately equal to log (SSR^c/SSR^u). Inference with the F statistic in the case of over 100 degrees of freedom involves approximately the comparison of $df[\log(SSR^c/SSR^u)]$ with the $\chi^2(q)$ distribution. Inference with the likelihood ratio statistic on the other hand involves the comparison of $n[\log(SSR^c/SSR^u)]$ with the $\chi^2(q)$ distribution. Even in the case where df is large, if n/df is substantially greater than one, the likelihood ratio statistic will reject the null hypothesis far more often than will the F. In the case of the freely estimated unemployment or output model in Appendix 6.3 and $N = 20$, the degrees of freedom of the unconstrained model for the joint or rationality tests is 111, while the number of observations is 184. The n/df of 1.7 in this case demonstrates that there is a potentially serious small sample bias in the likelihood ratio test when this many degrees of freedom are used up.

To make certain that rejections are valid, the output and unemployment models are estimated both with and without the smoothness restriction that the anticipated and unanticipated money growth coefficients (δ_i and β_i) lie along a fourth-order polynomial with an endpoint constraint. This particular polynomial distributed lag (PDL) specification was chosen because it is rarely rejected by the data and it has the advantage of using up few degrees of freedom.[2]

The anticipated aggregate demand X variable is constructed so that it will be serially uncorrelated, so that a smoothness restriction is not required to make coefficients on unanticipated aggregate demand intelligible. However, anticipated aggregate demand variables are highly

---

2. The PDL constraints are not rejected in models where money growth or inflation are the aggregate demand X variable. E.g., in model 2.1, $\chi^2(4) = 3.34$, while the critical value at 5 percent is 9.49; in model 4.1, $\chi^2(17) = 12.94$, while the critical value at 5 percent is 27.59; and in model A9.1, $\chi^2(14) = 20.54$, while the critical value at 5 percent is 23.7. The PDL constraints receive somewhat less support in the models using nominal GNP as the X variable. They are not rejected for the A5.1 output model at the 5 percent level, but are nearly so: $\chi^2(17) = 26.95$, while the critical $\chi^2(17)$ at 5 percent is 27.6. However, they are rejected at the 1 percent level in the unemployment model: $\chi^2(17) = 34.91$, while the critical $\chi^2(17)$ at 1 percent is 33.4. I experimented with an eighth-order PDL to see if this would fit the data substantially better, but it did not. Although this rejection of the PDL constraints is bothersome, the fact that the unrestricted models in Appendix 6.3 yield results so similar to those in tables 6.A.5 and 6.A.6 indicates that, imposing or not imposing, the PDL constraints yields the same conclusions.

serially correlated, and the use of PDLs has the advantage of providing more intelligible and more easily interpretable estimates of the anticipated aggregate demand coefficients, δ_i. The main results reported in this chapter thus are based on a PDL restriction. Comparing the main results with those in Appendix 6.3 obtained without a PDL restriction demonstrates that estimating with or without the restriction yields similar β coefficients and similar statistical inference on the validity of the MRE hypothesis. Therefore, we can be confident that any rejections of the MRE hypothesis are not due to small sample bias.

The specifications of the forecasting equations needed to estimate the MRE model are derived with the multivariate Granger (1969) procedure outlined in Chapter 2. The policy variable, X_t, is regressed on its own four lagged values (to insure white noise residuals) as well as on four lagged values of the following set of macrovariables: the quarterly $M1$ and $M2$ growth rate, the inflation rate, nominal GNP growth, the unemployment rate, the Treasury Bill rate, the growth rate of real government expenditure, the high employment surplus, the growth rate of the federal debt, and the balance of payments on current account. The four lagged values of each variable are retained in the equation only if they are jointly significant at the 5 percent level. This results in a specification of the money growth forecasting equation, for example, which is quite different from that used by Barro (1977, 1978) and Barro and Rush (1980): in addition to past money growth, past Treasury Bill rates and high employment budget surpluses appear as explanatory variables. Weintraub (1980) also finds significant explanatory power of short-term interest rates in the money growth equation, and the magnitude of his coefficients is similar to that found here. The specifications for the forecasting equations can be found in Appendix 6.4 as well as the F statistics for significant explanatory power of the four lagged values of each variable in these specifications.[3]

Earlier research on the MRE hypothesis (e.g., Barro 1977, 1978, 1979; Barro and Rush 1980; Grossman 1979; Leiderman 1980) uses a fairly short lag length—two years or less—on the anticipated and unanticipated X variables. This chapter looks at longer lag lengths for two reasons. Experimenting with plausible, less restrictive models that have longer lag lengths is appropriate for analyzing the robustness of results because this strategy has the disadvantage only of a potential decrease in the power of

---

3. Chow (1960) tests that split the sample into equal halves indicate that both the money growth and nominal GNP growth equations have the desirable property that the stability of the coefficients cannot be rejected. However, stability of the coefficients is rejected for the inflation equation. For the $M1$ growth equation, $F(13,66) = 1.37$, while the critical F at 5 percent is 1.88; for the nominal GNP equation, $F(9,74) = .60$, while the critical F at 5 percent is 2.0; and for the inflation equation, $F(13,55) = 3.40$, while the critical F at 5 percent is 1.9.

tests, but not of incorrect test statistics. In addition, estimates in this chapter and in Gordon (1979) find that unanticipated and anticipated aggregate demand variables lagged as far back as twenty quarters are significantly correlated with output and unemployment.

6.3   The Empirical Results

The tests of the MRE hypothesis in the text use seasonally adjusted, postwar quarterly data over the 1954–1976 period. The sample starts with 1954—the earliest possible starting date if models with long lags are to be estimated.[4] An advantage of excluding the early postwar years from the sample is that the potential change in policy regime occurring with the Fed-Treasury Accord in 1951 is avoided. In pursuit of information on robustness, both output and unemployment models are estimated, with $M1$ growth, nominal GNP growth, and inflation as the aggregate demand variable. The natural level of unemployment or output, $\tilde{y}_t$, is estimated as a time trend here, as in Barro (1978). A more complicated Barro (1977) specification has been avoided because, as Small (1979) and Barro (1979) indicate, its validity is doubtful.

6.3.1   The Data

The definitions and the sources of data used in this chapter are as follows:

$M1G$ = average growth rate (quarterly rate) of $M1$, calculated as the change in the log of quarterly $M1$, from the NBER data bank.

$M2G$ = average growth rate (quarterly rate) of $M2$, calculated as the change in the log of quarterly $M2$, from the NBER data bank.

RTB = average treasury bill rate at an annual rate (in fractions), from the MPS data bank.

π = inflation (quarterly rate), calculated as the changes in the log of the GNP deflator, from the MPS data bank.

GNP = real GNP ($billions 1972), from the MPS data bank.

UN = average quarterly unemployment rate, from the MPS data bank.

$NGNP$ = growth rate (quarterly) of nominal GNP, calculated as the change in the log of nominal GNP, from the MPS data bank.

The other variables used in the search procedure for the forecasting equations were obtained from the NBER data bank.

---

4. Quarterly data on such variables as SURP do not become available until 1947. With twenty lags on anticipated or unanticipated X_t, the additional four lags in the forecasting equation and another four lags due to the fourth-order AR correction, the first twenty-eight observations are used up. This leaves us with a 1954:1 start date.

6.3.2   Results with Money Growth as the
        Aggregate Demand Variable

The text will focus its attention on results obtained when money growth is the aggregate demand variable in the MRE model. However, results with inflation and nominal GNP growth as the aggregate demand variable are presented in Appendix 6.2 and they are consistent with the money growth results. The money growth results deserve more attention for two reasons. Research with money growth as the aggregate demand variable (e.g., Barro 1977, 1978, 1979; Barro and Rush 1980; Leiderman 1980; Germany and Srivastava 1979; Small 1979) is more common in the literature and produces results most favorable to the MRE hypothesis. The methodology employed in this research has been criticized, however, and another look at the question of whether anticipated monetary policy matters to the business cycle is called for. Furthermore, the identifying assumption used to estimate the MRE model, that it is a true reduced form, is on firmer ground when money growth is the aggregate demand variable. Although the exogeneity of money growth in output or unemployment equations is still controversial, economists are more willing to accept the exogeneity of money growth than the exogeneity of nominal GNP growth or inflation.

Table 6.1 summarizes the major findings by presenting the likelihood ratio tests of the MRE hypothesis with $M1$ growth as the aggregate demand variable. It tells the following story: When the lag length on unanticipated and anticipated money growth is only seven, the lag length used by Barro and Rush (1980), the likelihood ratio tests are not unfavorable to the MRE hypothesis. The joint hypothesis of neutrality and rationality is not rejected at the 5 percent level in either the output or unemployment models, 2.1 and 2.2. Separate tests of the rationality and the neutrality hypotheses reject only in one case—neutrality in the employment model 2.2—and even here the rejection is barely at the 5 percent level. However, when the lag length is allowed to be longer—up to twenty lags in the other models of the table—strong rejections of the MRE hypothesis occur. The output model displays especially strong rejections of the joint hypothesis—the probability of finding that value of the likelihood ratio statistic or higher under the null hypothesis is as low as 1 in 10,000. Here, both sets of constraints contribute to this rejection, with the neutrality and rationality hypothesis rejected at the 1 percent level. The long lag, unemployment models are also unfavorable to the joint MRE hypothesis, with the rejection at the 1 percent level. However, here the neutrality constraints are rejected far more strongly than the rationality constraints.

Excluding relevant variables from a model results in incorrect test statistics, and including irrelevant variables will at worst only reduce the power of tests and make rejections even more telling. The table 6.1

Table 6.1   Likelihood Ratio Tests of the MRE Hypothesis with $M1$ Growth as the Aggregate Demand Variable

Model:	2.1	2.2	4.1	4.2
Dependent Variable:	$Log(GNP_t)$	UN_t	$log(GNP_t)$	UN_t
Description:	7 Lags of $M1G_t - M1G_t^e$	7 Lags of $M1G_t - M1G_t^e$	20 lags of $M1G_t - M1G_t^e$	20 lags of $M1G_t - M1G_t^e$
Joint hypothesis:				
Likelihood ratio statistic	$\chi^2(15) = 22.69$	$\chi^2(15) = 22.80$	$\chi^2(15) = 43.83$**	$\chi^2(15) = 31.54$**
Marginal significance level	.0909	.0885	.0001	.0074
Neutrality:				
Likelihood ratio statistic	$\chi^2(4) = 3.36$	$\chi^2(4) = 9.67$*	$\chi^2(4) = 15.45$**	$\chi^2(4) = 12.08$*
Marginal significance level	.4993	.0464	.0039	.0168
Rationality:				
Likelihood ratio statistic	$\chi^2(11) = 19.44$	$\chi^2(11) = 13.31$	$\chi^2(11) = 29.17$**	$\chi^2(11) = 19.89$*
Marginal significance level	.0536	.2735	.0021	.0469

Note: Marginal significance level = the probability of getting that value of the likelihood ratio statistic or higher under the null hypothesis.

*Significant at the 5 percent level.

**Significant at the 1 percent level.

results therefore raise questions about previous empirical evidence from shorter lag models that supports the MRE hypothesis, neutrality in particular. Indeed, it appears that the shorter lag models are more favorable to the MRE hypothesis only because misspecification yields incorrect test statistics.

A look at the estimates of unemployment and output equations from these models leads to a deeper understanding of the test results. Table 6.2 contains the output, and unemployment equations with short lags, jointly estimated from the (2) and (4) system which impose the cross-equation rationality constraints. The resulting γ estimates for the models of table 6.2 and the following tables are in Appendix 6.4.

The table 6.2 models fit the data well, and the unanticipated money growth variables have significant explanatory power: many of their coefficients' asymptotic *t* statistics are greater than four in absolute value. The test results in table 1 become clearer when we study the estimated output and unemployment equations where current and lagged anticipated money growth are added as explanatory variables. The table 6.3 results illustrate why the neutrality proposition is not rejected for the output equation. The coefficients on anticipated money growth have no obvious pattern, are never significantly different from zero, and, in seven out of eight cases, are smaller in absolute value than their asymptotic standard errors. However, in the unemployment equation some coefficients on anticipated money growth are significantly different from zero at the 5 percent level, and this is enough to reject neutrality. Here, the last two lag coefficients on anticipated money growth are the most significant, with asymptotic *t* statistics exceeding 2.5. This creates the suspicion that even longer lag lengths for unanticipated and anticipated money growth may lead to strong rejections of the MRE hypothesis.

Table 6.4 contains estimates of the output and unemployment equations in which longer lags (twenty) of unanticipated money growth are used as explanatory variables. Tables 6.5 and 6.6 demonstrate why strong rejections of the MRE hypothesis now occur. Many of the coefficients on anticipated money growth are now significantly different from zero at the 1 percent level, with some asymptotic *t* statistics even exceeding four in absolute value. Of course these coefficients may be statistically significant and still unimportant from an economic viewpoint; but this is clearly not the case. The unanticipated coefficients not only tend to be greater in absolute value than their unanticipated counterparts, but generally they have higher asymptotic *t* statistics as well. In fact, only one out of twenty-one β coefficients is statistically significant, as opposed to nearly half of the δ coefficients. Contrary to what is implied by the MRE hypothesis, anticipated monetary policy does not appear to be less important than unanticipated monetary policy. In fact, the opposite seems to be the case.

Table 6.2 Nonlinear Estimates of Output and Unemployment Equations
Explanatory Variables: Unanticipated Money Growth, Seven Lags (PDL)

$$y_t = c + \tau \text{TIME} + \sum_{i=0}^{7} \beta_i (M1G_{t-i} - M1G^e_{t-i}) + \rho_1 \epsilon_{t-1} + \rho_2 \epsilon_{t-2} + \rho_3 \epsilon_{t-3} + \rho_4 \epsilon_{t-4} + \eta_{it}$$

Model:	2.1		2.2	
Dependent Variable:	$\log(\text{GNP}_t)$		UN_t	
	$c = 6.178(.047)^{**}$	$\tau = .008(.0005)$	$c = 3.55(1.54)^{*}$	$\tau = .024(.018)$
	$\beta_0 = .715(.230)^{**}$		$\beta_0 = -20.01(\,8.69)^{**}$	
	$\beta_1 = 1.617(.340)^{**}$		$\beta_1 = -43.21(15.38)^{**}$	
	$\beta_2 = 2.196(.414)^{**}$		$\beta_2 = -70.04(17.94)^{**}$	
	$\beta_3 = 2.412(.467)^{**}$		$\beta_3 = -87.80(19.63)^{**}$	
	$\beta_4 = 2.273(.485)^{**}$		$\beta_4 = -89.58(20.20)^{**}$	
	$\beta_5 = 1.835(.449)^{**}$		$\beta_5 = -74.20(18.30)^{**}$	
	$\beta_6 = 1.262(.371)^{**}$		$\beta_6 = -46.27(14.23)^{**}$	
	$\beta_7 = .524(.255)^{*}$		$\beta_7 = -16.16(\,9.04)$	
	$\rho_1 = 1.109(.117)^{**}$	$\rho_3 = .162(.169)$	$\rho_1 = 1.464(.112)^{**}$	$\rho_3 = .077(.202)$
	$\rho_2 = -.345(.172)^{*}$	$\rho_4 = .002(.115)$	$\rho_2 = -.763(.201)^{**}$	$\rho_4 = .144(.115)$
	$R^2 = .9988 \quad SE = .00851 \quad D\text{-}W = 2.02$		$R^2 = .9507 \quad SE = .3049 \quad D\text{-}W = 2.18$	

Note: Estimated from the (2) and (4) system, imposing the cross-equation constraints that γ is equal in (2) and (4). The β_i are constrained to lie along a fourth-order polynomial with the endpoint constrained. Asymptotic standard errors are in parentheses. SE = standard error of the equation (the unbiased estimate) = the square root of the sum of squared residuals (SSR) divided by $\frac{1}{2}$ the degrees of freedom, e.g., it equals $\sqrt{2(\text{SSR})/161}$ in tables 6.2 and 6.4; TIME = time trend = 29 in 1954:1 ... 120 in 1976:4; $M1G - M1G^e$ = unanticipated $M1$ growth; $\log(\text{GNP}_t)$ = log of real GNP; UN_t = average quarterly unemployment rate.

*Significant at the 5 percent level.
**Significant at the 1 percent level.

Table 6.3   Nonlinear Estimates of Output and Unemployment Equations
Explanatory Variables: Unanticipated and Anticipated Money Growth, Seven Lags (PDL)

$$y_t = c + \tau TIME + \sum_{i=0}^{7} \beta_i (M1G_{t-i} - M1G_{t-i}^e) + \sum_{i=0}^{7} \delta_i M1G_{t-i}^e + \rho_1 \epsilon_{t-1} + \rho_2 \epsilon_{t-2} + \rho_3 \epsilon_{t-3} + \rho_4 \epsilon_{t-4} + \eta_t$$

Model: Dependent Variable:	3.1 $\log(GNP_t)$			3.2 UN_t		
	$c = 6.194(.060)^{**}$	$\tau = .008(.0008)$		$c = 3.00(1.74)$	$\tau = .04(.025)$	
	$\beta_0 = .660(.243)^{**}$	$\delta_0 = .402(.564)$		$\beta_0 = -14.90(8.70)$	$\delta_0 = -10.82(15.43)$	
	$\beta_1 = 1.263(.599)^{*}$	$\delta_1 = -.211(.669)$		$\beta_1 = 25.16(19.53)$	$\delta_1 = 6.32(19.82)$	
	$\beta_2 = 2.191(.814)^{**}$	$\delta_2 = -.568(.753)$		$\beta_2 = -61.33(24.90)^{*}$	$\delta_2 = 12.72(23.43)$	
	$\beta_3 = 2.953(.993)^{**}$	$\delta_3 = -.621(.776)$		$\beta_3 = -96.52(30.34)^{**}$	$\delta_3 = -7.47(25.55)$	
	$\beta_4 = 3.240(1.097)^{**}$	$\delta_4 = -.397(.720)$		$\beta_4 = -113.59(34.07)^{**}$	$\delta_4 = -7.12(24.10)$	
	$\beta_5 = 2.932(1.046)^{**}$	$\delta_5 = -.002(.606)$		$\beta_5 = -105.18(32.60)^{**}$	$\delta_5 = -25.52(19.10)$	
	$\beta_6 = 2.092(.841)^{*}$	$\delta_6 = .382(.542)$		$\beta_6 = -73.70(25.42)^{**}$	$\delta_6 = -38.98(15.20)^{*}$	
	$\beta_7 = .967(.533)$	$\delta_7 = .495(.483)$		$\beta_7 = -31.33(14.51)^{*}$	$\delta_7 = -35.54(13.33)^{**}$	
	$\rho_1 = 1.121(.119)^{**}$	$\rho_3 = .075(.193)$		$\rho_1 = 1.450(.111)^{**}$	$\rho_3 = -.031(.205)$	
	$\rho_2 = -.350(.176)^{*}$	$\rho_4 = .091(.128)$		$\rho_2 = -.740(.199)^{**}$	$\rho_4 = -.250(.120)$	
	$R^2 = .9989$ SE = .00845 D-W = 2.01			$R^2 = .9543$ SE = .2970 D-W = 2.20		

Note: Estimated from the (2) and (6) system, imposing $\gamma = \gamma^*$. The β_i and δ_i are constrained to lie along a fourth-order polynomial with the endpoint constrained.

*Significant at the 5 percent level.

**Significant at the 1 percent level.

Table 6.4   **Nonlinear Estimates of Output and Unemployment Equations**
Explanatory Variables: Unanticipated Money Growth, Twenty Lags (PDL)

$$y_t = c + \tau \text{TIME} + \sum_{i=0}^{20} \beta_i (M1G_{t-i} - M1G^e_{t-i}) + \rho_1 \epsilon_{t-1} + \rho_2 \epsilon_{t-2} + \rho_3 \epsilon_{t-3} + \rho_4 \epsilon_{t-4} + \eta_t$$

Model:	4.1		4.2	
Dependent Variable:	$\log(GNP_t)$		UN_t	
	$c = 6.181(.053)^{**}$ $\tau = .008(.0005)$		$c = 3.94(1.85)^{*}$ $\tau = .019(.21)$	
$\beta_0 =$	$.751(.230)^{**}$	$\beta_{11} = .076(.682)$	$-25.30(\ 7.94)^{**}$	$\beta_{11} = \ 8.07(26.27)$
$\beta_1 =$	$1.578(.328)^{**}$	$\beta_{12} = -.154(.682)$	$-53.64(12.97)^{**}$	$\beta_{12} = 15.83(25.57)$
$\beta_2 =$	$2.060(.440)^{**}$	$\beta_{13} = -.313(.645)$	$-69.55(17.46)^{**}$	$\beta_{13} = 20.79(24.39)$
$\beta_3 =$	$2.266(.519)^{**}$	$\beta_{14} = -.398(.599)$	$-75.53(20.28)^{**}$	$\beta_{14} = 22.88(22.85)$
$\beta_4 =$	$2.255(.573)^{**}$	$\beta_{15} = -.414(.549)$	$-73.85(21.92)^{**}$	$\beta_{15} = 22.30(21.11)$
$\beta_5 =$	$2.086(.612)^{**}$	$\beta_{16} = -.370(.498)$	$-66.55(22.97)^{**}$	$\beta_{16} = 19.42(19.29)$
$\beta_6 =$	$1.806(.645)^{**}$	$\beta_{17} = -.281(.447)$	$-55.47(23.83)^{*}$	$\beta_{17} = 14.87(17.38)$
$\beta_7 =$	$1.459(.674)^{*}$	$\beta_{18} = -.169(.387)$	$-42.23(24.69)$	$\beta_{18} = \ 9.48(15.12)$
$\beta_8 =$	$1.084(.697)$	$\beta_{19} = -.061(.307)$	$-28.21(25.51)$	$\beta_{19} = \ 4.31(12.00)$
$\beta_9 =$	$.712(.713)$	$\beta_{20} = .008(.185)$	$-14.56(26.15)$	$\beta_{20} = \ \ .65(\ 7.27)$
$\beta_{10} =$	$.370(.716)$		$-2.23(26.45)$	
	$\rho_1 = 1.140(.117)^{**}$	$\rho_3 = .130(.171)$	$\rho_1 = \ 1.460(.113)^{**}$	$\rho_3 = .063(.204)$
	$\rho_2 = -.333(.174)$	$\rho_4 = -.011(.116)$	$\rho_2 = -.720(.202)^{**}$	$\rho_4 = .124(.133)$
	$R^2 = .9987$ $SE = .00872$ D-W = 2.00		$R^2 = .9493$ $SE = .3089$ D-W = 2.13	

Note: Estimated from the (2) and (4) system, imposing the cross-equation constraints that γ is equal in (2) and (4). The β_i are constrained to lie along a fourth-order polynomial with the endpoint constrained.
*Significant at the 5 percent level.
**Significant at the 1 percent level.

Table 6.5 **Nonlinear Estimates of Output Equation**

Explanatory Variables: Unanticipated and Anticipated Money Growth, Twenty Lags (PDL)

$$Log(GNP_t) = c + \tau TIME + \sum_{i=0}^{20} \beta_i(M1G_{t-i} - M1G^e_{t-i}) + \sum_{i=0}^{20} \delta_i M1G^e_{t-i} + \rho_1\epsilon_{t-1} + \rho_2\epsilon_{t-2} + \rho_3\epsilon_{t-3} + \rho_4\epsilon_{t-4} + \eta_t$$

Model: 5.1

Dependent Variable: $\log(GNP_t)$

$c = 6.212(.032)^{**}$ $\qquad \tau = .007(.0006)$

β	δ
$\beta_0 = .645(.237)^{**}$	$\delta_0 = 1.293(.365)^{**}$
$\beta_1 = .402(.405)$	$\delta_1 = 1.733(.388)^{**}$
$\beta_2 = .305(.570)$	$\delta_2 = 1.944(.429)^{**}$
$\beta_3 = .316(.666)$	$\delta_3 = 1.972(.446)^{**}$
$\beta_4 = .400(.713)$	$\delta_4 = 1.858(.440)^{**}$
$\beta_5 = .525(.736)$	$\delta_5 = 1.639(.419)^{**}$
$\beta_6 = .666(.756)$	$\delta_6 = 1.351(.393)^{**}$
$\beta_7 = .800(.780)$	$\delta_7 = 1.023(.370)^{**}$
$\beta_8 = .909(.811)$	$\delta_8 = .682(.354)$
$\beta_9 = .980(.840)$	$\delta_9 = .349(.345)$
$\beta_{10} = 1.004(.861)$	$\delta_{10} = .044(.339)$
$\beta_{11} = .978(.865)$	$\delta_{11} = -.219(.333)$
$\beta_{12} = .899(.849)$	$\delta_{12} = -.429(.326)$
$\beta_{13} = .773(.813)$	$\delta_{13} = -.578(.322)$
$\beta_{14} = .608(.761)$	$\delta_{14} = -.664(.322)^{*}$
$\beta_{15} = .417(.700)$	$\delta_{15} = -.686(.329)^{*}$
$\beta_{16} = .217(.630)$	$\delta_{16} = -.649(.338)$
$\beta_{17} = .030(.561)$	$\delta_{17} = -.561(.342)$
$\beta_{18} = -.117(.483)$	$\delta_{18} = -.435(.328)$
$\beta_{19} = -.196(.382)$	$\delta_{19} = -.285(.278)$
$\beta_{20} = -.170(.232)$	$\delta_{20} = -.133(.176)$

$\rho_1 = 1.051(.115)^{**}$ $\qquad \rho_3 = .081(.169)$

$\rho_2 = -.238(.171)$ $\qquad \rho_4 = -.106(.111)$

$R^2 = .9989$ $\qquad SE = .00838$ $\qquad D\text{-}W = 2.16$

Note: Estimated from the (2) and (6) system, imposing $\gamma = \gamma^*$. The β_i and δ_i are constrained to lie along a fourth-order polynomial with the endpoint constrained.

*Significant at the 5 percent level.

**Significant at the 1 percent level.

Table 6.6   **Nonlinear Estimates of Unemployment Equation**
Explanatory Variables: Unanticipated and Anticipated Money Growth, Twenty Lags (PDL):

$$UN_t = c + \tau TIME + \sum_{i=0}^{20} \beta_i (M1G_{t-i} - M1G^e_{t-i}) + \sum_{i=0}^{20} \delta_i M1G^e_{t-i} + \rho_1 \epsilon_{t-1} + \rho_2 \epsilon_{t-2} + \rho_3 \epsilon_{t-3} + \rho_4 \epsilon_{t-4} + \eta_t$$

Model:

Dependent Variable:

6.1

UN_t

$c = 3.28(1.79)$ $\tau = .067(.031)^*$

$\beta_0 = -18.38(\ 8.36)^*$	$\beta_{11} = 21.29(33.69)$	$\delta_0 = -17.09(12.27)$
$\beta_1 = -25.41(14.34)$	$\beta_{12} = 25.28(32.55)$	$\delta_1 = -38.80(12.87)^{**}$
$\beta_2 = -28.09(19.95)$	$\beta_{13} = 27.83(30.59)$	$\delta_2 = -52.16(14.38)^{**}$
$\beta_3 = -27.30(23.51)$	$\beta_{14} = 28.84(27.98)$	$\delta_3 = -58.66(15.37)^{**}$
$\beta_4 = -28.85(25.74)$	$\beta_{15} = 28.30(25.00)$	$\delta_4 = -59.67(15.70)^{**}$
$\beta_5 = -18.50(27.40)$	$\beta_{16} = 26.24(21.96)$	$\delta_5 = -56.43(15.56)^{**}$
$\beta_6 = -11.89(28.98)$	$\beta_{17} = 22.79(19.05)$	$\delta_6 = -50.10(15.18)^{**}$
$\beta_7 = -4.65(30.62)$	$\beta_{18} = 18.14(16.18)$	$\delta_7 = -41.69(14.69)^{**}$
$\beta_8 = 2.71(32.71)$	$\beta_{19} = 12.56(12.76)$	$\delta_8 = -32.10(14.17)^*$
$\beta_9 = 9.73(33.36)$	$\beta_{20} = 6.37(\ 7.78)$	$\delta_9 = -22.13(13.61)$
$\beta_{10} = 16.02(33.93)$		$\delta_{10} = -12.44(12.96)$

$\delta_{11} = -3.59(12.22)$	
$\delta_{12} = 3.98(11.47)$	
$\delta_{13} = 9.95(10.84)$	
$\delta_{14} = 14.11(10.52)$	
$\delta_{15} = 16.39(10.58)$	
$\delta_{16} = 16.80(10.91)$	
$\delta_{17} = 15.48(11.13)$	
$\delta_{18} = 12.71(10.75)$	
$\delta_{19} = 8.86(\ 9.19)$	
$\delta_{20} = 4.42(\ 5.82)$	

$\rho_1 = 1.442(.112)^{**}$ $\rho_3 = -.008(.202)$

$\rho_2 = -.690(.199)^{**}$ $\rho_4 = .171(.113)$

$R^2 = .9539$ $SE = .2983$ $D\text{-}W = 2.26$

Note: See table 6.5.

*Significant at the 5 percent level.

**Significant at the 1 percent level.

Interpreting the δ coefficients of anticipated money growth poses some difficulties. One natural tendency is to make inferences about long-run neutrality by testing whether the sum of the δ coefficients differs from zero. The following implicit question is being asked: What will be the output or unemployment response to a permanent increase of 1 percent in the expected rate of money growth? Lucas (1976), Sargent (1971, 1977), and Mishkin (1979) show that this question cannot be answered with reduced-form models, of which the MRE model is one example. The parameters of the MRE model are not invariant to changes in the time-series process of money growth and thus cannot yield reliable inferences about what will happen when the time-series process of money growth differs from that in the sample period. As the money growth equations in the appendices in this and in Chapter 5 indicate, the time-series process of money growth is stationary and is quite different from a random walk. Yet a permanent increase in expected money growth is consistent only with a random walk time-series process. Trying to use the estimated MRE model here to make inferences about the response to a permanent increase in expected money growth is thus inappropriate.

Furthermore, most structural macroeconometric models in use do not distinguish between anticipated and unanticipated monetary policy and are incapable of interpreting the lag patterns of the δ's versus the β's in tables 6.5 and 6.6. It is not obvious what form these lag patterns should take in a model where expectations are rational, yet anticipated monetary policy matters. Econometric models of this type are only now being developed—Taylor (1979), for example—but to my knowledge simulation results displaying the reduced-form β and δ coefficients are not yet available.

Output and unemployment models were also estimated using $M2$ growth rather than $M1$ growth as the policy variable. Here the Granger (1969) criterion generates a specification of the $M2$ equation that includes only past $M2$ growth and Treasury Bill rates as explanatory variables. The results are not reported here in the interests of brevity, but they indicate that using $M1$ rather than $M2$ in the estimated models does not change the conclusions.[5] However, using unanticipated $M2$ growth rather than $M1$ growth does lead to some deterioration in the fit of the equations as well as lower asymptotic t statistics.

It does not seem to matter, either, whether seasonally adjusted or seasonally unadjusted data are used in the empirical work here. Season-

---

5. E.g., the freely estimated A14.1 $M2$ model does not lead to rejection of the joint hypothesis. The likelihood statistic is $\chi^2(15) = 18.1$ with a marginal significance level of .26. However, the $M2$ results for the longer lag models explored in this chapter are just as negative to the MRE hypothesis. E.g., the freely estimated A15.1 model with $M2$ data leads to a likelihood ratio statistic for the joint hypothesis of $\chi^2(28) = 58.90$ with a marginal significance level of .0006.

ally unadjusted $M1$ data in output and unemployment models give results not appreciably different from seasonally adjusted data.[6] The empirical work in Chapters 4 and 5 that use models resembling the one here also find results not appreciably affected by the choice of seasonally adjusted over unadjusted data.

The money growth results here are much less favorable to the MRE hypothesis than previous work. Which of the several differences in the analysis here from that of earlier work might explain the less favorable results? As pointed out in Chapter 2, the joint nonlinear estimation procedure used here is even more favorable to the null hypothesis than the two-step procedure used in previous work, so this procedure cannot be the cause of the rejections. Polynomial distributed lags have been used in order to insure that rejections of the MRE hypothesis are not spurious. They have made very little difference to the results and do not appear to be a factor in the rejections.

The money growth specifications yielded by the procedure used here is substantially different from specifications in previous studies. In contrast to those, neither real government expenditures nor unemployment are explanatory variables in the money growth equation. Because so much of the debate on the MRE hypothesis has focused on the specification of the money growth equation (see Barro 1977; Small 1979; Germany and Srivastava 1979; Blinder 1980; Weintraub 1980), we may wonder whether this different specification is central to the findings. A comparison of the findings here with those from the other study that analyzes postwar quarterly data, Barro and Rush (1980), should help answer this question.

The models of table 6.2 that have the same seven-quarter lag length used in Barro and Rush yield results very similar to theirs, even though they use a different specification for the money growth equation. As in Barro and Rush, the models in this study fit the data well, the unanticipated money growth variables have significant explanatory power, and the tests of the rationality and neutrality constraints are not unfavorable to the MRE hypothesis. Most striking is the similarity of the parameter estimates. Not only do the table 6.2 models display the same pattern of serial correlation in the residuals as the Barro and Rush results, but the lag structure has the same humped pattern and peaks at identical lags.

---

6. Because a fourth-order autoregression is not sufficient to reduce the seasonally unadjusted $M1$ growth to white noise, values of the unadjusted $M1$ growth for lags five through eight replaced the SURP variables in the forecasting equation specification. The coefficients and asymptotic standard errors of the freely estimated A14.1 model estimated with unadjusted data are close to those using the adjusted data. In this case the likelihood ratio statistic of the joint hypothesis is $\chi^2(19) = 29.75$ with a marginal significance level of .0551. The unadjusted results for the long lag A15.1 model are unfavorable to the MRE hypothesis. So are the results using adjusted data: the likelihood ratio statistic for the joint hypothesis is $\chi^2(32) = 62.65$ with a marginal significance level of .0010.

The close resemblance between the table 6.2 results and those of Barro and Rush is an important finding. Although misspecification of the money growth forecasting equation would lead to an error-in-variables bias in the coefficients of the unemployment or output equation, the preceding chapter has argued and found evidence that the bias should not be severe. The similarity of the results in table 6.2 to those of Barro and Rush lends support to this view, and further support comes from the similarity of the $M2$ and $M1$ results where the specification of the money growth forecasting equation also differs.

The similarity of the table 6.2 and Barro-Rush results certainly shows that using a different sample period from Barro and Rush's is not what caused the MRE hypothesis to be rejected. By a process of elimination, we are left with the longer lag lengths as the key reason why this chapter contains results so much more unfavorable to the MRE hypothesis. However, there are three other minor differences between the models here and those in Barro and Rush: (1) a fourth-order AR serial correlation correction rather than a second-order AR correction, (2) exclusion of government expenditure variables from the output and employment equations, and (3) a different definition of the unemployment variable. Could these differences lead to the rejections found here? To ascertain the effect of these differences, the long lag models were reestimated so that the output and unemployment equations conformed to the Barro and Rush specification. The resulting models are found in Appendix 6.1.

As Barro and Rush found, the coefficient on their government expenditure variables do have the expected sign, indicating that a rise in government expenditure is associated with higher output and lower unemployment. Although the government expenditure variable does not exhibit significant additional explanatory power in the unemployment equation, it does so in the output equation. There the coefficient on the log of government expenditure is significantly different from zero at the 1 percent level: it is over three times its standard error. However, it is not clear that actual government expenditure belongs in an output or unemployment equation consistent with the MRE hypothesis. Some distinction between anticipated and unanticipated seems called for in this case. An attempt was made to estimate models that make this distinction, but the attempt was not very successful: the Granger criterion led to a specification of the government expenditure forecasting equation where the identification condition discussed in Chapter 2 was not satisfied: that is, no other variables besides past government expenditure were found to be significant explanatory variables in this equation. This is the reason why, despite its use by Barro and Rush, no form of government expenditure was included as an explanatory variable in the models of tables 6.1–6.6.

The basic finding in Appendix 6.1 is that the three changes in specification suggested by Barro and Rush (1980) do not appreciably affect the results. The test statistics are quite close to those found for the models in tables 6.1–6.6. The strong rejections of the MRE hypothesis hold up. Furthermore, contrary to the MRE hypothesis, anticipated monetary policy continues to be more important than unanticipated monetary policy in these results. As in tables 6.5 and 6.6, the coefficients on anticipated money growth are larger and more statistically significant than those of unanticipated money growth.

6.4   Conclusions

This chapter asks the question, "Does Anticipated Aggregate Demand Policy Matter?" The reported findings answer this question with a strong "yes": anticipated policy does seem to matter.

The most important results are those with money growth as the aggregate demand variable. These results strongly reject the neutrality proposition of the MRE hypothesis. Furthermore, contrary to the implications of the MRE hypothesis, unanticipated movements in monetary policy do not have a larger impact on output and unemployment than anticipated movements. The other proposition embodied in the MRE hypothesis, that expectations are rational, fares better in the empirical tests here. When the MRE component hypotheses of rationality and neutrality are tested jointly, strong rejections occur in both the output and unemployment models. In one case, the probability of finding the same or higher value of the likelihood ratio statistic under the null hypothesis is only 1 in 10,000. The crucial factor in the unfavorable findings on the MRE hypothesis appears to be the inclusion of long lags in the output and unemployment equations. The results here thus give further impetus to theoretical research (see Blinder's 1980 discussion) that is currently exploring why long lags may exist in rational expectations models of the business cycle.

Models with longer lags are less restrictive. The rejections in these models are therefore very damaging to earlier evidence in support of the MRE hypothesis obtained from models with shorter lags. As discussed in Chapter 2, the only cost to estimating the models with longer lags is a potential decrease in the power of the test statistics. Rejections in this case are thus even more telling. The failure to reject the MRE hypothesis in shorter lag models appears to be the result of an overly restrictive specification that leads to inconsistent parameter estimates and incorrect test statistics.

There is one qualification of the results that warrants further discussion. The methodology used here follows previous research in this area by using the identifying assumption that the output and unemployment equations are true reduced forms. It is not clear whether, if this assumption proved invalid, it might lead to rejections of the MRE hypothesis even if the hypothesis was true. The money growth results here are then by no means a definitive rejection of this hypothesis. However, this work does cast doubt on the previous evidence, also of a reduced-form nature, marshaled to support the view that only unanticipated monetary policy is relevant to the business cycle.

The above qualification is even more important for the results in Appendix 6.3 where the aggregate demand variables are nominal GNP growth or inflation, both of which are less likely to be exogenous. However, these results confirm the money growth results. Rejections of neutrality are extremely strong. In one case, for example, the probability of finding that value of the likelihood ratio statistic under the null hypothesis of neutrality is only 1 in 200,000. The hypothesis of rational expectations fares much better in these tests. Although the rationality hypothesis does not come out unscathed—there is one rejection at the 5 percent level, but just barely—it is not rejected in any other tests in this appendix at the 5 percent level.[7] This result might encourage those who are willing to assume rationality of expectations in constructing their macro models, yet are unwilling to assert the short-run neutrality of policy.

---

7. I do not cite the rationality test results in Appendix 6.3. In Chapter 2 I explain why they may not be reliable because of small sample bias.

Appendix 6.1: Output and Unemployment Models with Barro and Rush Specification

Table 6.A.1 Nonlinear Estimates of Output and Unemployment Equations

Explanatory Variables: Unanticipated Money Growth, Twenty Lags (PDL) and Government Expenditure Variables

$$y_t = c + \tau \text{TIME} + \theta G_t + \sum_{i=0}^{20} \beta_i (M1G_{t-i} - M1G^e_{t-i}) + \rho_1 \epsilon_{t-1} + \rho_2 \epsilon_{t-2} + \eta_t$$

Model:	A1.1			A1.2		
Dependent Variable:	$\log(GNP_t)$			$\log[UN_t/(1-UN_t)]$		
	$c = 5.579(.140)^{**}$	$\tau = .008(.0003)^{**}$	$\theta = .139(.030)^{**}$	$c = -2.86(.53)^{**}$	$\tau = .006(.004)$	$\theta = -4.30(2.46)^{*}$
	$\beta_0 = .736(.218)^{**}$	$\beta_{11} = .530(.340)$		$\beta_0 = -4.98(1.58)^{**}$	$\beta_{11} = -12.67(6.43)^{*}$	
	$\beta_1 = 1.523(.269)^{**}$	$\beta_{12} = .426(.324)$		$\beta_1 = -9.38(2.82)^{**}$	$\beta_{12} = -11.27(6.26)$	
	$\beta_2 = 1.974(.345)^{**}$	$\beta_{13} = .386(.309)$		$\beta_2 = -12.65(3.78)^{**}$	$\beta_{13} = -9.84(5.93)$	
	$\beta_3 = 2.162(.389)^{**}$	$\beta_{14} = .403(.300)$		$\beta_3 = -14.93(4.34)^{**}$	$\beta_{14} = -8.43(5.48)$	
	$\beta_4 = 2.152(.405)^{**}$	$\beta_{15} = .464(.297)$		$\beta_4 = -16.37(4.69)^{**}$	$\beta_{15} = -7.06(4.96)$	
	$\beta_5 = 2.004(.403)^{**}$	$\beta_{16} = .546(.303)$		$\beta_5 = -17.10(4.97)^{**}$	$\beta_{16} = -5.76(4.42)$	
	$\beta_6 = 1.767(.392)^{**}$	$\beta_{17} = .619(.307)^{*}$		$\beta_6 = -17.24(5.27)^{**}$	$\beta_{17} = -4.51(3.89)$	
	$\beta_7 = 1.485(.381)^{**}$	$\beta_{18} = .649(.296)^{*}$		$\beta_7 = -16.90(5.62)^{**}$	$\beta_{18} = -3.34(3.34)$	
	$\beta_8 = 1.195(.371)^{**}$	$\beta_{19} = .591(.254)^{*}$		$\beta_8 = -16.19(5.97)^{**}$	$\beta_{19} = -2.21(2.64)$	
	$\beta_9 = .926(.363)^{*}$	$\beta_{20} = .394(.162)^{*}$		$\beta_9 = -15.20(6.26)^{*}$	$\beta_{20} = -1.11(1.60)$	
	$\beta_{10} = .699(.353)^{*}$			$\beta_{10} = -14.00(6.42)^{*}$		
	$\rho_1 = .993(.110)^{**}$			$\rho_1 = 1.460(.089)^{**}$		
	$\rho_2 = -.273(.110)^{*}$			$\rho_2 = -.628(.087)^{**}$		
	$R^2 = .9989$ $SE = .00808$ D-W = 2.02			$R^2 = .9512$ $SE = .0588$ D-W = 2.14		

Note: Estimates from (2) and (4) system (where [4] includes the θG_t term) imposing the cross-equation constraints that γ is equal in (2) and (4). The β_i are constrained to lie along a fourth-order polynomial with the endpoint constrained. $G_t = \log(GEXP_t)$ in A1.1, where $GEXP_t$ is real federal government expenditure for quarter t, and $G_t = GEXP_t/GNP_t$ in A1.2.

*Significant at the 5 percent level.
**Significant at the 1 percent level.

Table 6.A.2   **Likelihood Ratio Tests for the Models of Table 6.A.1**

	Model	
	A1.1	A1.2
Joint hypothesis:		
Likelihood ratio statistic	$\chi^2(15) = 43.02^{**}$	$\chi^2(15) = 31.26^{**}$
Marginal significance level	.0002	.0081
Neutrality:		
Likelihood ratio statistic	$\chi^2(4) = 13.13^{*}$	$\chi^2(4) = 13.78^{**}$
Marginal significance level	.0106	.0081
Rationality		
Likelihood ratio statistic	$\chi^2(11) = 30.45^{**}$	$\chi^2(11) = 18.80$
Marginal significance level	.0013	.0648

*Significant at the 5 percent level.
**Significant at the 1 percent level.

Table 6.A.3   **Nonlinear Estimate of Output Equation**
Explanatory Variables: Unanticipated and Anticipated Money Growth, Twenty Lags (PDL), and Government Expenditure Variable

$$\text{Log(GNP}_t) = c + \tau \text{ TIME} + \theta G_t + \sum_{i=0}^{20} \beta_i (M1G_{t-i} - M1G^e_{t-i}) + \sum_{i=0}^{20} \delta_i M1G^e_{t-i} + \rho_1 \epsilon_{t-1} + \rho_2 \epsilon_{t-2} + \eta_t$$

Model:
Dependent Variable:

A3.1
$\log(\text{GNP}_t)$

$c = 5.570(.184)^{**}$ $\tau = .007(.0006)^{**}$ $\theta = .129(.038)^{**}$

$\beta_0 = .566(.225)^*$	$\beta_{11} = -.742(.945)$	$\delta_0 = 1.321(.337)^{**}$	$\delta_{11} = .204(.313)$
$\beta_1 = .184(.366)$	$\beta_{12} = -.771(.909)$	$\delta_1 = 1.690(.337)^{**}$	$\delta_{12} = .010(.282)$
$\beta_2 = -.098(.536)$	$\beta_{13} = -.799(.854)$	$\delta_2 = 1.881(.372)^{**}$	$\delta_{13} = -.143(.252)$
$\beta_3 = -.300(.660)$	$\beta_{14} = -.822(.785)$	$\delta_3 = 1.926(.402)^{**}$	$\delta_{14} = -.250(.226)$
$\beta_4 = -.440(.748)$	$\beta_{15} = -.834(.706)$	$\delta_4 = 1.856(.416)^{**}$	$\delta_{15} = -.311(.211)$
$\beta_5 = -.535(.813)$	$\beta_{16} = -.825(.623)$	$\delta_5 = 1.701(.418)^{**}$	$\delta_{16} = -.328(.207)$
$\beta_6 = -.597(.865)$	$\beta_{17} = -.785(.538)$	$\delta_6 = 1.485(.411)^{**}$	$\delta_{17} = -.304(.209)$
$\beta_7 = -.638(.908)$	$\beta_{18} = -.699(.449)$	$\delta_7 = 1.232(.399)^{**}$	$\delta_{18} = -.248(.203)$
$\beta_8 = -.667(.940)$	$\beta_{19} = -.552(.344)$	$\delta_8 = .961(.384)^*$	$\delta_{19} = -.170(.177)$
$\beta_9 = -.692(.959)$	$\beta_{20} = -.326(.203)$	$\delta_9 = .691(.364)$	$\delta_{20} = -.082(.114)$
$\beta_{10} = -.716(.961)$		$\delta_{10} = .434(.341)$	

$$\rho_1 = .967(.113)^{**}$$
$$\rho_2 = -.164(.109)$$

$R^2 = .9990$ $SE = .00779$ $D\text{-}W = 2.08$

Note: Estimated from the (2) and (6) system (where [6] includes the θG_t term), imposing $\gamma = \gamma^*$. The β_i and δ_i are constrained to lie along a fourth-order polynomial with the endpoint constrained. $G_t = \log(\text{GEXP}_t)$, where GEXP_t = real federal government expenditure for quarter t.

*Significant at the 5 percent level.

**Significant at the 1 percent level.

Table 6.A.4 **Nonlinear Estimate of Unemployment Equation**
Explanatory Variables: Unanticipated and Anticipated Money Growth, Twenty Lags (PDL), and Government Expenditure Variable

$$\text{Log}[UN_t/(1 - UN_t)] = c + \tau\,\text{TIME} + \theta G_t + \sum_{i=0}^{20} \beta_i(M1G_{t-i} - M1G_{t-i}^e) + \sum_{i=0}^{20} \delta_i M1G_{t-i}^e + \rho_1\epsilon_{t-1} + \rho_2\epsilon_{t-2} + \eta_t$$

Model:
Dependent Variable:

A4.1
log $[UN_t/(1 - UN_t)]$

$c = -2.64(.47)^{**}$ $\qquad \tau = .011(.004)^{**}$ $\qquad \theta = -4.51(2.49)$

$\beta_0 = -4.32(1.53)^{**}$	$\beta_{11} = -3.19(5.87)$	$\delta_0 = -3.34(2.38)$	$\delta_{11} = .04(2.21)$
$\beta_1 = -5.71(2.75)^{*}$	$\beta_{12} = -2.51(5.78)$	$\delta_1 = -8.05(2.63)^{**}$	$\delta_{12} = 1.74(2.13)$
$\beta_2 = -6.60(3.79)$	$\beta_{13} = -1.88(5.54)$	$\delta_2 = -10.95(2.97)^{**}$	$\delta_{13} = 3.08(2.10)$
$\beta_3 = -7.05(4.36)$	$\beta_{14} = -1.34(5.17)$	$\delta_3 = -12.34(3.13)^{**}$	$\delta_{14} = 4.02(2.16)$
$\beta_4 = -7.16(4.61)$	$\beta_{15} = -.89(4.73)$	$\delta_4 = -12.53(3.12)^{**}$	$\delta_{15} = 4.51(2.30)$
$\beta_5 = -6.99(4.74)$	$\beta_{16} = -.54(4.26)$	$\delta_5 = -11.80(2.99)^{**}$	$\delta_{16} = 4.57(2.47)$
$\beta_6 = -6.59(4.88)$	$\beta_{17} = -.29(3.79)$	$\delta_6 = -10.37(2.82)^{**}$	$\delta_{17} = 4.22(2.58)$
$\beta_7 = -6.04(5.10)$	$\beta_{18} = -.12(3.27)$	$\delta_7 = -8.49(2.66)^{**}$	$\delta_{18} = 3.50(2.52)$
$\beta_8 = -5.38(5.37)$	$\beta_{19} = -.03(2.60)$	$\delta_8 = -6.35(2.52)^{*}$	$\delta_{19} = 2.49(2.17)$
$\beta_9 = -4.66(5.63)$	$\beta_{20} = .00(1.58)$	$\delta_9 = -4.12(2.41)$	$\delta_{20} = 1.28(1.37)$
$\beta_{10} = -3.92(5.82)$		$\delta_{10} = -1.95(2.31)$	

$$\rho_1 = 1.372(.094)$$
$$\rho_2 = -.526(.090)^{**}$$

$R^2 = .9572 \qquad SE = .0558 \qquad \text{D-W} = 2.14$

Note: Estimated from the (2) and (6) system (where [6] includes the θG_t term), imposing $\gamma = \gamma^*$. The β_i and δ_i are constrained to lie along a fourth-order polynomial with the endpoint constrained. $G_t = GEXP_t/GNP_t$, where $GEXP_t$ = real federal government expenditure for quarter t.
*Significant at the 5 percent level.
**Significant at the 1 percent level.

Appendix 6.2:   Results with Nominal GNP Growth and Inflation as the Aggregate Demand Variable

Nominal GNP Growth as the Aggregate Demand Variable

The models here follow Gordon (1979) and Grossman (1979) in using nominal GNP growth as the aggregate demand variable in the output and unemployment equations. We should be cautious in interpreting the results because the assumptions that nominal GNP growth is exogenous and that the models are reduced forms are questionable. Nevertheless, these results will shed light on previous evidence on the MRE hypothesis using nominal GNP growth as the X variable. Table 6.A.5 reports the output and unemployment equations that have been estimated from the (2) and (4) system, imposing the cross-equation constraints that the γ are equal in both equations. Twenty lagged quarters of unanticipated nominal GNP growth have been included in the models because coefficients on lags as far back as this are significantly different from zero at the 5 percent level—a result confirmed by Gordon (1979).[8]

The signs and shape of the A5.1 and A5.2 models are sensible, showing an increase in unanticipated nominal GNP growth usually associated with an increase in output or a decrease in unemployment. The fit of these equations is good too—compare them, for example, with the results in table 6.2 and table 6.A.9—and several of the coefficients on unanticipated nominal GNP growth even exceed their asymptotic standard errors by a factor of 10. The good fit is not surprising because we would expect nominal GNP fluctuations to track short-run movements accurately in real GNP or unemployment if price level movements are smooth.

Despite these attractive results, table 6.A.6 indicates that the MRE hypothesis is not supported. Both the unemployment and output models lead to strong rejections of the joint hypothesis. Rejection in the output model is at the .00001 level; in the unemployment model it is at the .0009 level.[9] One reason for the stronger rejections here with nominal GNP growth as the aggregate demand variable may be that the higher correlation of this aggregate demand variable with output or unemployment leads to tests with greater power. The most interesting aspect of these results is that the rationality constraints contribute very little to these rejections. In both models, the data do not reject the rationality of expectations. The culprit behind the rejections of the joint hypothesis is

8. See McCallum (1979b) for a critique of the Gordon (1979) study.

9. As in the money growth results, the long lags for the unanticipated and anticipated nominal GNP variables are critical to the negative findings on the MRE hypothesis. E.g., an output model with only seven lags of nominal GNP growth and the lag coefficients freely estimated does not reject the joint hypothesis: $\chi^2(15) = 23.07$ with a marginal significance level of .0827.

Table 6.A.5 **Nonlinear Estimates of Output and Unemployment Equations**
Explanatory Variables: Unanticipated Nominal Income Growth, Twenty Lags, Polynomial Distributed Lags

$$y_t = c + \tau\,\text{time} + \sum_{i=0}^{20}\beta_i(NGNP_{t-i} - NGNP^e_{t-i}) + \rho_1\epsilon_{t-1} + \rho_2\epsilon_{t-2} + \rho_3\epsilon_{t-3} + \rho_4\epsilon_{t-4} + \eta_t$$

	Model:	A5.1		A5.2
Dependent Variable:		$\log(GNP_t)$		UN_t

A5.1 $c = 6.191(.043)^{**}$ $\tau = .008(.0005)$

$\beta_0 = .927(.043)^{**}$			$\beta_{11} = .351(.279)$	
$\beta_1 = 1.134(.106)^{**}$			$\beta_{12} = .229(.258)$	
$\beta_2 = 1.246(.171)^{**}$			$\beta_{13} = .126(.233)$	
$\beta_3 = 1.281(.220)^{**}$			$\beta_{14} = .044(.203)$	
$\beta_4 = 1.253(.256)^{**}$			$\beta_{15} = -.016(.172)$	
$\beta_5 = 1.178(.280)^{**}$			$\beta_{16} = -.053(.139)$	
$\beta_6 = 1.067(.296)^{**}$			$\beta_{17} = -.069(.107)$	
$\beta_7 = .933(.305)^{**}$			$\beta_{18} = -.067(.077)$	
$\beta_8 = .786(.307)^{*}$			$\beta_{19} = -.051(.052)$	
$\beta_9 = .636(.304)^{*}$			$\beta_{20} = -.027(.028)$	
$\beta_{10} = .488(.294)$				

$\rho_1 = 1.285(.110)^{**}$ $\rho_3 = -.086(.179)$
$\rho_2 = -.073(.179)$ $\rho_4 = -.165(.110)$

$R^2 = .9998$ $SE = .00350$ $D\text{-}W = 1.89$

A5.2 $c = -138.011(1840)$ $\tau = .519(3.408)$

$\beta_0 = -25.529(\ 2.626)^{**}$			$\beta_{11} = -32.213(13.077)^{*}$	
$\beta_1 = -53.559(\ 5.102)^{**}$			$\beta_{12} = -24.676(12.297)^{*}$	
$\beta_2 = -71.535(\ 7.559)^{**}$			$\beta_{13} = -18.593(11.236)$	
$\beta_3 = -81.300(\ 9.409)^{**}$			$\beta_{14} = -14.057(\ 9.948)$	
$\beta_4 = -84.534(10.785)^{**}$			$\beta_{15} = -11.000(\ 8.519)$	
$\beta_5 = -82.760(11.831)$			$\beta_{16} = -\ 9.199(\ 7.057)$	
$\beta_6 = -77.342(12.633)^{**}$			$\beta_{17} = -\ 8.268(\ 5.670)$	
$\beta_7 = -69.486(13.225)^{**}$			$\beta_{18} = -\ 7.664(\ 4.424)$	
$\beta_8 = -60.237(13.595)^{**}$			$\beta_{19} = -\ 6.685(\ 3.253)^{*}$	
$\beta_9 = -50.483(13.715)^{**}$			$\beta_{20} = -\ 4.470(\ 1.911)^{*}$	
$\beta_{10} = -40.952(13.549)^{**}$				

$\rho_1 = 1.227(.112)^{**}$ $\rho_3 = .058(.179)$
$\rho_2 = -.300(.178)$ $\rho_4 = .012(.115)$

$R^2 = .9754$ $SE = .21267$ $D\text{-}W = 2.01$

Note: Estimated from the (2) and (4) system, imposing the cross-equation constraints that γ is equal in (2) and (4). The β_i are constrained to lie along a fourth-order polynomial with the endpoint constrained.
*Significant at the 5 percent level.
**Significant at the 1 percent level.

Table 6.A.6   **Likelihood Ratio Tests for the Models of Table 6.A.5**

	Model	
Model	A5.1	A5.2
Joint hypothesis:		
Likelihood ratio statistic	$\chi^2(11) = 43.19$**	$\chi^2(11) = 31.69$**
Marginal significance level	1.01×10^{-5}	.0009
Neutrality:		
Likelihood ratio statistic	$\chi^2(4) = 30.22$**	$\chi^2(4) = 19.90$**
Marginal significance level	4.41×10^{-6}	.0005
Rationality:		
Likelihood ratio statistic	$\chi^2(7) = 12.86$	$\chi^2(7) = 11.28$
Marginal significance level	.0756	.1269

*Significant at the 5 percent level.
**Significant at the 1 percent level.

the neutrality proposition. These neutrality rejections are exceedingly strong: the probability of finding the same or higher value of the likelihood ratio statistic under the null hypothesis of neutrality is 1 in 2,000 for the unemployment model and 1 in 200,000 for the output model! Clearly, in these models, anticipated nominal GNP growth does matter, and rejection of the neutrality constraints cannot be blamed on the failure of the maintained hypothesis of rationality. These results then lend some support to modeling strategies in which expectations are assumed to be rational.

Tables 6.A.7 and 6.A.8 contain the results from the (2) and (6) system with rational expectations imposed. As we would expect from table 6.A.6, many of the coefficients on anticipated nominal GNP growth are significantly different from zero at the 1 percent level, with some asymptotic t statistics even exceeding 7 in absolute value. The coefficients on anticipated nominal GNP growth are of a similar magnitude to the coefficients on unanticipated nominal GNP growth. Contrary to what is implied by the MRE hypothesis, anticipated aggregate demand policy as represented by nominal GNP growth is not obviously less important than unanticipated aggregate demand policy.

Inflation as the Aggregate Demand Variable

The next set of results explores á Lucas (1973) supply function where inflation is the aggregate demand variable. We should be cautious in interpreting these results, not only because the assumption that inflation is exogenous is tenuous, but also because the γ coefficients in the inflation-forecasting equation were not found to be stable. Table 6.A.9 presents the output and unemployment equations estimated from the constrained (2) and (4) system. The seventeen-quarter lag length on

Table 6.A.7 Nonlinear Estimates of Output Equations

Explanatory Variables: Unanticipated and Anticipated Nominal GNP Growth, Twenty Lags (PDL)

$$\text{Log}(GNP_t) = c + \tau\text{TIME} + \sum_{i=0}^{20} \beta_i(NGNP_{t-i} - NGNP^e_{t-i}) + \sum_{i=0}^{20} \delta_i NGNP^e_{t-i} + \rho_1\epsilon_{t-1} + \rho_2\epsilon_{t-2} + \rho_3\epsilon_{t-3} + \rho_4\epsilon_{t-4} + \eta_t$$

Model: A7.1
Dependent Variable: $\log(GNP_t)$

$c = 6.127(.049)^{**}$ $\qquad \tau = .009(.0007)$

$\beta_0 = .913(.040)^{**}$	$\delta_0 = .744(.098)^{**}$	$\delta_{11} = -.415(.257)$
$\beta_1 = .815(.058)^{**}$	$\delta_1 = .745(.104)^{**}$	$\delta_{12} = -.460(.248)$
$\beta_2 = .725(.075)^{**}$	$\delta_2 = .688(.126)^{**}$	$\delta_{13} = -.477(.214)^{*}$
$\beta_3 = .640(.090)^{**}$	$\delta_3 = .588(.150)^{**}$	$\delta_{14} = -.467(.214)^{*}$
$\beta_4 = .560(.101)^{**}$	$\delta_4 = .460(.173)^{**}$	$\delta_{15} = -.431(.191)^{*}$
$\beta_5 = .486(.110)^{**}$	$\delta_5 = .315(.195)$	$\delta_{16} = -.374(.166)^{*}$
$\beta_6 = .415(.117)^{**}$	$\delta_6 = .163(.215)$	$\delta_{17} = -.301(.139)^{*}$
$\beta_7 = .349(.123)^{**}$	$\delta_7 = .014(.233)$	$\delta_{18} = -.218(.111)^{*}$
$\beta_8 = .286(.127)^{*}$	$\delta_8 = -.123(.247)$	$\delta_{19} = -.134(.081)$
$\beta_9 = .227(.130)$	$\delta_9 = -.244(.256)$	$\delta_{20} = -.058(.046)$
$\beta_{10} = .172(.130)$	$\delta_{10} = -.342(.266)$	
$\beta_{11} = .121(.128)$		
$\beta_{12} = .075(.124)$		
$\beta_{13} = .034(.117)$		
$\beta_{14} = -.002(.109)$		
$\beta_{15} = -.031(.098)$		
$\beta_{16} = -.052(.087)$		
$\beta_{17} = -.064(.074)$		
$\beta_{18} = -.067(.061)$		
$\beta_{19} = -.058(.045)$		
$\beta_{20} = -.036(.026)$		

$\rho_1 = 1.207(.105)^{**}$ $\qquad \rho_3 = .030(.170)$

$\rho_2 = .009(.171)$ $\qquad \rho_4 = -.273(.106)^{*}$

$R^2 = .9998 \qquad SE = .00332 \qquad \text{D-W} = 1.95$

Note: Estimates from the (2) and (6) system imposing $\gamma = \gamma^{*}$. The β_i and δ_i are constrained to lie along a fourth-order polynomial with the endpoint constrained.

*Significant at the 5 percent level.
**Significant at the 1 percent level.

Table 6.A.8   **Nonlinear Estimates of Unemployment Equation**
Explanatory Variables: Unanticipated and Nominal GNP Growth, Twenty Lags (PDL)

$$UN_t = c + \tau TIME + \sum_{i=0}^{20} \beta_i(NGNP_{t-i} - NGNP^e_{t-i}) + \sum_{i=0}^{20} \delta_i NGNP^e_{t-i} + \rho_1\epsilon_{t-1} + \rho_2\epsilon_{t-2} + \rho_3\epsilon_{t-3} + \rho_4\epsilon_{t-4} + \eta_t$$

Model: A8.1
Dependent Variable: UN_t

$c = -168.2(2420)$ $\tau = .575(3.85)$

$\beta_0 = -23.90(2.64)^{**}$	$\beta_{11} = -11.35(5.38)^{*}$	$\delta_0 = -36.46(5.78)^{**}$
$\beta_1 = -35.22(4.00)^{**}$	$\beta_{12} = -8.70(5.14)$	$\delta_1 = -40.33(5.36)^{**}$
$\beta_2 = -41.42(5.33)^{**}$	$\beta_{13} = -7.08(4.88)$	$\delta_2 = -42.27(5.97)^{**}$
$\beta_3 = -43.60(6.14)^{**}$	$\beta_{14} = -6.41(4.64)$	$\delta_3 = -42.58(6.71)^{**}$
$\beta_4 = -42.72(6.51)^{**}$	$\beta_{15} = -6.50(4.41)$	$\delta_4 = -41.55(7.32)^{**}$
$\beta_5 = -39.67(6.58)^{**}$	$\beta_{16} = -7.09(4.20)$	$\delta_5 = -39.44(7.80)^{**}$
$\beta_6 = -35.21(6.46)^{**}$	$\beta_{17} = -7.78(3.95)^{*}$	$\delta_6 = -36.51(8.19)^{**}$
$\beta_7 = -30.01(6.26)^{**}$	$\beta_{18} = -8.06(3.57)^{*}$	$\delta_7 = -32.99(8.50)^{**}$
$\beta_8 = -24.62(6.04)^{**}$	$\beta_{19} = -7.35(2.92)^{*}$	$\delta_8 = -29.07(8.73)^{**}$
$\beta_9 = -19.50(5.82)^{**}$	$\beta_{20} = -4.93(1.79)^{***}$	$\delta_9 = -24.94(8.86)^{**}$
$\beta_{10} = -15.00(5.61)^{**}$		$\delta_{10} = -20.78(8.86)^{*}$

$\delta_{11} = -16.73(8.73)$		
$\delta_{12} = -12.91(8.47)$		
$\delta_{13} = -9.44(8.11)$		
$\delta_{14} = -6.39(7.69)$		
$\delta_{15} = -3.84(7.24)$		
$\delta_{16} = -1.82(6.77)$		
$\delta_{17} = -.37(6.24)$		
$\delta_{18} = .51(5.50)$		
$\delta_{19} = .84(4.39)$		
$\delta_{20} = .65(2.65)$		

$\rho_1 = 1.222(.112)^{**}$ $\rho_3 = -.007(.179)$
$\rho_2 = -.324(.180)$ $\rho_4 = .106(.112)$

$R^2 = .9766$ $SE = .20999$ $D\text{-}W = 2.06$

Note: See table 6.A.7.
*Significant at the 5 percent level.
**Significant at the 1 percent level.

Table 6.A.9   **Nonlinear Estimates of Output and Unemployment Equations**

Explanatory Variables: Unanticipated Inflation, Seventeen Lags, Polynomial Distributed Lags

$$y_t = c + \tau \text{TIME} + \sum_{i=0}^{17} \beta_i(\pi_{t-i} - \pi_{t-i}^e) + \rho_1 \epsilon_{t-1} + \rho_2 \epsilon_{t-2} + \rho_3 \epsilon_{t-3} + \rho_4 \epsilon_{t-4} + \eta_t$$

Model:	A9.1		A9.2	
Dependent Variable:	$\log(\text{GNP}_t)$		UN_t	
	$c = 6.159(.035)^{**}$	$\tau = .009(.0004)$	$c = 4.176(1.124)^{**}$	$\tau = .016(.013)$
	$\beta_0 = -.523(.322)$	$\beta_9 = -1.316(.701)$	$\beta_0 = 2.509(10.799)$	$\beta_9 = 67.993(25.671)^{**}$
	$\beta_1 = -.843(.520)$	$\beta_{10} = -1.308(.676)$	$\beta_1 = 2.501(19.858)$	$\beta_{10} = 69.993(26.068)^{**}$
	$\beta_2 = -1.057(.667)$	$\beta_{11} = -1.295(.636)^*$	$\beta_2 = 7.360(24.992)$	$\beta_{11} = 69.012(25.512)^{**}$
	$\beta_3 = -1.192(.736)$	$\beta_{12} = -1.220(.583)^*$	$\beta_3 = 15.519(26.368)$	$\beta_{12} = 65.044(23.988)^{**}$
	$\beta_4 = -1.270(.753)$	$\beta_{13} = -1.221(.524)^*$	$\beta_4 = 25.589(25.553)$	$\beta_{13} = 58.255(21.715)^{**}$
	$\beta_5 = -1.309(.746)$	$\beta_{14} = -1.135(.464)^*$	$\beta_5 = 36.349(24.121)$	$\beta_{14} = 48.987(19.013)^{**}$
	$\beta_6 = -1.324(.733)$	$\beta_{15} = -.994(.403)^*$	$\beta_6 = 46.755(23.308)^*$	$\beta_{15} = 37.753(16.076)^*$
	$\beta_7 = -1.326(.723)$	$\beta_{16} = -.775(.326)^*$	$\beta_7 = 55.934(23.603)^*$	$\beta_{16} = 25.242(12.646)^*$
	$\beta_8 = -1.322(.715)$	$\beta_{17} = -.453(.205)^*$	$\beta_8 = 63.189(24.639)^*$	$\beta_{17} = 12.313(7.796)$
	$\rho_1 = 1.320(.112)^{**}$	$\rho_3 = .021(.185)$	$\rho_1 = 1.601(.112)^{**}$	$\rho_3 = .055(.208)$
	$\rho_2 = -.419(.186)^*$	$\rho_4 = -.044(.112)$	$\rho_2 = -.855(.210)^{**}$	$\rho_4 = .056(.106)$
	$R^2 = .9986$ $SE = .00942$ $D\text{-}W = 2.02$		$R^2 = .9435$ $SE = .32652$ $D\text{-}W = 2.15$	

Note: See table 6.A.5.

*Significant at the 5 percent level.

**Significant at the 1 percent level.

unanticipated inflation has been included in the models again because coefficients on lags as far back as this are significantly different from zero at the 5 percent level.

The suprising result of table 6.A.9 is that the coefficients on unanticipated inflation are often significantly different from zero and yet they have the opposite sign to what we would expect from a Lucas supply function. These results contradict Sargent's (1976a) finding of a negative correlation between unanticipated inflation and employment, but are in agreement with Fair (1979). Our results may contradict Sargent because 1973–1975 data are included in the sample period. Sargent takes unanticipated inflation to be a response to aggregate demand shifts, possibly a more reasonable assumption for the sample period he used in estimation. However, it is plausible that the supply shock effect of a decreased supply of food and energy—which would be linked to an unanticipated upward movement in the U.S. inflation rate coupled with an output decline—is dominating the aggregate demand effects on unanticipated inflation in the data used here. Thus the estimated coefficients on unanticipated inflation may not contradict the MRE hypothesis, but they certainly do not support it.

The likelihood ratio tests in table 6.A.10 indicate that the MRE hypothesis is not supported for the models with inflation as the aggregate demand variable. The joint hypothesis is rejected for both models at the 5 percent significance level, with the neutrality hypothesis the major contributor to these rejections. The neutrality constraints are rejected at the .001 marginal significance level for the output model and .01 for the unemployment model. The rationality constraints again fare better with the marginal significance levels equaling .51 for the output model and .04 for the unemployment model. The evidence, as before, seems to be

Table 6.A.10   **Likelihood Ratio Tests for Models of Table 6.A.9**

	Model	
	A9.1	A9.2
Joint hypothesis:		
Likelihood ratio statistic	$\chi^2(15) = 28.45^*$	$\chi^2(15) = 32.34^{**}$
Marginal significance level	.0189	.0058
Neutrality:		
Likelihood ratio statistic	$\chi^2(4) = 18.52^{**}$	$\chi^2(4) = 13.20^*$
Marginal significance level	.0010	.0104
Rationality:		
Likelihood ratio statistic	$\chi^2(11) = 10.23$	$\chi^2(11) = 20.16^*$
Marginal significance level	.5098	.0432

*Significant at the 5 percent level.

**Significant at the 1 percent level.

negative on the neutrality implications of the MRE hypothesis, but far less so on the rationality implication.

Tables 6.A.11 and 6.A.12 show that, contrary to the MRE hypothesis, the effects from unanticipated inflation are not stronger than from anticipated inflation. Not only are the coefficients on anticipated inflation substantially larger than the unanticipated coefficients, but their asymptotic t statistics are substantially larger as well. Overall, the Lucas supply model estimated here is not successful. Its coefficients have the "wrong" signs, it fits the data worse than a corresponding model with money growth as the aggregate demand variable, and it strongly rejects neutrality, with anticipated inflation proving to be more significantly correlated with output and unemployment than unanticipated inflation.

Table 6.A.11   Nonlinear Estimates of Output Equation

Explanatory Variables: Unanticipated and Anticipated Inflation, Seventeen Lags (PDL)

$$\text{Log(GNP}_t) = c + \tau\text{TIME} + \sum_{i=0}^{17} \beta_i(\pi_{t-i} - \pi^e_{t-i}) + \sum_{i=0}^{17} \delta_i \pi^e_{t-i} + \rho_1\epsilon_{t-1} + \rho_2\epsilon_{t-2} + \rho_3\epsilon_{t-3} + \rho_4\epsilon_{t-4} + \eta_t$$

Model:
Dependent Variable: $\log(\text{GNP}_t)$

A11.1

$c = 6.089(.068)^{**}$ $\tau = .011(.001)$

$\beta_0 = -.082(.311)$	$\beta_{11} = -.293(.803)$	$\delta_0 = .128(.538)$
$\beta_1 = .032(.466)$	$\beta_{12} = -.589(.748)$	$\delta_1 = -.994(.397)^*$
$\beta_2 = .192(.624)$	$\beta_{13} = -.856(.680)$	$\delta_2 = -1.544(.390)^{**}$
$\beta_3 = .358(.730)$	$\beta_{14} = -1.052(.600)$	$\delta_3 = -1.682(.391)^{**}$
$\beta_4 = .498(.800)$	$\beta_{15} = -1.126(.507)^*$	$\delta_4 = -1.547(.378)^{**}$
$\beta_5 = .589(.836)$	$\beta_{16} = -1.021(.389)^{**}$	$\delta_5 = -1.258(.369)^{**}$
$\beta_6 = .615(.861)$	$\beta_{17} = -.669(.228)^{**}$	$\delta_6 = -.912(.373)^*$
$\beta_7 = .566(.875)$		$\delta_7 = -.588(.386)$
$\beta_8 = .441(.879)$		$\delta_8 = -.342(.393)$
$\beta_9 = -.246(.869)$		$\delta_9 = -.211(.384)$
$\beta_{10} = -.006(.844)$		$\delta_{10} = -.210(.361)$

$\delta_{11} = -.334(.343)$	
$\delta_{12} = -.559(.354)$	
$\delta_{13} = -.838(.405)^*$	
$\delta_{14} = -1.104(.469)^*$	
$\delta_{15} = -1.272(.508)^*$	
$\delta_{16} = -1.233(.475)^{**}$	
$\delta_{17} = -.858(.323)^{**}$	

$\rho_1 = 1.092(.121)^{**}$ $\rho_3 = .202(.172)$

$\rho_2 = -.312(.171)$ $\rho_4 = -.067(.119)$

$R^2 = .9988$ SE = .00855   D-W = 1.99

Note: Estimates from the (2) and (6) system imposing $\gamma = \gamma$. The β_1 and δ_i are constrained to lie along a fourth-order polynomial with the endpoint constrained.

*Significant at the 5 percent level.
**Significant at the 1 percent level.

Table 6.A.12   Nonlinear Estimates of Unemployment Equation

Explanatory Variables: Unanticipated and Anticipated Inflation, Seventeen Lags (PDL)

$$UN_t = c + \tau\, TIME + \sum_{i=0}^{20} \beta_i(\pi_{t-i} - \pi_{t-i}^e) + \sum_{i=0}^{20} \delta_i \pi_{t-i}^e + \rho_1 \epsilon_{t-1} + \rho_2 \epsilon_{t-2} + \rho_3 \epsilon_{t-3} + \rho_4 \epsilon_{t-4} + \eta_t$$

Model:
Dependent Variable:

A12.1
UN_t

$c = 6.981(2.687)^{**}$ $\tau = -.068(.045)$

$\beta_0 = 4.54(10.27)$	$\delta_0 = -42.90(26.23)$	$\delta_{11} = 13.52(13.83)$
$\beta_1 = 12.65(18.50)$	$\delta_1 = 11.15(16.72)$	$\delta_{12} = 15.84(14.71)$
$\beta_2 = 13.15(25.01)$	$\delta_2 = 43.03(15.77)^{**}$	$\delta_{13} = 20.45(17.19)$
$\beta_3 = 8.66(28.65)$	$\delta_3 = 58.14(15.99)^{**}$	$\delta_{14} = 25.75(20.23)$
$\beta_4 = 1.47(30.32)$	$\delta_4 = 61.24(15.28)^{**}$	$\delta_{15} = 29.53(22.05)$
$\beta_5 = -6.55(30.89)$	$\delta_5 = 56.47(14.34)^{**}$	$\delta_{16} = 28.93(20.73)$
$\beta_6 = -13.86(31.00)$	$\delta_6 = 47.31(14.04)^{**}$	$\delta_{17} = 20.46(14.15)$
$\beta_7 = -19.32(30.96)$	$\delta_7 = 36.62(14.44)^{*}$	
$\beta_8 = -22.14(30.83)$	$\delta_8 = 26.63(14.89)$	
$\beta_9 = -21.91(30.47)$	$\delta_9 = 18.92(14.83)$	
$\beta_{10} = -18.61(29.73)$	$\delta_{10} = 14.44(14.24)$	
$\beta_{11} = -12.57(28.53)$		
$\beta_{12} = -4.50(26.86)$		
$\beta_{13} = 4.52(24.77)$		
$\beta_{14} = 13.04(22.27)$		
$\beta_{15} = 19.23(19.19)$		
$\beta_{16} = 20.89(15.05)$		
$\beta_{17} = 15.46(9.04)$		

$\rho_1 = 1.410(.122)^{**}$ $\rho_3 = .016(.201)$

$\rho_2 = -.665(.203)^{**}$ $\rho_4 = .161(.115)$

$R^2 = .9530$ $SE = .30255$ $D\text{-}W = 2.10$

Note: See table 6.A.11.

*Significant at the 5 percent level.

**Significant at the 1 percent level.

Appendix 6.3: Results Not Using Polynominal Distributed Lags

Table 6.A.13   Likelihood Ratio Tests of the MRE Hypothesis with *M*1 Growth as the Aggregate Demand Variable

	Model				
	A14.1	A14.2	A15.1	A15.2
Joint hypothesis:				
Likelihood ratio statistic	$\chi^2(19) = 22.37$	$\chi^2(19) = 31.55^*$	$\chi^2(32) = 66.90^{**}$	$\chi^2(32) = 54.06^{**}$
Marginal significance level	.2662	.0351	.0003	.0087
Neutrality:				
Likelihood ratio statistic	$\chi^2(8) = 9.53$	$\chi^2(8) = 11.97$	$\chi^2(21) = 45.22^{**}$	$\chi^2(21) = 36.47$
Marginal significance level	.2996	.1524	.0016	.0830
Rationality:				
Likelihood ratio statistic	$\chi^2(11) = 12.34$	$\chi^2(11) = 20.14^*$	$\chi^2(11) = 27.10^{**}$	$\chi^2(11) = 27.01^{**}$
Marginal significance level	.3386	.0435	.0044	.0046

Note: The tables here correspond to previous tables as follows: 6.A.13 to 6.1, 6.A.14 to 6.2, 6.A.15 to 6.4, 6.A.16 to 6.A.5, 6.A.17 to 6.A.6, 6.A.18 to 6.A.9, 6.A.19 to 6.A.10.

Table 6.A.14 **Nonlinear Estimates of Output and Unemployment Equations**

Explanatory Variables: Unanticipated Money Growth, Seven Lags, Freely Estimated

$$y_t = c + \tau TIME + \sum_{i=0}^{7} \beta_i (M1G_{t-i} - M1G_{t-i}^e) + \rho_1 \epsilon_{t-1} + \rho_2 \epsilon_{t-2} + \rho_3 \epsilon_{t-3} + \rho_4 \epsilon_{t-4} + \eta_t$$

Model:	A14.1	A14.2
Dependent Variable:	$\log(GNP_t)$	UN_t

A14.1

$c = 6.175(.046)^{**}$ $\quad \tau = .008(.0005)$

$\beta_0 = .743(.247)^{**}$
$\beta_1 = 1.616(.375)^{**}$
$\beta_2 = 2.065(.444)^{**}$
$\beta_3 = 2.450(.484)^{**}$
$\beta_4 = 2.244(.501)^{**}$
$\beta_5 = 1.812(.484)^{**}$
$\beta_6 = .996(.421)^{*}$
$\beta_7 = .509(.269)$

$\rho_1 = 1.138(.119)^{**}$ $\quad \rho_3 = .195(.177)$
$\rho_2 = -.379(.177)^{*}$ $\quad \rho_4 = -.027(.119)$

$R^2 = .9989 \quad SE = .0085 \quad D\text{-}W = 1.97$

A14.2

$c = 3.563(1.590)^{*}$ $\quad \tau = .024(.018)$

$\beta_0 = -18.73(9.03)^{*}$
$\beta_1 = -40.73(16.05)^{*}$
$\beta_2 = -69.01(19.33)^{**}$
$\beta_3 = -86.41(20.40)^{**}$
$\beta_4 = -92.79(20.85)^{**}$
$\beta_5 = -72.45(20.32)^{**}$
$\beta_6 = -42.26(16.53)^{*}$
$\beta_7 = -15.14(9.26)$

$\rho_1 = 1.474(.114)$ $\quad \rho_3 = .072(.208)$
$\rho_2 = -.777(.206)$ $\quad \rho_4 = .156(.118)$

$R^2 = .9514 \quad SE = .3062 \quad D\text{-}W = 2.05$

Note: Estimated from the (2) and (4) system, imposing the cross-equation constraints that γ is equal in (2) and (4). Note that the β_i are estimated without constraints.

*Significant at the 5 percent level.
**Significant at the 1 percent level.

Table 6.A.15   **Nonlinear Estimates of Output and Unemployment Growth**
Explanatory Variables: Unanticipated Money Growth, Twenty Lags, Freely Estimated

$$y_t = c + \tau \text{TIME} + \sum_{i=0}^{20} \beta_i (M1G_{t-i} - M1G_{t-i}^e) + \rho_1 \epsilon_{t-1} + \rho_2 \epsilon_{t-2} + \rho_3 \epsilon_{t-3} + \rho_4 \epsilon_{t-4} + \eta_t$$

Model:	A15.1		A15.2	
Dependent Variable:	$\log(GNP_t)$		UN_t	
	$\tau = .008(.0005)$		$\tau = .026(.023)$	
	$c = 6.195(.048)^{**}$		$c = 3.375(2.064)$	
	$\beta_0 = .850(.275)^{**}$	$\beta_{11} = .200(.640)$	$\beta_0 = -11.73(9.92)$	$\beta_{11} = 6.66(27.18)$
	$\beta_1 = 1.784(.430)^{**}$	$\beta_{12} = .482(.620)$	$\beta_1 = -21.61(18.24)$	$\beta_{12} = 10.64(26.63)$
	$\beta_2 = 2.320(.523)^{**}$	$\beta_{13} = .625(.616)$	$\beta_2 = -52.81(22.04)^{*}$	$\beta_{13} = 10.52(26.20)$
	$\beta_3 = 2.935(.614)^{**}$	$\beta_{14} = .624(.631)$	$\beta_3 = -83.72(23.14)^{**}$	$\beta_{14} = 4.85(25.94)$
	$\beta_4 = 2.989(.722)^{**}$	$\beta_{15} = .751(.640)$	$\beta_4 = -103.18(25.16)^{**}$	$\beta_{15} = 6.02(25.22)$
	$\beta_5 = 2.605(.796)^{**}$	$\beta_{16} = .889(.616)$	$\beta_5 = -91.00(27.33)^{**}$	$\beta_{16} = 1.33(24.09)$
	$\beta_6 = 1.637(.822)^{*}$	$\beta_{17} = .882(.574)$	$\beta_6 = -72.77(28.43)^{*}$	$\beta_{17} = -14.13(22.76)$
	$\beta_7 = 1.103(.802)$	$\beta_{18} = .512(.534)$	$\beta_7 = -50.06(28.90)$	$\beta_{18} = -24.56(21.36)$
	$\beta_8 = .677(.764)$	$\beta_{19} = .300(.444)$	$\beta_8 = -25.47(29.57)$	$\beta_{19} = -17.22(17.07)$
	$\beta_9 = .496(.719)$	$\beta_{20} = .099(.277)$	$\beta_9 = -5.44(29.28)$	$\beta_{20} = -2.57(9.49)$
	$\beta_{10} = .166(.675)$		$\beta_{10} = 3.16(24.15)$	
	$\rho_1 = 1.098(.127)^{**}$	$\rho_3 = .184(.184)$	$\rho_1 = 1.463(.117)^{**}$	$\rho_3 = -.070(.217)$
	$\rho_2 = -.338(.184)$	$\rho_4 = -.042(.129)$	$\rho_2 = -.708(.212)^{**}$	$\rho_4 = .249(.126)^{*}$
	$R^2 = .9989$ SE = .0086 D-W = 1.97		$R^2 = .9564$ SE = .3027 D-W = 2.09	

Note: See table 6.A.14.

*Significant at the 5 percent level.

**Significant at the 1 percent level.

Table 6.A.16   Nonlinear Estimates of Output and Unemployment Equations Explanatory Variables: Unanticipated Nominal GNP Growth, Twenty Lags, Freely Estimated

$$y_t = c + \tau TIME + \sum_{i=0}^{20} \beta_i (NGNP_{t-i} - NGNP_{t-i}^e) + \rho_1 \epsilon_{t-1} + \rho_2 \epsilon_{t-2} + \rho_3 \epsilon_{t-3} + \rho_4 \epsilon_{t-4} + \eta_t$$

Model:	A16.1	A16.2
Dependent Variable:	$\log(GNP_t)$	UN_t
	$c = 6.176(.034)^{**}$ $\tau = .008(.0004)$	$c = -208.831(3501.00)$ $\tau = .682(5.828)$

A16.1 ($\log(GNP_t)$):

$\beta_0 = .893(.045)^{**}$
$\beta_1 = 1.142(.125)^{**}$
$\beta_2 = 1.060(.191)^{**}$
$\beta_3 = .971(.234)^{**}$
$\beta_4 = .704(.267)^{**}$
$\beta_5 = .448(.283)$
$\beta_6 = .260(.282)$
$\beta_7 = .157(.275)$
$\beta_8 = .043(.262)$
$\beta_9 = .014(.252)$
$\beta_{10} = .002(.245)$

$\beta_{11} = -.035(.237)$
$\beta_{12} = -.028(.225)$
$\beta_{13} = -.001(.210)$
$\beta_{14} = -.026(.191)$
$\beta_{15} = -.094(.168)$
$\beta_{16} = -.101(.144)$
$\beta_{17} = -.034(.118)$
$\beta_{18} = -.071(.090)$
$\beta_{19} = -.074(.067)$
$\beta_{20} = -.015(.039)$

$\rho_1 = 1.410(.119)^{**}$ $\rho_3 = -.191(.204)$
$\rho_2 = -.150(.203)$ $\rho_4 = -.110(.123)$

$R^2 = .9998$ $SE = .00340$ D-W = 1.82

A16.2 (UN_t):

$\beta_0 = -24.549(2.614)^{**}$
$\beta_1 = -52.080(5.058)^{**}$
$\beta_2 = -63.001(7.881)^{**}$
$\beta_3 = -66.126(10.215)^{**}$
$\beta_4 = -59.198(11.931)^{**}$
$\beta_5 = -48.080(12.763)^{**}$
$\beta_6 = -43.597(12.635)^{**}$
$\beta_7 = -39.639(11.906)^{**}$
$\beta_8 = -31.964(10.624)^{**}$
$\beta_9 = -26.995(9.200)^{**}$
$\beta_{10} = -21.845(8.313)^{**}$

$\beta_{11} = -15.367(7.713)^{*}$
$\beta_{12} = -12.427(7.046)$
$\beta_{13} = -14.263(6.821)^{*}$
$\beta_{14} = -14.319(6.523)$
$\beta_{15} = -12.399(6.009)^{*}$
$\beta_{16} = -7.101(5.555)$
$\beta_{17} = -10.166(4.975)^{*}$
$\beta_{18} = -9.791(4.262)^{*}$
$\beta_{19} = -7.402(3.647)^{*}$
$\beta_{20} = -5.610(2.216)^{*}$

$\rho_1 = 1.357(.119)^{**}$ $\rho_3 = .055(.194)$
$\rho_2 = -.404(.197)^{*}$ $\rho_4 = -.010(.118)$

$R^2 = .9816$ $SE = .19424$ D-W = 1.94

Note: See table 6.A.14.
*Significant at the 5 percent level.
**Significant at the 1 percent level.

Table 6.A.17   Likelihood Ratio Tests for Models of Table 6.A.16

	Model	
	A16.1	A16.2
Joint hypothesis:		
Likelihood ratio statistic	$\chi^2(28) = 57.89^{**}$	$\chi^2(28) = 71.21^{**}$
Marginal significance level	.0008	1.25×10^{-5}
Neutrality:		
Likelihood ratio statistic	$\chi^2(21) = 56.11^{**}$	$\chi^2(21) = 64.04^{**}$
Marginal significance level	4.86×10^{-5}	3.07×10^{-6}
Rationality:		
Likelihood ratio statistic	$\chi^2(7) = 1.85$	$\chi^2(7) = 4.20$
Marginal significance level	.9674	.7561

*Significant at the 5 percent level.
**Significant at the 1 percent level.

Table 6.A.18   **Nonlinear Estimates of Output and Unemployment Equations**

Explanatory Variables: Unanticipated Inflation, Seventeen Lags, Freely Estimated

$$y_t = c + \tau\text{TIME} + \sum_{i=0}^{17} \beta_i(\pi_{t-i} - \pi_{t-i}^e) + \rho_1\epsilon_{t-1} + \rho_2\epsilon_{t-2} + \rho_3\epsilon_{t-3} + \rho_4\epsilon_{t-4} + \eta_t$$

Model: Dependent Variable:	A18.1 $\log(\text{GNP}_t)$			A18.2 UN_t	
	$c = 6.155(.040)^{**}$	$\tau = .009(.0005)$		$c = 4.143(1.207)^{**}$	$\tau = .017(.014)$
$\beta_0 = -.634(.344)$	$\beta_9 = -1.400(.921)$		$\beta_0 = 4.399(12.251)$	$\beta_9 = 79.022(36.798)^{*}$
$\beta_1 = -1.067(.565)$	$\beta_{10} = -1.131(.855)$		$\beta_1 = 12.877(22.979)$	$\beta_{10} = 76.155(37.139)^{*}$
$\beta_2 = -1.012(.695)$	$\beta_{11} = -1.034(.745)$		$\beta_2 = 11.192(31.350)$	$\beta_{11} = 70.156(37.001)$
$\beta_3 = -.778(.759)$	$\beta_{12} = -1.376(.660)^{*}$		$\beta_3 = 11.586(35.338)$	$\beta_{12} = 73.634(37.472)^{*}$
$\beta_4 = -1.434(.815)$	$\beta_{13} = -1.255(.574)^{*}$		$\beta_4 = 10.521(35.997)$	$\beta_{13} = 60.702(37.027)$
$\beta_5 = -2.021(.870)^{*}$	$\beta_{14} = -.758(.511)$		$\beta_5 = 31.214(35.693)$	$\beta_{14} = 43.523(33.948)$
$\beta_6 = -1.828(.904)^{*}$	$\beta_{15} = -1.147(.466)^{*}$		$\beta_6 = 43.389(35.602)$	$\beta_{15} = 25.826(28.163)$
$\beta_7 = -1.173(.936)$	$\beta_{16} = -1.400(.388)^{**}$		$\beta_7 = 55.321(36.368)$	$\beta_{16} = 25.187(19.344)$
$\beta_8 = -1.608(.939)$	$\beta_{17} = -.852(.242)^{**}$		$\beta_8 = -67.247(36.701)$	$\beta_{17} = 10.284(9.580)$
$\rho_1 = 1.370(.117)^{**}$	$\rho_3 = -.0385(.198)$		$\rho_1 = 1.650(.117)^{**}$	$\rho_3 = .028(.229)$
$\rho_2 = -.440(.198)^{*}$	$\rho_4 = .001(.121)$		$\rho_2 = -.891(.228)^{**}$	$\rho_4 = .086(.114)$
$R^2 = .9989$	$SE = .00876$	$\text{D-W} = 1.95$	$R^2 = .9493$ $SE = .32333$	$\text{D-W} = 2.05$

Note: See table 6.A.14.

*Significant at the 5 percent level.

**Significant at the 1 percent level.

Table 6.A.19   **Likelihood Ratio Tests for Models of Table 6.A.18**

	Model	
	A18.1	A18.2
Joint hypothesis:		
Likelihood ratio statistic	$\chi^2(29) = 64.38^{**}$	$\chi^2(29) = 57.03^{**}$
Marginal significance level	.0002	.0014
Neutrality:		
Likelihood ratio statistic	$\chi^2(18) = 43.51^{**}$	$\chi^2(18) = 33.93^{*}$
Marginal significance level	.0007	.0129
Rationality:		
Likelihood ratio statistic	$\chi^2(11) = 22.33^{*}$	$\chi^2(11) = 32.01^{*}$
Marginal significance level	.0219	.0008

*Significant at the 5 percent level.
**Significant at the 1 percent level.

Appendix 6.4: Jointly Estimated Forecasting Equations

Table 6.A.20   **Money Growth Equations Estimated Jointly with Output and Unemployment Equations in Text**

	Model							
	2.1	2.2	3.1	3.2	4.1	4.2	5.1	6.1
Constant term	.002	.003	.002	.002	.002	.002	.003	.003
	(.001)	(.001)	(.001)	(.001)	(.001)	(.001)	(.001)	(.001)
$M1G_{t-1}$	.768	.712	.770	.730	.740	.676	.672	.690
	(.110)	(.111)	(.113)	(.112)	(.112)	(.112)	(.113)	(.112)
$M1G_{t-2}$	−.018	−.052	−.006	.024	−.010	−.024	.039	.028
	(.143)	(.142)	(.147)	(.138)	(.143)	(.142)	(.143)	(.142)
$M1G_{t-3}$	−.116	−.058	−.073	−.032	−.092	−.042	−.012	−.004
	(.130)	(.130)	(.131)	(.119)	(.130)	(.129)	(.129)	(.132)
$M1G_{t-4}$	−.161	−.133	−.149	−.116	−.055	−.065	−.016	−.026
	(.101)	(.105)	(.102)	(.098)	(.106)	(.108)	(.107)	(.115)
RTB_{t-1}	−.319	−.379	−.265	−.350	−.273	−.349	−.408	−.425
	(.089)	(.092)	(.088)	(.093)	(.093)	(.094)	(.099)	(.101)
RTB_{t-2}	.628	.634	.558	.583	.560	.590	.541	.597
	(.161)	(.162)	(.166)	(.159)	(.163)	(.160)	(.163)	(.163)
RTB_{t-3}	−.237	−.258	−.237	−.219	−.188	−.188	−.210	−.205
	(.169)	(.170)	(.167)	(.161)	(.171)	(.169)	(.170)	(.171)
RTB_{t-4}	.002	.070	−.000	.031	−.057	−.030	.082	.036
	(.098)	(.102)	(.091)	(.094)	(.104)	(.105)	(.104)	(.109)
$SURP_{t-1}$	−.140	−.143	−.152	−.156	−.156	−.165	−.197	−.176
	(.067)	(.070)	(.061)	(.065)	(.069)	(.070)	(.070)	(.075)
$SURP_{t-2}$	.132	.099	.185	.153	.118	.093	.128	.072
	(.082)	(.082)	(.080)	(.079)	(.082)	(.081)	(.082)	(.083)
$SURP_{t-3}$	.042	.047	−.006	.021	.048	.062	.018	.046
	(.086)	(.086)	(.085)	(.083)	(.086)	(.085)	(.086)	(.087)
$SURP_{t-4}$	−.147	−.120	−.126	−.115	−.113	−.097	−.066	−.068
	(.069)	(.071)	(.067)	(.066)	(.069)	(.070)	(.070)	(.075)
R^2	.6290	.6369	.6284	.6469	.6322	.6475	.6548	.6584
SE	.00437	.00432	.00443	.00432	.00435	.00427	.00427	.00425
D-W	1.95	1.92	1.97	1.99	1.94	1.90	2.02	2.03

Note: Forecasting equations were estimated with the output or unemployment equation imposing the cross-equation constraints that γ is equal in both equations. For purposes of comparison, OLS column shows the estimate of the unconstrained forecasting equation. Note that SE is the unbiased standard error and is calculated as described in the note to table 6.2.

	Model								
A1.1	A1.2	A3.1	A4.1	A14.1	A14.2	A15.1	A15.2	OLS
.002	.002	.003	.003	.002	.003	.002	.002	.003
(.001)	(.001)	(.001)	(.001)	(.001)	(.001)	(.001)	(.601)	(.001)
.741	.696	.699	.685	.755	.718	.810	.735	.673
(.111)	(.111)	(.114)	(.110)	(.111)	(.113)	(.118)	(.119)	(.113)
−.060	−.034	.056	.006	−.002	−.045	.022	−.007	.047
(.141)	(.139)	(.143)	(.138)	(.145)	(.145)	(.154)	(.151)	(.143)
−.095	−.005	.005	.017	−.131	−.078	−.108	−.091	−.035
(.130)	(.127)	(.130)	(.129)	(.130)	(.132)	(.138)	(.136)	(.136)
−.150	−.053	.064	−.080	−.154	−.124	−.232	−.115	−.039
(.105)	(.106)	(.107)	(.112)	(.102)	(.107)	(.110)	(.113)	(.118)
−.260	−.376	−.433	−.417	−.313	−.370	−.331	−.336	−.404
(.092)	(.092)	(.100)	(.099)	(.091)	(.093)	(.092)	(.094)	(.103)
.574	.597	.533	.605	.613	.613	.657	.572	.592
(.162)	(.157)	(.165)	(.159)	(.162)	(.164)	(.163)	(.163)	(.164)
−.216	−.236	−.206	−.220	−.229	−.231	−.247	−.165	−.190
(.170)	(.166)	(.170)	(.167)	(.170)	(.173)	(.172)	(.173)	(.173)
−.024	.052	.087	.054	.003	.055	−.013	−.013	.009
(.102)	(.103)	(.102)	(.108)	(.100)	(.103)	(.104)	(.106)	(.113)
−.147	−.134	−.190	−.168	−.157	−.152	−.164	−.137	−.206
(.069)	(.069)	(.068)	(.073)	(.067)	(.070)	(.069)	(.070)	(.076)
.123	.099	.155	.075	.147	.108	.150	.009	.100
(.082)	(.080)	(.082)	(.081)	(.080)	(.082)	(.085)	(.083)	(.084)
.054	.047	.019	.055	.042	.046	.064	.040	.039
(.087)	(.084)	(.086)	(.085)	(.085)	(.082)	(.090)	(.088)	(.088)
−.137	−.105	−.013	−.095	−.149	−.119	−.175	−.101	−.078
(.069)	(.070)	(.070)	(.073)	(.069)	(.071)	(.073)	(.071)	(.076)
.6231	.6504	.6397	.6568	.6306	−.6370	.6263	.6426	.6601
.00440	.00424	.00435	.00424	.00441	.00438	.00466	.00453	.00422
1.87	1.95	2.03	1.98	1.93	1.90	2.00	2.09	1.98

Table 6.A.21 Nominal GNP Growth Forecasting Equations, Estimated Jointly with Output and Unemployment Equations in Text

	Model						
	A5.1	A5.2	A7.1	A8.1	A16.1	A16.2	OLS
Constant Term	.0084**	.0079**	.0068**	.0076**	.0113**	.0116**	.0068**
	(.0022)	(.0017)	(.0024)	(.0025)	(.0025)	(.0024)	(.0025)
$NGNP_{t-1}$	.3139**	.4437**	.1481	.2645**	.3293**	.3000**	.2209*
	(.0952)	(.1007)	(.0956)	(.0934)	(.1112)	(.1120)	(.1047)
$NGNP_{t-2}$	.0587	−.0062	−.1712	−.1470	−.1141	−.1390	−.1368
	(.0485)	(.0959)	(.0943)	(.0908)	(.1104)	(.1135)	(.1086)
$NGNP_{t-3}$	.0643	.1448	−.0131	.1082	.0995	.1540	.0407
	(.0456)	(.0894)	(.0911)	(.0902)	(.1081)	(.1112)	(.1071)
$NGNP_{t-4}$	.0177	−.0900	−.1054	−.2256**	−.1898**	−.2061*	−.1774
	(.0444)	(.0752)	(.0843)	(.0864)	(.0958)	(.0993)	(.0997)
$M2G_{t-1}$	−.0040	.2049	.2222	.1618	.0833	.1891	.3549
	(.0808)	(.1294)	(.1667)	(.1603)	(.0790)	(.1211)	(.1898)
$M2G_{t-2}$	−.0051	−.3015	.0074	.2755	.0307	−.1168	.0085
	(.1040)	(.2196)	(.2245)	(.2115)	(.1038)	(.1886)	(.2841)
$M2G_{t-3}$	.2141*	.4024	.5786*	.1877	.1828	.2397	.4365
	(.1037)	(.2210)	(.2312)	(.2092)	(.1035)	(.1874)	(.2598)
$M2G_{t-4}$	−.1332	−.2474	.0180	−.0120	−.0631	−.0778	−.0799
	(.0895)	(.1422)	(.1806)	(.1775)	(.0885)	(.1362)	(.2103)
R^2	.2017	.2341	.3453	.3552	.2943	.2874	.3712
SE	.00994	.00974	.00912	.00905	.00987	.00992	.00880
D-W	1.86	2.14	1.93	2.22	2.10	2.04	2.11

Note: See table 6.A.20.

*Significant at the 5 percent level.

**Significant at the 1 percent level.

Table 6.A.22   Inflation Forecasting Equations, Estimated Jointly with Output and Unemployment Equations

	Model						
	A9.1	A9.2	A11.1	A12.1	A18.1	A18.2	OLS
Constant Term	−.0011	−.0012	−.0005	−.0005	−.0011	−.0012	−.0008
	(.0010)	(.0010)	(.0011)	(.0011)	(.0011)	(.0011)	(.0011)
π_{t-1}	.2040*	.2405*	.2408*	.2225**	.2126*	.2343*	.2477*
	(.1030)	(.1039)	(.0953)	(.0861)	(.1028)	(.1088)	(.1054)
π_{t-2}	.1259	.1314	.1491	.1710	.0976	.1580	.1598
	(.1053)	(.1067)	(.0993)	(.0804)	(.1056)	(.1100)	(.1087)
π_{t-3}	.2280*	.2087*	.2249*	.2196*	.1810	.2271*	.2744*
	(.1048)	(.1057)	(.0999)	(.0815)	(.1034)	(.1088)	(.1089)
π_{t-4}	.0888	.0240	.0549	.0913	.1541	−.0019	.0466
	(.1003)	(.1020)	(.0953)	(.0803)	(.0957)	(.1039)	(.1036)
RTB_{t-1}	.2284**	.2280**	.2890**	.2269**	.2400**	.2432**	.2513**
	(.0802)	(.0804)	(.0747)	(.0656)	(.0701)	(.0804)	(.0816)
RTB_{t-2}	−.1093	−.1208	−.1563	−.1018	−.0490	−.1378	−.1311
	(.1308)	(.1323)	(.1273)	(.0987)	(.1092)	(.1303)	(.1324)
RTB_{t-3}	.1819	.1832	.1824	.1849	.0250	.1806	.1684
	(.1471)	(.1488)	(.1385)	(.1154)	(.1242)	(.1464)	(.1490)

Table 6.A.22 (continued)

	Model						
	A9.1	A9.2	A11.1	A12.1	A18.1	A18.2	OLS
RTB_{t-4}	-.2408*	-.2134*	-.2366*	-.2530**	-.1549	-.2107*	-.2423*
	(.0991)	(.0991)	(.0936)	(.0845)	(.0894)	(.0996)	(.1018)
$M2G_{t-1}$	.1271	.1147	.0889	.0238	.1432	.1249	.1234
	(.0907)	(.0915)	(.0819)	(.0734)	(.0842)	(.0906)	(.0935)
$M2G_{t-2}$	.0083	-.0042	-.0238	.0886	-.0364	.0052	.0051
	(.1188)	(.1201)	(.1104)	(.0846)	(.1073)	(.1167)	(.1104)
$M2G_{t-3}$	.2093*	.1982	.2082*	.0948	.2029*	.1678	.1874
	(.1067)	(.1079)	(.1025)	(.0797)	(.0984)	(.1060)	(.1090)
$M2G_{t-4}$	-.2212**	-.1964*	-.2513**	-.1464*	-.1844*	-.1845*	-.2240**
	(.0845)	(.0853)	(.0778)	(.0704)	(.0793)	(.0858)	(.0868)
R^2	.7369	.7367	.7359	.7306	.7263	.7371	.7411
SE	.00347	.00347	.00352	.00355	.00370	.00363	.00347
D-W	1.92	1.99	2.01	1.92	1.65	1.70	1.74

Note: See table 6.A.20.
*Significant at the 5 percent level.
**Significant at the 1 percent level.

Table 6.A.23 **F Statistics for Significant Explanatory Power in Forecasting Equations of Four Lags of Each Variable**

Variable	$M1G$ Forecasting Equation	NGNP Forecasting Equation	π Forecasting Equation
NGNP	1.09	2.24	1.44
π	1.69	.96	8.38**
RTB	5.28**	.11	5.01**
$M2G$	1.25	5.65**	3.04*
$M1G$	15.80**	.48	.60
UN	1.66	1.62	.76
RGNP	.82	.94	1.44
G	.13	2.47	1.55
BOP	1.28	.61	2.26
GDEBT	1.52	.92	.61
SURP	2.56*	1.66	1.35

Note: The F statistics test the null hypothesis that the coefficients on the four lagged values of each of these variables equals zero. The F statistics are distributed asymptotically as $F(4,x)$ where x runs from 75 to 83. The critical F at the 5 percent level is 2.5 and at the 1 percent level is 3.6. NGNP = quarterly rate of growth of real GNP, π = quarterly rate of growth of the GNP deflator, RTB = average 90-day treasury bill rate, $M2G$ = quarterly rate of growth of average $M2$, $M1G$ = quarterly rate of growth of average $M1$, UN = average unemployment rate, RGNP = quarterly rate of growth of real GNP, G = quarterly rate of growth of real federal government expenditure, BOP = average balance of payments on current account, GDEBT = quarterly rate of growth of government debt, SURP = high employment surplus.

*Significant at the 5 percent level.

**Significant at the 1 percent level.

7   Concluding Remarks

Rather than recount the empirical results already adequately summarized at the end of each chapter, now is the appropriate time to provide a general perspective on the methods used in this book. A general view will be worthwhile particularly because, although the empirical studies in the preceding chapters analyze quite different issues, certain patterns of results recur in all of them. These patterns say something important about the line of research pursued here, and they deserve to be emphasized.

The models analyzed in this book which stress the distinction between effects from unanticipated and anticipated movements in variables require measures of expectations in order to be estimated. Life is hard for the econometrician because unfortunately the real world rarely supplies him with the data he needs, in this case measures of expectations. The solution to the problem here is first to specify forecasting equations and then to use the assumption of rational expectations to generate the required expectations measures. The danger in this approach is that misspecification of the expectations measures can lead to seriously biased results, which lead in turn to inappropriate conclusions.

A surprising finding—at least at first—arises in all the empirical studies in this book. The specification of equations describing expectations does not seem to matter very much. Results in Chapter 4 with an efficient-markets model, where the expectations of short-rates are a function of lagged short rates, are very close to results with a similar efficient-markets model in Mishkin (1978), where, in contrast, the short-rate expectations are described by a forward rate measure. In Chapter 5 and its Appendix 5.2, changing the specifications of the expectations equations does not appreciably affect the results and conclusions. In Chapter 6, although the specification of money growth expectations is quite different from that of Barro and Rush (1980), the results are strikingly similar.

The robustness of the results in these studies to changes in the specification of expectations is too consistent to be mere coincidence. It appears that in models of the type discussed here, where the effects of unanticipated movements in variables are emphasized, the danger from misspecification of expectations is not very severe. Paradoxically, the explanation for this good news might be simply that macro variables are extremely hard to forecast. Thus forecast errors may be so large relative to the error in specifying expectations that any resulting errors-in-variables bias is quite small.

Another potential problem in the empirical analysis here is the failure of theory to indicate whether economic agents focus on seasonally adjusted or on unadjusted data. All the empirical studies in this book indicate that this problem, too, is not severe. Results from either adjusted or unadjusted data are similar, except that results from unadjusted data do appear to be somewhat stronger. Possibly the unadjusted data are "cleaner": that is, they are not filtered as occurs with seasonal adjustment using such programs as Census X-11.

On balance the results in the preceding chapters justify using the assumption of rational expectations in empirical work, especially when financial markets are studied. Chapter 4 finds that, except for inflation during the unusual 1959–1969 period, forecasts in the bond market appear to be rational. The long bond results in Chapter 5 are also favorable to the rational expectations hypothesis, and the rejections of constraints in the short-rate models can be attributed plausibly to an inappropriate model of market equilibrium. The results of the rationality tests in Chapter 6 are somewhat mixed. However, the null hypothesis of rationality is accepted more often than it is rejected, and, of the two component hypotheses of the MRE hypothesis, rationality fares substantially better than neutrality.

This is the good news about the use of rational expectations models of the type discussed in this book; there is, however, some bad news as well. The hypothesis of rational expectations has nothing to say about whether the models estimated here are true reduced forms where the error term is uncorrelated with the explanatory variables. Only when there is further information to identify the models as reduced forms is the interpretation of the empirical results clear-cut. If this information is not available, very different inferences are possible. This unsatisfactory situation is not specific to the models estimated here. As Sims (1980) has noted, the same problem plagues all macroeconometric modeling, and it is one reason why understanding the macro economy is such a difficult task.

So called "causality" or "exogeneity" tests based on the work of Granger (1969) or Sims (1972) do not help remedy the problem encountered here. If we could determine that our unanticipated variables are exogenous, then we would be more willing to believe that our models are true reduced forms, and interpreting empirical results would be much simpler. Unfortunately, Granger-"causality" tells us nothing about the kind of exogeneity most relevant to the analysis here, the potential contemporaneous correlation of unanticipated variables with the error term. This is not to say that Granger-causality is a useless concept for rational expectations econometrics. Certain rational expectations models lead to testable implications about Granger-causal relations among the data. Even more important, the use of the Granger concept can tell us what information belongs in equations describing expectations formation and therefore in the decision rules of economic agents. The concept of Granger-causality has often been misused in the literature (see Zellner 1979), but it does have a real, though limited, role to play in the kind of econometrics described in this book.

The preceding chapters should have convinced the reader of the value of using the rational expectations hypothesis to analyze important empirical issues in macroeconomics. The research in this book is only a start in this direction. The approach used here is applicable to a wider range of problems, several of which have been mentioned in Chapter 1. It is to be hoped that this book will stimulate research that makes further use of the techniques described in the preceding pages.

References

Abel, A., and Mishkin, F. S. 1980. "On the Econometric Testing of Rationality and Market Efficiency." Unpublished paper. University of Chicago.

———. 1983. "An Integrated View of Tests of Rationality, Market Efficiency and the Short-Run Neutrality of Monetary Policy." *Journal of Monetary Economics* 9 (forthcoming).

Anderson, L. C., and Jordan, J. L. 1968. "Monetary and Fiscal Actions: A Test of Their Relative Importance in Economic Stabilization." *St. Louis Federal Reserve Bank Review* 50:11–24.

———. 1969. "Monetary and Fiscal Actions: A Test of Their Relative Importance in Economic Stabilization—Reply." *St. Louis Federal Reserve Bank Review* 51:12–16.

Barro, R. J. 1977. "Unanticipated Money Growth and Unemployment in the United States." *American Economic Review* 67:101–115.

———. 1978. "Unanticipated Money, Output, and the Price Level in the United States." *Journal of Political Economy* 86:549–580.

———. 1979. "Unanticipated Money Growth and Unemployment in the United States: Reply." *American Economic Review* 69:1004–1009.

Barro, R. J., and Hercowitz, Z. 1980. "Money Stock Revisions and Unanticipated Money Growth." *Journal of Monetary Economics* 6:257–268.

Barro, R. J., and Rush, M. 1980. "Unanticipated Money and Economic Activity." In *Rational Expectations and Economic Policy*, edited by S. Fischer, pp. 23–48. Chicago: University of Chicago Press for the National Bureau of Economic Research.

Bernanke, B. 1982. "The Financial Collapse as a Direct Cause of the Great Depression." Unpublished paper. Stanford University, Graduate School of Business.

Bilson, J. F. O. 1980. "The Rational Expectations Approach to the Consumption Function: A Multi-Country Study." *European Economic Review* 13:273–308.

Björklund, A., and Holmlund, B. 1981. "The Duration of Unemployment and Unexpected Inflation." *American Economic Review* 71:121–131.

Blinder, A. 1980. "Comment" (on Barro and Rush). In *Rational Expectations and Economic Policy*, edited by S. Fischer, pp. 48–54. Chicago: University of Chicago Press for the National Bureau of Economic Research.

Bodie, Z. 1976. "Common Stocks as a Hedge against Inflation." *Journal of Finance* 31:459–470.

Brainard, W. C., and Cooper, R. N. 1976. "Empirical Monetary, Macroeconomics: What Have We Learned in the Last 25 Years." *American Economic Review* 65:167–175.

Cagan, P. 1956. "The Monetary Dynamics of Hyperinflation." In *Studies in the Quantity Theory of Money*, edited by M. Friedman. Chicago: University of Chicago Press.

———. 1972. *The Channels of Monetary Effects on Interest Rates*. New York: National Bureau of Economic Research.

Carlson, J. A. 1977. "A Study of Price Forecasts." *Annals of Economic and Social Measurement* 6:27–56.

Carr, J., and Darby, M. R. 1981. "The Role of Money Supply Shocks in the Short-Run Demand for Money." *Journal of Monetary Economics* 8:183–200.

Chow, G. C. 1960. "Tests of Equality between Sets of Coefficients in Two Linear Regressions." *Econometrica* 28:591–605.

———. 1980. "Estimation of Rational Expectations Models." *Journal of Economic Dynamics and Control*, vol. 2.

De Leeuw, F., and Kalchenbrenner, J. 1969. "Monetary and Fiscal Actions: A Test of Their Relative Importance in Economic Stabilization—Comment." *St. Louis Federal Reserve Bank Review* 51:6–11.

Dornbusch, R. 1980. "Exchange Rate Economics: Where Do We Stand?" *Brookings Papers on Economic Activity* 1:143–183.

Engle, R. F. 1980. "A General Approach to the Construction of Model Diagnostics Based Upon the Lagrange Multiplier Principle." Discussion Paper 79–43. University of California at San Diego.

Fair, R. 1978. "The Sensitivity of Fiscal-Policy Effects to Assumptions about the Behavior of the Federal Reserve." *Econometrica* 46:1165–1179.

———. 1979. "An Analysis of the Accuracy of Four Macroeconometric Models." *Journal of Political Economy* 87:701–719.

Fama, E. F. 1970. "Efficient Capital Markets: A Review of Theory and Empirical Work." *Journal of Finance* 25:283–417.

————. 1975. "Short-Term Interest Rates as Predictors of Inflation." *American Economic Review* 65:269–282.

————. 1976a. *Foundations of Finance*. New York: Basic.

————. 1976b. "Forward Rates as Predictors of Future Spot Rates." *Journal of Financial Economics* 3:361–377.

Fama, E. F., and Schwert, G. W. 1977. "Asset Returns and Inflation." *Journal of Financial Economics* 5:115–146.

————. 1979. "Inflation, Interest, and Relative Prices." *Journal of Business* 52:183–209.

Feige, E. L., and Pearce, D. K. 1976. "Economically Rational Expectations: Are Innovations in the Rate of Inflation Independent of Innovations in Measures of Monetary and Fiscal Policy?" *Journal of Political Economy* 84:499–522.

Feldstein, M. S., and Eckstein, O. 1970. "The Fundamental Determinants of the Interest Rate." *Review of Economics and Statistics* 52:363–375.

Fischer, S. 1977. "Long Term Contracts, Rational Expectations, and the Optimal Money Supply Rule." *Journal of Political Economy* 85:191–206.

————. 1981. "Relative Price Variability and Inflation in the United States and Germany." National Bureau of Economic Research, Conference Paper no. 135. *European Economic Review* (forthcoming).

Fisher, I. 1930. *The Theory of Interest*. New York: Macmillan.

Fisher, L., and Lorie, J. H. 1977. *A Half Century of Returns on Stocks and Bonds*. Chicago: University of Chicago Press.

Flavin, M. A. 1981. "The Adjustment of Consumption to Changing Expectations about Future Income." *Journal of Political Economy* 89:974–1009.

French, K. R.; Ruback, R. S.; and Schwert, G. W. 1981. "Effects of Nominal Contracting on Stock Returns." Working Paper series no. MERC 81–07. University of Rochester, Managerial Economics Research Center, Graduate School of Management.

Frenkel, J. A. 1977. "The Forward Exchange Rate Expectations, and the Demand for Money: The German Hyperinflation." *American Economic Review* 67:653–670.

————. 1981. "Flexible Exchange Rates, Prices, and the Role of 'News': Lessons from the 1970's." *Journal of Political Economy* 89:665–705.

Friedman, B. 1980. "Survey Evidence on the 'Rationality' of Interest Rate Expectations." *Journal of Monetary Economics* 6:753–766.

Friedman, M. 1956. "The Quantity Theory of Money—a Restatement." In *Studies in the Quantity Theory of Money*, edited by M. Friedman. Chicago: University of Chicago Press.

————. 1959. "The Demand for Money—Some Theoretical and Empirical Results." *Journal of Political Economy* 67:327–351.

————. 1968. "The Role of Monetary Policy." *American Economic Review* 58:1–17.

————. 1969. "Factors Affecting the Level of Interest Rates." *Proceedings of the 1968 Conference on Savings and Residential Financing.* Sponsored by the United States Savings and Loan League (The League).

Germany, J. D., and Srivastava, S. 1979. "Empirical Estimates of Unanticipated Policy: Issues in Stability and Identification." Unpublished paper. Massachusetts Institute of Technology.

Gibson, W. E. 1970. "Interest Rates and Monetary Policy. *Journal of Political Economy* 78:431–455.

Gibson, W. E., and Kaufman, G. G. 1968. "The Sensitivity of Interest Rates to Changes in Money and Income." *Journal of Political Economy* 76:472–478.

Glesjer, H. 1969. "A New Test for Heteroscedasticity." *Journal of the American Statistical Association* 64:316–323.

Goldfeld, S. M. 1973. "The Demand for Money Revisited. *Brookings Papers on Economic Activity* 3:577–638.

Goldfeld, S. M., and Quandt, R. E. 1965. "Some Tests for Homoscedasticity." *Journal of the American Statistical Association* 60:539–547.

————. 1972. *Non-Linear Methods in Econometrics.* Amsterdam: North-Holland.

Goldsmith-Nagan Bond and Money Market Letter. Washington, D.C., various issues.

Gordon, R. J. 1979. "New Evidence That Fully Anticipated Monetary Changes Influence Real Output after All." Discussion Paper no. 369. Northwestern University, Center for Mathematical Studies in Economics and Management Science.

Granger, C. W. J. 1969. "Investigating Causal Relations by Econometric Models and Cross-Spectral Methods. *Econometrica* 37:424–438.

Granger, C. W. J., and Newbold, P. 1974. "Spurious Regressions in Econometrics." *Journal of Econometrics* 2:111–120.

Grossman, J. 1979. "Nominal Demand Policy and Short-Run Fluctuations in Unemployment and Prices in the United States." *Journal of Political Economy* 87:1063–1085.

Grossman, S. J., and Stiglitz, J. E. "Information and Competitive Price Systems." *American Economic Review* 66:246–253.

Hansen, L. P., and Sargent, T. J. 1980. "Formulating and Estimating Dynamic Linear Rational Expectations Models." *Journal of Economic Dynamics and Control* 2:7–46.

Hartley, P. 1983. "Rational Expectations and the Foreign Exchange Market." In *Exchange Rates and International Macroeconomics,* edited by J. Frenkel. Chicago: University of Chicago Press for the National Bureau of Economic Research, forthcoming.

Hoffman, D. L., and Schlagenhauf, D. E. 1981a. "An Econometric Investigation of Monetary Neutrality and Rationality Propositions from an International Perspective." Unpublished paper. Arizona State University.

———. 1981b. "Rational Expectations, the Role of 'News,' and Exchange Market Efficiency." Faculty Working Papers no. EC 81–102. Arizona State University.

Jacobs, R. L.; Leamer, R. E.; and Ward, M. P. 1979. "Difficulties in Testing for Causation." *Economic Inquiry* 17:401–413.

Jaffe, J., and Mandelkar, G. 1976. "The 'Fisher' Effect for Risky Assets: An Empirical Investigation." *Journal of Finance* 31:447–458.

Kmenta, J. 1971. *Elements of Econometrics*. New York: Macmillan.

Kohn, R. 1979. "Asymptotic Estimation and Hypothesis Testing Results for Vector Linear Time Series Models." *Econometrica* 47:1005–1030.

Laidler, D. 1977. *The Demand for Money: Theories and Evidence*, pp. 119–152. New York: Dun-Donnelly.

Leamer, E. 1978. *Specification Searches: Ad Hoc Inference with Nonexperimental Data*. New York: Wiley.

Leiderman, L. 1979. "Expectations and Output-Inflation Tradeoffs in a Fixed-Exchange-Rate Economy." *Journal of Political Economy* 87:1285–1306.

———. 1980. "Macroeconometric Testing of the Rational Expectations and Structural Neutrality Hypothesis for the United States." *Journal of Monetary Economics* 6:69–82.

Levich, R. 1979. "On the Efficiency of Markets for Foreign Exchange." In *International Economic Policy*, edited by R. Dornbusch and J. A. Frenkel. Baltimore: Johns Hopkins University Press.

Livingston, J. A. Survey published twice yearly in *Philadelphia Sunday Bulletin* (1948–1971) and *Philadelphia Inquirer* (1972–).

Ljung, C. M., and Box, G. E. P. 1978. "Measure of Lack of Fit in Time Series Models." *Biometrika* 65:297–303.

Lucas, R. E., Jr. 1972. "Econometric Testing of the Natural Rate Hypothesis." In *The Econometrics of Price Determination*, edited by O. Eckstein, pp. 5–15. Washington, D.C.: Board of Governors of the Federal Reserve System.

———. 1973. "Some International Evidence on Output-Inflation Tradeoffs." *American Economic Review* 63:326–334.

———. 1976. "Econometric Policy Evaluation: A Critique." In *The Phillips Curve and Labor Markets*, edited by K. Brunner and A. H. Meltzer, pp. 19–46. Carnegie-Rochester Conference Series on Public Policy, vol. 1. Amsterdam: North-Holland.

Lucas, R. E., Jr., and Sargent, T. J., eds. 1981. *Rational Expectations and Econometric Practice*. Minneapolis: University of Minnesota Press.

McCallum, B. T. 1979a. "On the Observational Inequivalence of Classical and Keynesian Models." *Journal of Political Economy* 87:394–402.

———. 1979b. "Topics Concerning the Formulation, Estimation, and Use of Macroeconometric Models with Rational Expectations." *American Statistical Association Proceedings of the Business and Economic Statistics Section.*

Makin, J. H. 1981. "Real Interest, Money Surprises and Anticipated Inflation." Working Paper no. 818. National Bureau of Economic Research.

———. 1982. "Anticipated Money, Inflation Uncertainty and Real Economic Activity." *Review of Economics and Statistics* 64:126–134.

Mishkin, F. S. 1978. "Efficient-Markets Theory: Implications for Monetary Policy." *Brookings Papers on Economic Activity* 3:707–752.

———. 1979. "Simulation Methodology in Macroeconomics: An Innovation Technique." *Journal of Political Economy*, 87:816–836.

———. 1981a. "Monetary Policy and Long-Term Interest Rates: An Efficient Markets Approach." *Journal of Monetary Economics* 7:29–55.

———. 1981b. "Are Market Forecasts Rational?" *American Economic Review* 71:295–306.

———. 1982a. "Does Anticipated Monetary Policy Matter? An Econometric Investigation." *Journal of Political Economy* 90:22–51.

———. 1982b. "Does Anticipated Aggregate Demand Policy Matter? Further Econometric Results." *American Economic Review* 72.

———. 1982c. "Monetary Policy and Short-Term Interest Rates: An Efficient Markets-Rational Expectations Approach." *Journal of Finance* 67:63–72.

MIT-Penn-SSRC. 1977. "Quarterly Econometric Model." Unpublished paper. Board of Governors of the Federal Reserve System, Washington, D.C.

Modigliani, F. 1974. "The Channels of Monetary Policy in the FMP Econometric Model of the U.S." In *Modelling the Economy*, edited by G. Renton. London: Heineman Educational Books.

———. 1977. "The Monetarist Controversy or, Should We Forsake Stabilization Policies?" *American Economic Review* 67:1–19.

Modigliani, F., and Shiller, R. J. 1973. "Inflation, Rational Expectations, and the Term Structure of Interest Rates." *Economica* 40:12–43.

Mullineaux, D. J. 1978. "On Testing for Rationality: Another Look at the Livingston Price Expectations Data." *Journal of Political Economy* 86:329–336.

Mussa, M. 1979. "Empirical Regularities in the Behavior of Exchange Rates and Theories of Foreign Exchange Market." In *Policies for Employment Prices, and Exchange Rates*, edited by K. Brunner and A.

H. Meltzer, pp. 9–58. Carnegie-Rochester Conference Series on Public Policy, vol. 11. Amsterdam: North-Holland.

Muth, J. F. 1961. "Rational Expectations and the Theory of Price Movements." *Econometrica* 29:315–335.

Nelson, C. R. 1972. *The Term Structure of Interest Rates.* New York: Basic.

———. 1976. "Inflation and Rates of Return on Common Stock." *Journal of Finance* 31:421–483.

———. 1979. "Granger Causality and the Natural Rate Hypothesis." *Journal of Political Economy* 87:390–394.

Nelson, C. R., and Schwert, G. W. 1977. "Short-Term Interest Rates as Predictors of Inflation: On Testing the Hypothesis That the Real Rate is Constant." *American Economic Review* 67:478–486.

Pagan, A. 1981. "Econometric Issues in the Analysis of Regressions with Generated Regressors." Unpublished paper. Australian National University. Center for Economic Policy Research.

Pesando, J. E. 1975. "A Note on the Rationality of the Livingston Price Expectations." *Journal of Political Economy* 83:849–858.

———. 1978. "On the Efficiency of the Bond Market: Some Canadian Evidence." *Journal of Political Economy* 86:1057–1076.

Phelps, E. S. 1967. "Phillips Curves, Expectations of Inflation, and Optimal Unemployment Over Time," *Economica* 34:254–281.

Phelps, E. S., and Taylor, J. B. 1977. "Stabilizing Powers of Monetary Policy under Rational Expectations," *Journal of Political Economy* 85:163–190.

Plosser, C. I. 1982. "Government Financing Decisions on Asset Returns." *Journal of Monetary Economics* 9:325–352.

Plosser, C. I., and Schwert, G. W. 1978. "Money, Income and Sunspots: Measuring Economic Relationships and the Effects of Differencing." *Journal of Monetary Economics* 4:637–660.

Poole, W. 1976. "Rational Expectations in the Macro Model." *Brookings Papers on Economic Activity* 2:463–505.

Rozeff, M. S. 1974. "Money and Stock Prices: Market Efficiency and the Lag in Effect of Monetary Policy." *Journal of Financial Economics* 1:245–302.

Sargent, T. J. 1971. "A Note on the 'Accelerationist' Controversy." *Journal of Money, Credit and Banking* 3:721–725.

———. 1973. "Rational Expectations, the Real Rate of Interest, and the Natural Rate of Unemployment." *Brookings Papers on Economic Activity* 2:429–472.

———. 1976a. "A Classical Macroeconometric Model for the United States." *Journal of Political Economy* 84:207–237.

———. 1976b. "The Observational Equivalence of Natural and Unnatural Rate Theories of Macroeconomics." *Journal of Political Economy* 84:631–640.

———. 1977. "Observations on Improper Methods of Simulating and Teaching Friedman's Time Series Consumption Model." *International Economic Review* 18:445–462.

———. 1978. "Estimation of Dynamic Labor Demand Schedules under Rational Expectations." *Journal of Political Economy* 86:1009–1044.

———. 1979. "A Note on Maximum Likelihood Estimation of the Rational Expectations Model of the Term Structure." *Journal of Monetary Economics* 5:133–144.

———. 1981. "Interpreting Economic Time Series." *Journal of Political Economy* 89:213–248.

Sargent, T. J., and Wallace, N. 1975. "Rational Expectations, the Optimal Monetary Instrument and the Optimal Money Supply Rule." *Journal of Political Economy* 83:241–254.

SAS Institute. 1979. *SAS User's Guide, 1979 Edition*. Raleigh, N.C.: SAS Institute.

Schwert, G. W. 1977*a*. "Stock Exchange Seats as Capital Assets." *Journal of Financial Economics* 4:51–78.

———. 1977*b*. "Public Regulation of National Securities Exchanges: A Test of the Capture Hypothesis." *Bell Journal of Economics* 8:128–150.

———. 1981. "The Adjustment of Stock Prices to Information about Inflation." *Journal of Finance* 36:15–29.

Sheffrin, S. M. 1979. "Unanticipated Money Growth and Output Fluctuations." *Economic Inquiry* 17:1–13.

Shiller, R. J. 1979. "The Volatility of Long-Term Interest Rates and Expectations Models of the Term Structure." *Journal of Political Economy* 87:1190–1219.

———. 1980. "Can the Fed Control Real Interest Rates?" In *Rational Expectations and Economic Policy*, edited by S. Fischer, pp. 117–167. Chicago: University of Chicago Press for the National Bureau of Economic Research.

Sims, C. A. 1972. "Money, Income, and Causality." *American Economic Review* 62:540–552.

———. 1977. "Relationships and the Lack Thereof between Economic Time Series, with Special Reference to Money and Interest Rates: Comment." *Journal of the American Statistical Association* 72:23–24.

———. 1980. "Macroeconomics and Reality." *Econometrica* 48:1–48.

Small, D. H. 1979. "Unanticipated Money Growth and Unemployment in the United States: Comment." *American Economic Review* 69:996–1003.

Taylor, J. B. 1979. "Estimation and Control of a Macroeconomic Model with Rational Expectations." *Econometrica* 47:1267–1286.

Urich, T., and Wachtel, P. 1981. "Market Response to the Weekly Money Supply Announcements in the 1970's." *Journal of Finance* 36:1063–1072.

Wallace, N. 1976. "Microeconomic Theories of Macroeconomic Phenomena and Their Implications for Monetary Policy." In *A Prescription for Monetary Policy: Proceedings from a Seminar Series*, pp. 87–97. Minneapolis: Federal Reserve Bank of Minneapolis.

Wallis, K. F. 1980. "Econometric Implications of the Rational Expectations Hypothesis." *Econometrica* 48:49–72.

Weintraub, R. 1980. "Comment" (on Barro and Rush). In *Rational Expectations and Economic Policy*, edited by S. Fischer. Chicago: University of Chicago Press.

Wogin, G. 1980. "Unemployment and Monetary Policy under Rational Expectations: Some Canadian Evidence." *Journal of Monetary Economics* 6:59–68.

Working, H. 1960. "Note on the Correlation of First Differences of Averages in a Random Chain." *Econometrica* 28:916–918.

Zellner, A. 1962. "An Efficient Method of Estimating Seemingly Unrelated Regressions and Tests for Aggregation Bias." *Journal of the American Statistical Association* 57:348–368.

———. 1979. "Causality and Econometrics." In *Three Aspects of Policy and Policy Making: Knowledge, Data and Institutions*, edited by K. Brunner and A. H. Meltzer, pp. 9–54. Carnegie-Rochester Conference Series vol. 10. Amsterdam: North-Holland.

Index